Ranked Choice Voting

Ranked Choice Voting

JAMES W. ENDERSBY
MICHAEL J. TOWLE

OXFORD
UNIVERSITY PRESS

Oxford University Press is a department of the University of Oxford.
It furthers the University's objective of excellence in research, scholarship,
and education by publishing worldwide. Oxford is a registered trade mark of
Oxford University Press in the UK and in certain other countries.

Published in the United States of America by Oxford University Press
198 Madison Avenue, New York, NY 10016, United States of America.

© Oxford University Press 2025

All rights reserved. No part of this publication may be reproduced, stored in a retrieval system, transmitted, used for text and data mining, or used for training artificial intelligence, in any form or by any means, without the prior permission in writing of Oxford University Press, or as expressly permitted by law, by license or under terms agreed with the appropriate reprographics rights organization. Inquiries concerning reproduction outside the scope of the above should be sent to the Rights Department, Oxford University Press, at the address above.

You must not circulate this work in any other form
and you must impose this same condition on any acquirer.

CIP data is on file at the Library of Congress

ISBN 9780197798911
ISBN 9780197798928 (pbk.)

DOI: 10.1093/9780197798959.001.0001

Paperback printed by Marquis, Canada
Hardback printed by Bridgeport National Bindery, Inc., United States of America

Contents

List of Figures	vi
List of Tables	vii
Acknowledgments	viii
Introduction	1
1. Ranked Choice Voting and Election Reform	8
2. Ranked Choice Voting in the Family of Electoral Systems	26
3. Local Elections and Ranked Choice	48
4. RCV in Partisan and State Elections	74
5. RCV in State and Federal Elections	89
6. Evaluation of RCV Elections	106
7. Completing and Counting Ballots	132
8. Evaluating RCV	158
Appendices	170
Interviews	173
Notes	174
References	195
Index	209

List of Figures

1.1.	Academy Award Nomination Ballot	20
2.1.	Ballot for Australian House of Representatives	37
2.2.	Ballot for Australian Senate	38
4.1.	Conservative Party of Canada Leadership Election, 2017	87
4.2.	Conservative Party of Canada Leadership Election, 2020	88
5.1.	Maine Certification of 2018 Election for 2nd congressional district	94
6.1.	Average number of candidates competing by office	113
6.2.	Percent turnout among registered voters in four cities adopting RCV	117
6.3.	Percent nontransferable votes by count single-member election (IRV/AV)	120
6.4.	Percent nontransferable votes by count multimember election (STV)	121
B.1.	Ballots for the Australian House of Representatives	171
B.2.	Ballot for the Australian Senate	172

List of Tables

0.1.	Election results for the US Congress from Maine, 2018	4
1.1.	Recent elections with minority winners	9
1.2.	Hypothetical election with three candidates	13
2.1.	Electoral system taxonomy national parliaments	30
2.2.	Example of a Borda count	33
2.3.	Vegetable choice among five friends	41
2.4a.	Violation of monotonicity three alternatives, seventeen voters: Original initial preferences of all voters	44
2.4b.	Violation of monotonicity three alternatives, seventeen voters: Revised two preference reversals, voters 7 and 8	45
2.5.	Mayoral election in Burlington, Vermont, 2009	46
3.1.	Municipalities in the United States with preferential voting systems	52
3.2.	Municipalities in western Canada with preferential voting systems	55
3.3.	Ballot examples for the voter preferential and associated voting systems	69
4.1.	North Carolina Court of Appeals, 2010	81
4.2.	Electoral systems in western Canadian provinces	84
5.1.	Hypothetical presidential primary: Sixteen delegates assigned according to PR with threshold and RCV with next preference assigned	103
6.1.	Ranked choice elections in American cities: Cases in sample	110
6.2.	Average number of candidates per seat by election and office	112
6.3.	Average number of mayoral and council candidates, before and after ranked choice voting	114
6.4.	First count leader(s) that win election	123
6.5.	First count leader(s) that win election after more than one round	124
6.6.	RCV electoral success according to several methods of calculation	126
7.1.	Examples of correctly completed ballots	140
7.2.	Examples of how local rules could determine how ballots are counted	142
7.3.	Original tally and recount: Alameda County, California, 2022 General Election for School Director, District 4	144
7.4.	Examples of other marked ballots	145
8.1.	2020 Georgia runoffs for US Senate	160
A.1.	Preferential voting systems	170

Acknowledgments

Electoral reform has again risen to the top of the American agenda. One reform proposal, ranked choice voting (RCV), is the subject of this book. Although there are many works that discuss elements of this electoral system, few, we believe, offer a comprehensive and impartial presentation of the history, theory, and actual application of RCV. Our motivation for producing this work was to fill this gap by providing an accessible presentation about preferential elections.

Several years ago, one of us had the opportunity to lead a study-abroad trip to Ireland. The other suggested this as an opportunity to gather then-unavailable election data. In the days long before easy digital scanning and internet downloads, that intrepid scholar stood in a library and photocopied the rounds of ballot-counting in each of the thirty-nine constituencies from the then-recent general elections to the Dáil Éireann, the Irish parliament. Ireland elects its parliament in districts of three, four, or five members, using a rather complex form of RCV known as the single transferable vote (STV). We later poured over all these data. We began to think intently about the implications and consequences of RCV.

We have been friends since graduate school. Although we pursued different types of academic careers, we often discussed the different political topics we had been thinking about. These conversations led to several joint publications, including research on the use of the STV in Ireland. On a few of these occasions, our discussions of RCV produced scrawled outlines or bullet points of our ideas, often on cocktail napkins! Some of these ideas were worth further consideration and made back to our homes after conferences, while others have been swept away by waitstaff clearing tables. (We like to think that perhaps we gave some brilliant gems of insight that launched an academic career for whoever cleared our table, but our respective handwriting makes that highly unlikely.)

From the photocopies in Ireland, a fascination with preferential or RCV began, resulting in several conference papers. Some of our earlier work seems quaint now, given how much more we have read and pondered about these voting systems over the years. But we kept returning to the topic. For a long time, this seemed just an idiosyncratic interest of ours, but we began to follow the growing research by other scholars on this topic. While various forms of preferential voting had been used in the United States and Canada for many decades, more communities either newly adopted or considered the adoption of the most common form of RCV, the instant runoff. In 2018, Maine became the first state to implement it for federal elections. There is now both a vast amount of scholarly literature on the topic and subsets of the public that have strong feelings about ranked voting. Yet we realized that there was no single volume that succinctly summarized the growing canon of literature on the topic.

We decided to try to present a broad and objective description of RCV in North America. We appreciate the support of our respective institutions. Mount St. Mary's University granted Michael Towle a sabbatical to begin our research. The University of Missouri provided James Endersby with the Provost's Great Books Award to complete the project. What started with some musings and photocopies resulted in the completion of the volume that you see here.

Our gratitude goes to our families who put up with what many might consider boring dialogues about the nuances of RCV. At home and in the classroom, our families and students withstood endless exhortations about the importance of electoral systems. These discussions allowed us to solidify our ideas. We have many colleagues to recognize for helping us to complete this project. We appreciate the contributions and support of many colleagues. Gidong Kim, Steven Jokinsky, and Tyler Coleman assisted with quantitative data collection efforts on municipal election results, and Steven Jokinsky dug up electoral laws and regulations. Anne Frederick provided excellent support with the transcription of interviews. Kathleen Skeffington Murray and Linda Endersby helped with graphics. We thank scholars who took the time to read and comment on earlier drafts of parts of the manuscript including Andrea Benjamin, John Curiel, and Jessica Trounstine. Our colleagues at Missouri and Mount St. Mary's offered thoughtful comments and valuable insights. Editor David McBride, the reviewers, and Andrea Smith and the staff at Oxford University Press provided invaluable support and assistance.

We dedicate this book to our wives and children who support us always.

Introduction

For the 2018 midterm elections, the state of Maine offered its voters a new method to elect members of Congress. Rather than cast a single vote for one congressional candidate, the simple voting process used in most American elections, a Maine voter could rank candidates according to preference: first choice, second choice, third choice, and so forth. To be elected, a candidate had to win a majority—not just a plurality—of votes. If no candidate received a majority of first-choice votes, the candidate with the fewest votes would be eliminated and ballots for this candidate would be reassigned to the candidate ranked next (second choice) by each voter. If no candidate received a majority after this reassignment, the process is repeated. The candidate with the fewest votes is eliminated and ballots for this candidate are reassigned to the viable candidate ranked next, and so forth, until one candidate is elected with a majority of the remaining votes.

This electoral system, often referred to as ranked choice voting (RCV), is attracting attention as a possibility to improve the quality of elections. RCV is a reform with the proponents' intentions to enhance voter satisfaction with elections, to promote trust in government, and to increase voter turnout. These are laudable goals that nearly everyone wants to achieve. Critics of RCV, on the other hand, identify a number of other key problems. Voters, particularly citizens with less education, may have difficulty understanding how the electoral system works and dealing with the demands of creating a rank order among many candidates. In addition, there are new challenges for fair and equitable administration of elections as well as questions about whether the RCV can achieve its stated goals.

Decision-making can be challenging any time there are more than two alternatives. Elections with only two parties or only two candidates work predictably and well using the commonly used method of majority rule. An election with three or more candidates, however, introduces complications. With multiple candidates or options, there is no guarantee that any candidate will receive a majority, over half, of votes cast. For instance, if you go out to lunch with a group of friends or colleagues from work, all preferring one or the other of two restaurants, an informal majority vote satisfies at least half of the group.[1] Problems arise immediately if some members of the group

Ranked Choice Voting. James W. Endersby and Michael J. Towle, Oxford University Press.
© Oxford University Press (2025). DOI: 10.1093/9780197798959.003.0001

prefer three or four different restaurants and there is no majority agreement. No matter which restaurant is chosen, a majority of the group would rather eat somewhere else. Usually, rather than sacrificing friendships or workplace collegiality, we develop methods to resolve conflict and produce a consensus. One of these natural methods is to eliminate the alternative that the fewest group members support and consider which restaurant is their second choice. This method may produce a majority consensus, satisfying group members that their preferences have been considered and appreciated.[2]

This decision-making process is analogous to RCV in democratic elections. An electoral system is a social decision-making method for achieving consensus in a large group, encompassing anywhere from hundreds to many millions of group members. The reformers favoring RCV think it is better than our current electoral system. Majority rule, or plurality rule when there are more than two alternatives, works well much of the time. However, elections among more than two parties or candidates have the same difficulties as the lunch example, but without the social cohesion of a small group to encourage consensus-making. If no candidate receives an election majority, large numbers of voters may feel dissatisfaction from the absence of consensus. RCV is a reform proposed to increase the level of confidence and trust in government and elections. Whether RCV achieves this objective is less clear.

The purpose of this book is to provide a balanced description and evaluation of RCV and related concepts. Numerous examples from experiences of actual elections are given. Municipalities from California to Maine and from Minnesota to New Mexico hold RCV elections. Although this electoral reform seems new and innovative, the theory and practice of RCV have been around for centuries and are used around the world. This general system of election goes by many names, including instant runoff voting (IRV) and the alternative vote (AV). For instance, Australia uses AV for election to the federal House of Representatives and for the legislatures in most states, using a method that is essentially American IRV and RCV.

Related electoral systems such as the single transferable vote (STV) are often confused with RCV. In Ireland, a voter in an electoral constituency casts a single preferential ballot to elect from three to five members of the lower chamber of Irish parliament, the Dáil Éireann. Cambridge, Massachusetts, has used STV for citywide election of its nine-member council since World War II. What distinguishes AV/IRV from STV is the number of candidates elected from an electoral district. For RCV and sister methods, only one candidate wins, but multiple winners are elected with STV. In fact, there is an entire family of decision-making methods that ask voters to rank alternatives in order of preference from first onward. The term *preferential voting* may be used to encompass this entire family from the AV of Australia to the STV of Ireland as well as the current North American versions. The book will compare and contrast RCV, other forms of preferential voting, and other electoral systems, including the plurality system commonly used for elections in the United States, Britain, Canada, and many other countries.

Most Americans, indeed, most citizens in democratic countries, think of elections in a manner more consistent with the other forty-nine states in the 2018 midterms. To elect an officeholder, each voter casts one vote for a single candidate. One candidate wins by receiving more votes than any other, a *plurality*. The American colonies inherited this electoral system from the British. Scholars also use various terms to identify this electoral practice where one candidate needs to get more votes than any other, including the descriptive single-member district plurality (SMDP) elections or the racing analogy first-past-the-post (FPTP). These plurality contests characterize Anglo-American elections.

But on further reflection, Americans select officeholders through a wide variety of methods. Local elective offices, particularly those in smaller, rural communities, may be decided through at-large elections for which a voter may cast ballots for two, three, or more candidates for a council or similar office. Many states have a provision that if no candidate wins a *majority* (more than 50 percent) of ballots cast, a runoff election pairs the top two vote-getters. The development of party primaries produced another form of a two-stage election in which party nominees are selected and then face off in the general election. States from the Gulf Coast to the Pacific Coast have tried out changes to the system of primary and general elections. Voters in the United States have experience with a broad range of electoral types, including that uniquely American institution, the Electoral College. Indeed, the federal structure of the American government allows states to experiment and innovate with public policy, including the management of elections. American electoral innovation has led to many more historical and contemporary variations on the SMDP model.

Democratic countries generally have an even wider experience with electoral systems. A simple classification might include the traditional British and American forms of plurality elections, proportional representation where legislative seats are allocated in terms of the percentage of votes received by each political party, mixed systems that merge these two extreme methods, and a fourth category comprising other electoral innovations. The breadth of electoral systems is vast, and this book fits RCV within major theoretical and actual electoral systems.

However, as social scientists have shown, there is no best electoral system. RCV has some advantages and some disadvantages. An effective way to assess the performance of RCV, and to decide if it should be adopted more widely, is to thoughtfully consider the evidence for and against RCV in actual settings. The experience with the 2018 congressional election in Maine, for instance, led immediately and simultaneously to joyful enthusiasm with its implementation and strident calls for its repeal.

Results from the two congressional districts in Maine in 2018, shown in Table 0.1, reveal much about the implementation of RCV. In the first congressional district, five-term incumbent Chellie Pingree handily won reelection. She received nearly 59 percent, a clear majority. Under both

Table 0.1 Election results for the US Congress from Maine, 2018

	First District				
	Round 1				
Candidate	Votes		Transferred	Votes	
Pingree, Chellie (D)	201,195	58.8% W			
Holbrook, Mark I. (R)	111,118	32.5%			
Grohman, Martin J. (I)	29,670	8.7%			

	Second District				
	Round 1			Round 2	
Candidate	Votes	Percentage	Transferred	Votes	
Poliquin, Bruce (R)	134,184	46.3%	4,747	138,931	49.4%
Golden, Jared F. (D)	132,013	45.6%	10,427	142,440	50.6% W
Bond, Tiffany L. (I)	16,552	5.7%			
Hoar, William R. S. (I)	6,875	2.4%			
Nontransferable votes			8,253		

Source: State of Maine, Department of the Secretary of State, Bureau of Corporations, Elections & Commissions.

plurality and RCV, Pingree was elected over her two challengers. In the second district, covering most of the northern and eastern portions of the state, the outcome was quite different. Two-term incumbent Bruce Poliquin received 46.3 percent of the votes. His three challengers split the remainder, although one, Jared Golden, came in close with 45.6 percent. Poliquin received only 2,171 more votes than Golden in second place (out of nearly 290,000 votes cast). Under plurality vote, Poliquin would have been reelected. But since Maine's adoption of RCV, he would need a majority of first-place votes for election. What mattered next was the second or third preference of those voters who selected one of the two independent candidates, since these voters' first preferences did not count in determining a winner.

With RCV, Maine election officials examined each of these ballots to determine whether the voter preferred Poliquin or Golden. If an independent voter recorded a preference, that ballot would be transferred to count for one of the leading candidates. In the final tabulation, Poliquin picked up an additional 4,747 votes, but Golden gained 10,427. This margin gave Golden enough ballots to surpass Poliquin and to obtain a majority. Golden won and became the first member of Congress elected through RCV, with 50.6 percent of the votes. Golden and voters supporting him along with the two independent candidates cheered the result; Poliquin and his followers considered the outcome unfair. In any case, the difference between these two election outcomes in Maine's first and second districts illustrates the basics of how RCV works.[3]

Of course, there is also much more to RCV than the 2018 Maine results, and that is the subject of the following chapters. The book is not, however, a treatise either advocating or opposing RCV. To emphasize what we noted above, there is no "best" electoral system. The authors of this book are political scientists who are fascinated by RCV and its implications for democratic elections, as well as other electoral systems. Our hope is to provide some useful insights into RCV and perhaps into the nature of fair elections generally. Our approach is to provide an objective assessment of the pluses and minuses of RCV. Advocates tend to only focus on its advantages. Defenders of the status quo emphasize RCV's disadvantages and rarely confront the shortcomings of single-member districts with plurality elections. Our goal is to present enough information about RCV to allow informed decisions about the adoption and maintenance of this electoral system. As political scientists, our interest focuses on political elections, but RCV has other applications as well. We will sprinkle our discussion with examples from other group decision-making situations ranging from selecting recipients of the Academy Awards, the film industry's Oscars, to locations for future Olympic games. Nevertheless, our primary concern is the application of RCV for political elections.

Chapter 1 opens with an overview of RCV and compares it to plurality election. The goals and motivations behind RCV are presented, along with the potential drawbacks of RCV. Chapter 2 places RCV within the context of other electoral systems. Other potential election reforms have characteristics that are similar to RCV. Comparisons are made between RCV, STV, and alternative methods of election. Chapter 3 provides historical context and discusses the long, but often unrecognized, experience with electoral reform, particularly in North America. Most American experiences with RCV involve nonpartisan and municipal elections. Chapter 4 expands on the application of RCV in two ways, for partisan and other state-level contests. Based on the experience in Maine and elsewhere, the attention of electoral reformers focuses on the selection of party nominees and on partisan and other general elections for statewide office. In Chapter 5, this discussion is extended to state elections generally, including a description of RCV in Maine and Alaska, and the application of ranked choice methods for presidential elections. The potential applications of RCV are explored in these contexts.

The next chapters use the experience from hundreds of past contests with RCV. Chapter 6 examines the macro- or election-level effects of RCV. These effects include topics of candidate competition, so-called wasted votes, majoritarian outcomes, and voter turnout. Chapter 7 investigates the micro effects of RCV on individual voter behavior. This includes the information demands on a voter required by RCV, ballot completion, and how a voter may respond to those demands. Existing research on voter satisfaction and trust is discussed. This chapter also looks behind the scenes at a few select issues concerning election administration, such as voter education efforts. Since RCV can be more complicated than SMDP elections, communities must manage the added complexity of counting ranked votes. Experience suggests some important lessons for the implementation of RCV. Finally, Chapter 8 concludes by discussing some important things to remember concerning RCV and election reform. The goals and criticisms of RCV and plurality voting are reviewed in the context of election experience.

There is no perfect election system. RCV and related procedures have both advantages and disadvantages when compared to plurality, simple runoffs, and other frequently used election systems. We need to decide what we want to achieve as we consider election and decision-making procedures. A thoughtful evaluation of RCV may help us clarify what we want and expect from elections.

1
Ranked Choice Voting and Election Reform

Majority rule is a fundamental principle of democratic governance. This principle fits alongside a number of other core ideas central to democracy: individual freedom, free and fair elections, representative government, the rule of law, and the protection of minority rights. Majority rule works the majority of the time, but not always. The problem is that majority rule requires a very specific set of circumstances to work effectively. Those circumstances may not exist for popular elections. Some political reformers suggest alternatives that bring us closer to the core notion of majority rule.

A *majority* requires that the winning outcome receives more than half of the votes cast. A majority is guaranteed when there are only two alternatives, provided there is an odd number of voters. In other words, majority rule works for decisions between yes and no, pass and fail, Party D and Party R. However, there is no guarantee of a majority when there are three or more alternatives. Often, votes involve only two alternatives. Nearly all votes in the US Congress and other legislative bodies are between two options. Legislative votes may involve a sequence of paired alternatives, but only two options at a time.[1] Direct democracy devices such as the referendum and the initiative typically allow citizens to choose between two policy options, a proposition and the status quo. Controversies in these contests center on the wording and interpretation of the alternatives, but there are only two options—approving the ballot proposition or not. Likewise, a strict two-party system offers two alternatives. Popular elections, however, are not necessarily limited to two options.[2]

A *plurality*, in contrast with a majority election, selects the winning outcome with the most votes, even if it is under 50 percent. Elections frequently have three or more candidates running for public office. Although several states require runoffs between the top two candidates, many elected officials in the United States win with less than a majority of the vote. In plurality elections, the candidate with the most votes is the winner, no matter how small the proportion received by this winning candidate. For example, in 1994, Maine voters elected independent candidate Angus King as governor with only 35.4 percent, not much more than a third of the total votes cast. King was elected in a four-way race that also included Democrat, Republican, and Green Party candidates. Although winners elected with such a small proportion of the vote are unusual, these outcomes are possible with three or more candidates. Plurality elections, selecting a winner with the most votes, are more common in the United States than requirements for an absolute majority.

Plurality winners are common in the United States. In the November 2020 elections, winners in 5 of the 35 contests for US senator, 1 of 14 for state governor, and 8 of 435 for US representative received less than a majority. Similarly, 10 winning candidates received less than a majority in the 2022 midterm elections.[3] Table 1.1 shows these minority winners for elections from 2012 to 2022. These cases strike some political observers as unfair since a majority voted *against* the candidate elected. The criticism centers on the idea that outcomes are either indifferent to majority opinion or insufficiently reflective of the diversity of voters' viewpoints. Ranked choice voting (RCV)—or one of several other electoral alternatives, including a top-two

Table 1.1 Recent elections with minority winners

Election Year	US House of Representatives*	US Senate*	State Governors**
2012	9/435	3/33	3/15
2014	7/435	4/36	11/38
2016	9/435	9/34	3/15
2018	5/435	2/35	5/38
2020	8/435	5/35	1/14
2022	5/435	2/35	3/38

*California (fifty-three seats in the US House, fifty-two seats for 2022) and Washington (ten) limit to two candidates in the general election; Alaska (House & Senate 2022), Louisiana (six), Maine (two, 2018 and 2022), and Georgia (two Senate, 2020) hold a runoff if no candidate receives a majority in the general election. For the House of Representatives, only 366 seats (364 in 2018) have the possibility of a minority winner in the final round.
**As some states elect governors in off-year elections, results reported for the election cycle include the previous odd-numbered year.

runoff—has a majoritarian flavor. A candidate must receive a majority in the final round in order to be elected. Receiving a majority may be a common feature of plurality elections, but it is not required.[4]

For example, consider a hypothetical example of an election among three alternatives. The three candidates are Jane, Kate, and Luke. All 2,000 voters cast their ballots for the candidate they prefer most. In other words, they all vote, and they all vote sincerely—without any strategic considerations. As we will soon see, these assumptions may place unrealistic limits on voter decision-making, but it seems reasonable that voters should cast ballots for the candidate they like best. In this hypothetical plurality election, the result is 800 votes for Jane, 700 votes for Kate, and 500 votes for Luke. Jane wins the election with 40 percent of the total votes cast. Despite her plurality, Jane does not have a clear mandate as a majority (60 percent) of voters preferred someone else. Moreover, suppose the voters supporting Luke had Kate as their second preference. If the Luke supporters had foreseen the election outcome—that their candidate would come in third in the final tally—then they would have made a tactical decision to cast their ballots for Kate. Then Kate would have defeated Jane in the election, and 60 percent of voters—a clear majority—would be more satisfied with that outcome. Under this set of voter preferences among the candidates, either a traditional runoff or a ranked choice election would produce a majoritarian outcome. This emphasis on the majority is what some electoral reformers seek.

We focus on RCV and other proposed reforms concerning the electoral system. Contemporary discussion of political reform of voting and elections covers at least two broad types. One involves who votes. These involve traditional voting rights as well as protections against fraud. Voting reforms of this type include easing voter registration, allowing early voting and/or no-excuse absentee voting, requiring identification to reduce potential election fraud, simplifying the ballot to reduce voter mistakes, holding elections by mail or over the internet, improving security of the ballot, and so forth. Much of American political development involves the expansion of suffrage. States first expanded voting rights beyond property owners. Three Constitutional Amendments—the 15th, 19th, and 26th—extended voting rights across the nation to groups based on race, gender, and age. Congress and state legislatures passed many laws influencing voting rights. However, our concern here is not who casts votes, but how votes are cast.[5]

The second type of political reform involves the process of selecting the winner. The typical focus of reform is the system of single-member district plurality (SMDP) elections. RCV addresses common complaints about SMDP elections. The focus in this book is on this kind of reform: the electoral system, or how votes are counted and the election victors are selected.

There are yet other types of proposed reforms on a variety of factors such as electronic security of vote results; restrictions on campaign contributions, expenditures, and conduct of political campaigns; regulation of political parties; redistricting and related claims of racial or partisan gerrymandering; incumbent term limits; and so forth. Most of these other reforms are less focused on the electoral process than on related features in the electoral environment. The issue of drawing district lines, or gerrymandering, is somewhat related to our concerns because one method to reduce the impact of districting on outcomes is to utilize multimember districts. Multimember districts already occur for some city councils, school boards, county commissions, and so forth. We will discuss implications of other electoral systems such as the single transferable vote (STV) for these representative bodies. But issues of campaign finance, access to the ballot, redistricting, the role of the mass media, and so forth, are beyond the scope of the discussion here.

Plurality and Ranked Choice Elections

For purposes of clarity, there is an important distinction between single- and multimember districts. A single-member district occurs where a certain geographical area elects one representative. Currently, all 435 members of the US House of Representatives are elected through single-member districts. Most state legislators are elected as representatives uniquely representing a defined geographical district. Many local public officials are elected to represent a single constituency. For instance, city council members elected from wards represent single-member districts, though at-large council members may be elected separately or together. Governors and most state executives are elected in single-member districts consisting of the entire state. Often, cities and towns with mayors elect one person to represent the entire municipality. National and regional elections in Great Britain and Canada also involve single-member electoral districts (sometimes called ridings), although, as in the United States, there is considerable diversity in terms of local election methods. Outside the United States, the term typically used to describe SMDP elections is first-past-the-post (FPTP), but the concept is the same.[6]

If plurality elections lead to dissatisfaction about minority winners, one straightforward solution is to pair the top candidates in a runoff election. Two states—Louisiana and Georgia—allow a runoff for federal and state elections. If the leading candidate's vote exceeds 50 percent, the candidate is elected. If no candidate receives a majority in the general election, then the two candidates with the most votes are paired in a subsequent runoff election. Ten states require a runoff for primary elections, in which a political party's nominee is selected. Louisiana's system, the so-called jungle primary, has candidates from all parties compete in the general election rather than an earlier primary election. In Louisiana, if no candidate receives a majority, the top two candidates compete in a runoff election held several weeks later. Similarly, Washington and California adopted the "top two" primary system. Candidates of all parties compete in the primary election, and the top two candidates, regardless of political party affiliation, are paired in the general election. The justification for these various forms of runoffs is that a majority winner is produced between the top two candidates.[7]

Returning to the hypothetical three-candidate election, no candidate receives a majority. A runoff election would pair the top two candidates, Jane and Kate. Since those who supported Luke had Kate as their second choice, a runoff would allow those who initially supported Luke to change their votes to Kate. In the runoff, Kate would defeat Jane by a margin of 1,100 votes to 900. Of course, in an actual runoff, the campaigns for candidates Jane and Kate must mount significant get-out-the-vote efforts. There would be a natural tendency for potential voters to abstain from voting in the runoff (or in the initial campaign). The candidates may choose to adjust their stances in a runoff to appeal to a changed electorate.

However, there are drawbacks to runoff elections. A second election resulting from a traditional runoff adds cost for election administration. Election supervisors must print ballots, distribute information on the election, obtain polling sites and equipment, marshal an army of election workers, and so forth—all for two elections rather than one. The runoff campaign also may be costly as the two candidates compete for additional votes and fundraising dollars over a few more weeks. The second campaign may be more divisive as well. Although many voters cast ballots in both elections, holding two rounds also means there are two separate decision-making electorates, often of substantially different sizes. In the hypothetical example, all voters cast ballots in both elections, but in actual elections, more or fewer voters participate in the initial and runoff elections. Advocates for RCV suggest an "instant" runoff based on the preferences of the same voters at a single point in time. RCV asks each voter to provide a ranked preference ordering among the candidates, and election administrators then reassign and tabulate votes to determine a winner quickly and at a comparatively low cost. Moreover, there is no need for a separate election, nor for an additional campaign and the potential public dissatisfaction that may follow.

For example, in the hypothetical election between Jane, Kate, and Luke, each voter identifies their first and second (and third) choices. Table 1.2 outlines how an RCV election would proceed. Luke's supporters rank Kate second and Jane third. Also assume that Jane's supporters rank Luke second, and those favoring Kate rank Jane second. (This is just a simple example. Not all voters in a bloc have the same second and third preferences, but let's postpone that complication for now.) Since Jane does not reach a majority in the first round, Luke—the candidate with the fewest votes—is dropped as a viable alternative. A second round compares whether each voter prefers the remaining candidates—Jane or Kate. Jane's original 8,000 supporters remain, as do Kate's 7,000 voters. However, from ranking information on their original ballots, those 5,000 originally supporting Luke have their ballots transferred to Kate, their second choice. Kate wins the instant runoff with 12,000 votes to Jane's 8,000. There is no need for another campaign or another formal election.

The beauty of RCV grows from the full expression of preferences of voters and the efficient determination of majority winners from those preferences. Plurality election seems unattractive because Jane would win with only a

Table 1.2 Hypothetical election with three candidates

Voter's Most Preferred Candidate	Voter's Second Preference	Votes in Plurality Election	Votes in Runoff Election
Jane	Luke	8,000 ✓	8,000
Kate	Jane	7,000	12,000 ✓
Luke	Kate	5,000	

In a plurality election, candidate Jane would win with the most votes, 40 percent. In a runoff election, Jane and Kate would advance to a runoff as the top two candidates. Since voters initially casting ballots for Luke hold Kate as their second preference, Kate would win the runoff election with 60 percent of all votes.

minority of the vote. However, the selection of Kate as the majority winner, in this contrived example, is also an illusion. Kate received a majority over Jane, but among voters' first preferences, she polled only 35 percent. Moreover, Luke's supporters ranked Kate second, but Jane's supporters had Luke as their second choice, as can be seen in Table 1.2. If an election were held between Kate and Luke only, each would receive their first-place votes, 7,000 and 5,000, respectively. But voters favoring Jane rank Luke second, and they would provide an additional 8,000 votes for him. Luke would defeat Kate, 65 percent to 35 percent. This might suggest that Luke is the candidate who should win, although he was dropped as an alternative after the first round. To make matters even more complicated, in a pairwise contest, Jane would beat Luke, 75 percent to 25 percent. In this example, no candidate consistently outperforms the others. While majority rule works for choosing between two alternatives, in this example with three candidates, there is a cycle among majorities. Jane receives a majority over Luke, as Luke wins with a majority over Kate, and Kate defeats Jane with a majority.

The possibility of majority winner cycles was known as early as the eighteenth century. French philosopher and mathematician the Marquis de Condorcet (1785) suggested, as Nobel Prize-winning economist Kenneth Arrow (1963) later proved, that no electoral system or social decision-making system in general can overcome the case of a cycle of majority winners. Different methods of decision may produce different winners. With three or more alternatives and at least three voters, no method can satisfy a reasonable set of fairness criteria. While it may seem somewhat unsatisfactory to those seeking a definitively "best" outcome, ultimately there is no guarantee of a universally preferred winner in a free society. Subsequently, philosopher Allan Gibbard (1973) and economist Mark Satterthwaite (1975) independently demonstrated that every decision-making or electoral system may be subject to manipulation at some point. Arrow compared the problem to the Second Law of Thermodynamics, suggesting that no transformation from one form of energy to another can be fully efficient. No electoral system can be fair 100 percent of the time. Plurality election has the advantage of being a simple electoral system that we all understand. Other electoral systems may better provide descriptive representation (i.e., representing race/ethnicity, gender, geography, occupation, or the like). Runoff elections, whether two-stage or ranked choice, give voters the perceived satisfaction of a majority winner, even if that majority is created artificially through a forced procedure.

Thus, the fact that there is no "best" electoral system does not prevent us from selecting what criteria regarding elections we want to emphasize. The worst-case scenario is the situation of cycling majorities, such as the Jane–Kate–Luke example, and no decision-making method can save us from that. However, if we prefer our elections simple and expect to resolve inherent conflict through other means, then SMDP elections are an effective method of social decision-making. If we value the majoritarian impulse over the simplicity of plurality elections, then a runoff or an RCV system is a reasonable direction to go. But a runoff or a ranked choice election may violate our sense of fairness under some conditions. In our hypothetical example, Jane's followers are likely satisfied by plurality election. Kate's supporters see a runoff or preferential system as better. Luke's faction wants a different election system altogether.[8]

Multimember Elections and the Single Transferable Vote

At-large elections occur when everyone in an area or constituency can vote for an officeholder in an election. For at-large elections, voters are not subdivided into geographical districts; they all vote together. Some at-large elections could be single-member districts, for example, a town electing a mayor. Other at-large elections are in multimember districts, such as a town electing several members of a city council. Multimember districts are often used in local elections in the United States to elect councils, boards, or commissions. One common method used in the United States is to have all candidates on that ballot listed together and then allow voters to select as many candidates as there are seats. For example, a town might have its voters cast up to four votes for four candidates on a four-member town council, and voters can cast one vote for a mayor elected separately.

In this case, the municipal election would be a multimember, at-large election. At-large elections are an alternative to having a town divided into districts, with one elected official representing each district.[9] Drawing district lines is rather arbitrary for most communities, and redistricting may be fraught with problems of descriptive and partisan misrepresentation. In fact, one common objection to using SMDP elections for the US House of Representatives, state legislatures, and local officials is that they too easily lead to gerrymandering. Gerrymandering is a deliberate drawing of district lines in such a way as to maximize the electoral advantage for a party or group.

Redistricting can also be utilized to underrepresent populations according to race, ethnicity, or class. Issues pertaining to redistricting are not unlike the representational problems discussed here: there is no "best" method of drawing district lines.[10]

A key problem with at-large, multimember districts is that they often do not provide proportional representation (PR). The traditional American at-large election is plurality-based. For example, if there are two town council members to be elected,[11] each voter casts up to two votes for the at-large seats. This system is called plural at-large voting or block voting.[12] Suppose our hypothetical town of 1,000 total voters is divided between two factions, the Purples, comprising 60 percent of town residents, and the Lavenders, the other 40 percent. Each faction puts forward two candidates in the election: Peter and Patrick for the Purple group, and Liz and Linda for the Lavender group. Assuming all citizens vote and vote sincerely for their two most preferred candidates, then Peter and Patrick each win with 30 percent of the total vote. Liz and Linda both lose; each receives 20 percent of votes cast.[13] A potential problem with at-large, multimember elections is that a majority faction will win all seats, leaving the minority with no representation at all.[14]

Dividing those two multimember seats into single-member, at-large seats on separate ballots will not change the outcome. For instance, if Patrick faces Linda in the contest for At-Large Seat 1 and Peter runs against Liz for At-Large Seat 2, the outcome is similar: Patrick and Peter both win 60 percent –40 percent. Somehow, this result of a majority faction winning all the seats violates our sense of fairness. Minority groups are not allowed effective representation.[15] Earlier, we sought majority winners, but sometimes proportionality seems a better goal rather than majoritarianism.

Similarly, some object to SMDP systems because they cannot guarantee proportionality. Reconsidering the town example above, imagine the town divided into four single-member districts of equal population that perfectly represent the overall town's divisions. In other words, each ward or district contains 60 percent Purple voters and 40 percent Lavender voters.[16] Assuming all voters support their faction, each Purple candidate wins the district 60 percent –40 percent. Despite the fact that 40 percent of that region's voters are Lavender supporters, none of the four seats go to a Lavender candidate. Thus, some critics look fondly to other democratic countries that use PR systems. PR systems use an electoral system in which the partisan makeup of the legislature more closely mirrors the overall partisan preference of the voters; for example, if 40 percent of voters support a candidate from the Lavender

Party, then roughly 40 percent of the representatives elected should be from the Lavender Party.

Ranked choices on a ballot may provide one effective method to improve proportionality. However, voters would cast only a single vote in a multimember election, rather than the number of votes equal to the number of seats. Each ballot cast would numerically order the candidates according to the voter's preference. Each ballot would be applied to a candidate as needed for election so that most voters see that some candidate they prefer is elected.[17]

Suppose four council members are elected in our hypothetical town. The Purple Party names four candidates: Patrick, Peter, Pierre, and Placido. Likewise, the Lavender Party gives four nominees: Linda, Liz, Lucy, and Lykeisha. To keep things simple (for now), let's assume that all voters rank candidates in the same order; Purple voters rank Patrick first, Peter second, and so on. Of the 1,000 voters, 600 prefer the Purple slate and 400 the Lavender ticket. Since there are 1,000 votes and 4 seats, any candidate receiving 250 votes is elected. This threshold of 250 for election is known as the Hare quota. There are several alternative counting methods and quotas, but we want to keep it simple for now. On the first count, Patrick is elected because he receives 600 votes, well over the threshold of 250. The lead Lavender candidate, Linda, is also elected because she received 400 votes, again over the threshold of 250.

However, on this first count, there are surplus votes that do not elect a candidate. Of the 600 votes for Patrick, 350 (600- 250) are surplus votes. Rather than wasting those votes (remember, each voter only gets one vote!), they should be transferred to the voters' second preference. In our simple example, the second preference is Peter, and all 350 votes are transferred to him. Likewise, there are 150 excess votes for Linda; those surplus votes should be transferred to those voters' second choice, Liz. By the second count, Patrick and Linda are already elected, and Peter is elected with 350 votes, 100 of which are a surplus above the quota of 250. With three candidates now elected, the election goes to a third round. On this third count, Pierre has 100 transferred votes and Liz has 150. Liz does not reach the quota of 250, but she does have a majority of the remaining votes after the transfer. Since Liz has more votes than Pierre and any remaining candidates, Liz is elected in the third round.

Under this system of a STV, the election outcome is closer to the proportional ideal. Both the Purple partisans and the Lavender faction elect two seats on the four-member council, and, following the same logic, the Purples would elect the at-large mayor. In this admittedly contrived example, PR is achieved. The Lavender voters account for 40 percent of the electorate, and 2/5 of the City Council comprises Lavender-sponsored candidates. Proportionality is an important objective for the application of the STV. That objective can be somewhat difficult to achieve in practice, but the principle extends from the elected candidates reaching or surpassing a threshold.

RCV and the STV are similar in important ways. Both ask voters to order their preferred candidates from first downward, and in both cases, each voter has one vote. Candidates are elected by passing a defined threshold. The threshold for the above Purple–Lavender example was a convenient quota, defined as the total number of votes cast, V, divided by the number of candidates elected, C. This is the Hare quota, or V/C. Most political elections with majoritarian rules require a candidate's votes to exceed the Droop quota, the total votes cast divided by one more than the candidates elected, or V/(C+1). Exceeding the Droop quota meets the expectations of many observers.[18] For RCV, the traditional instant runoff variety, since one candidate is elected, votes should exceed the quota of 50 percent. For STV, a candidate should receive more than the total number of votes divided by one more than the number of candidates elected, or 33 1/3 percent for two candidates, more than 25 percent for three candidates, and so forth. RCV/instant runoff voting (IRV) and STV differ in terms of how many officials are elected. For traditional RCV, only one vote is elected while for STV multiple winners are determined. Many commentators on political reform often muddle RCV and STV together, but these two electoral systems are quite different and aim to achieve different objectives.

Decision-Making beyond Political Elections

Application of these decision-making systems is not limited to political elections. They can be applied to innumerable other collective decisions. Consider, for example, the task of finalizing nominations for the Academy Awards, the Oscars. Just like political campaigns, the decision-making process for these film awards involves rules concerning the eligibility of voters, the qualification of candidates, and how nominees and winners are selected.[19] The initial suggestions of individuals worthy of recognition for the various categories (Best Actor, Best Original Screenplay, Best

Cinematographer, and so forth) come from practitioners within those categories (actors, screenwriters, cinematographers, etc.). From the many possible nominations for each category, the Academy of Motion Picture Arts and Sciences (AMPAS) must cull the possibilities to a manageable number of nominees, typically five. There are several thousand Academy members, but the number within some of the branches is relatively small. Ultimately, a single winner will be chosen from the list of nominees for each category.

The process of nominee selection asks members of each branch of the Academy to rank order up to five submissions for nominees. Figure 1.1 shows an example of an AMPAS nomination ballot for Best Picture in the 55th Academy Awards in 1983, for which all Academy members were eligible to vote. The number of potential nominees can be quite large, so Academy voters receive a "reminder list" of eligible nominees. In 2019, there were 347 eligible films for Best Picture. Submissions become official nominees if the number of votes passes the threshold defined by the Droop quota. For the standard five award nominees, the threshold is 1/6 of the total number of votes. If a film reaches or exceeds the Droop quota on the first ballot, a nomination is secured. Excess ballots over the threshold are transferred proportionally to the voter's second ranking in the second round. If there are no excess ballots, films with the fewest number of votes are dropped in succession. Those ballots are also transferred to the next lower preference. The process is repeated, typically, until all nomination slots are filled. Rarely are there too few selected to fill the list of five nominees.

For most categories, winners among the nominees are selected by plurality vote, but Best Picture is now an exception. Since 2010, the number of Best Picture nominations can be as few as five or as high as ten. So, the threshold used is 1/11 of the total nomination ballots cast, and the Academy also requires that a nominee receive at least 5 percent of the ballots cast. These rules restrict the number of films nominated for Best Picture: a full ten nominees for the 94th Academy Awards presented in 2022 (for films released in 2021), nine nominees in 2021, and eight in 2020. With so many Best Picture nominations, a plurality winner could attract only a small percentage of the votes, so Academy rules use preferential or RCV for this category. Since ballots are secret, and because counts are considered proprietary, it is unknown whether all voters rank order the full list of their Best Picture contenders.[20] In any case, on their final ballot, Oscar voters may rank order their preferences among the nominated films. If no film receives a majority on the first ballot, then the picture with the lowest number of votes is dropped and those

20 RANKED CHOICE VOTING

Figure 1.1 Academy Award Nomination Ballots.

Copyright © Academy of Motion Picture Arts and Sciences. Reproduced with permission, courtesy of the Academy's Margaret Herrick Library.

ballots are transferred to their second preference. The process is repeated until a majority winner is obtained.[21]

The process of awarding nominations for the Oscars is a form of the STV. Since 2010, the Best Picture is decided through RCV—ranked choice or IRV. There are additional regulations for awards pertaining to specific Academy branches, but preferential voting is the primary selection method for nominees and the method for selecting the Oscar winner for Best Picture. Although Oscar recipients receive no explicitly political benefit, determination of award winners does produce political and social impacts articulated by commentators and sometimes the recipients themselves. Certainly, nominations and Oscars, for many in the film community, produce financial and reputational benefits.

Moreover, this example shows that electoral systems are really just decision-making processes when the number of participants is too large for direct coordination (such as a small group of friends selecting a restaurant for lunch). This decision-making generality is why we may often refer to objects of collective choice as alternatives rather than candidates or parties. The selection of public officials is the more prominent application of various electoral systems, but plurality, ranked choice, and other voting methods are general methods to produce collective decisions. Preferential voting in its various forms produces some advantages, in particular, the perceptions of a broad consensus and of representation of the preferences of a large group.

Advantages and Disadvantages of Ranking Choices

It should not be surprising that the current election methods used in the United States have their detractors, but proposals for electoral reform also have their critics. Proponents and opponents offer a wide array of reasons for and against the adoption or maintenance of RCV systems. A summary of key arguments includes the following goals and motivations for RCV (in no particular order).

1. *Majoritarianism.* A fundamental justification for RCV is the dissatisfaction with the plurality requirement for SMDP elections. Typical plurality elections offer no guarantee that the winner will have the support of more than half of the voters, but preferential voting methods lead to majority winners. Although not guaranteed, a majority outcome may also elect more centrist or less polarizing candidates.
2. *Runoff efficiency.* Runoff elections lead to majority winners, but there are other associated problems. The electorate in the first election and the runoff may have different compositions, particularly for political

elections. The original and runoff elections may have a completely different character. The 2020 runoff for the Georgia Senate, for example, arguably became a national campaign for control of the US Senate rather than a state election.[22] In addition, a separate runoff election requires extra cost to administer, perhaps doubling the costs of the election. A preferential election eliminates the second election, outcomes are determined quickly, with little additional cost, and is composed of the same voters as the first round. RCV offers a more streamlined process without campaigns begging for supporters to return to the polls.

3. *Higher voter turnout.* Another objection to plurality elections is that they are likely to produce "wasted votes." A voter casting a ballot for the winner has an effective vote, but voters casting ballots for losing candidates find their votes wasted and unrepresented in the outcome. Since voting is costly at some level, citizens who perceive their votes may be wasted simply skip the election. If voters perceive their votes are less likely to be wasted, they are more likely to turn out and participate in the election.

4. *Incentives for sincere voting.* The potential for wasted votes is particularly strong for those who cast ballots for likely third-place or lower-ranked candidates. Plurality elections provide an incentive for supporters of independent or minor party candidates to cast a ballot for their second choice. In other words, plurality elections encourage strategic or tactical voting. Voters abandon their first preference in favor of one of the perceived top two candidates. Single-member plurality elections tend to produce two-party systems because of this. RCV elections, however, encourage a sincere ordering of preferences.[23] Voters who prefer a (likely) lower-placed alternative sincerely identify their first choice with the knowledge that their vote may be transferred to an alternative with greater support in a subsequent round. Thus, preferential voting encourages voters to express their true preferences, rather than trying to game the system.

5. *Representation of marginal interests.* Again, the notion of wasted votes and strategic behavior suggests that some members of the electorate are less likely to have their true preferences represented. Often, these may be voters further to the left or to the right of the mainstream alternatives. However, in the current era of political polarization, moderate voters may be underrepresented by the two major party candidates. RCV allows some representation of unheard voices in the first round.

6. *Proportional representation (for STV).* For the selection of multiple winners, such as in an at-large "vote for three" election, plurality voting tends to select all winners from the same party, faction, or group. A preferential election selecting multiple alternatives allows more voters' ballots to count for electing at least one of the winners. As in the earlier example, the broader electorate is represented, and the outcome is closer to a proportional ideal. However, this goal is limited to STV and is not a feature of RCV. For all forms of preferential voting, however, advocates claim that outcomes are more representative of the population, enhancing the descriptive representation of women, ethnic, and racial minorities compared to plurality elections.
7. *Voter satisfaction.* Since citizens may express fuller preferences among the alternatives under RCV, an argument can be made that voters will feel that the political system is more legitimate compared to plurality or runoff. Voters should have higher levels of political efficacy and political trust. Moreover, political candidates should be motivated to conduct campaigns that are less negative toward their opponents. In addition to strong supporters, candidates may also need to appeal to voters as a second or third choice. They may promote more positive messages, thus reducing polarization and voter dissatisfaction with election campaigns.

Critics of RCV question whether these goals and motivations are actually achieved. In fact, a key disagreement between reformers and critics is whether these outcomes are likely. Furthermore, critics raise a number of additional disadvantages that may be associated with preferential voting systems. The points below summarize a few of these criticisms.

1. *Information demands on voters.* Plurality elections require voters to identify their first choice only, a relatively simple task. For preferential systems, voters are asked to identify their second, third, and perhaps subsequent choices, a more difficult exercise that may require much more information and thought. In a political environment where many voters do not identify their first preference, even in elections for prestigious offices, the demands for identifying correctly a third, or tenth, ranked preference may be too much.
2. *Formal or mathematical problems with counting.* Determining victory in plurality or runoff elections is simple and straightforward. Calculating the winner for ranked choice elections involves more complexity

and occurs somewhat behind the scenes. This is particularly the case for STV elections, for which different counting methods could produce different winners. Strategic behavior on the part of voters and candidates may still occur. Moreover, RCV elections are subject to unusual, logical flaws, such as a violation of monotonicity: a principle that an alternative gaining more support should not then do worse in the final outcome, and vice versa.

3. *Universal second/mediocre choice.* To the extent RCV succeeds with its goals, candidates for campaigns may exhibit less leadership and articulate less of a vision or issue platform.[24] In order to appeal to a broader spectrum of voters, candidates may target a common denominator—acceptable but nonspecific issue positions. For critics, RCV may result in even more voter uncertainty about what candidates would do if selected for office. Generally, RCV may substitute the bland for the bold.

4. *Deviations from runoff elections.* In traditional runoffs, narrowing the field to the two leading candidates may provide an opportunity for reevaluation and a growing consensus among voters. Relying on preferences, particularly if obscure or poorly informed at the time of the first election, may lead—if proponents are correct—to the selection of a third or fourth (or lower) place alternative. Some, unpersuaded by RCV proponents, see this distinction between a traditional runoff and an instant runoff as a challenge to effective democratic decisions rather than a strength.

5. *Prioritization of extremist voters.* Since the preferences of extremist or fringe voters, left and right, are likely to be transferred and counted, critics of RCV elections find the notion that more extremist voters are more likely to be decisive in elections troubling. The idea that elections should more frequently be determined by voters with less confidence in the status quo and/or in democratic decision-making is troublesome.

6. *Comparative lack of transparency.* In a plurality election, each voter knows whether their vote counted for a winning alternative or a loser. If the election goes beyond the first round in a preferential election, it may not be clear how an individual voter's ballot is cast. A voter would not know how their vote counted unless they followed the sequence of rounds. For STV elections with multiple alternatives, the ability to know how an individual ballot contributed to the outcome is particularly obscure.

The chapters that follow will assess many of these claims. Various forms of RCV have been used around the world (including in the United States) for over 100 years. Because of this, political scientists have gathered considerable evidence regarding the appeal of these types of elections, as well as some potential problems. It is our hope to present these in an accessible, objective, and useful way.

2
Ranked Choice Voting in the Family of Electoral Systems

Plurality elections are the most common form of political elections in the United States and many other countries. Selection of plurality winners is simple and straightforward, so the administration of elections is comparatively easy. An electoral system with plurality elections tends to reduce the number of political parties or factions to only a few, often just two. Of course, when there are three or more alternatives, the plurality winner may not receive a majority. Moreover, plurality elections may lead to results that are unrepresentative of the electorate overall.

To deal with the possibility of no single majority winner, alternative electoral systems, such as the runoff or ranked choice voting (RCV), involve a successive elimination procedure. Following a traditional election, if no candidate attracts a majority or some other quota of votes, then the field of candidates is narrowed in some predetermined fashion until a consensus alternative is selected. RCV or instant runoff voting (IRV) is not the only method of successive elimination of alternatives; however, it is one electoral system that follows this procedure.

To account for the lack of representation across many districts, other alternatives to plurality elections may focus less on a single winner. Instead, these alternatives emphasize the overall representative quality of a legislature—a national parliament, a state assembly, a city council, or a committee. Election outcomes might then represent the preferences of voters overall, voters in the minority as well as those in the majority. For instance, one objection to plurality (SMDP) elections is that many voters' preferences are not represented. A vote could be classified as either effective or wasted. Effective votes do contribute to a winner. Wasted votes are votes that do not contribute to a winning candidate. Plurality elections produce a high number of "wasted votes." For example, imagine a district that elects a Republican candidate with 60 percent of the vote, while the other 40 percent vote for a Democrat. In this situation, 60 percent of the votes are effective and 40 percent are wasted.[1] Furthermore, if there were ten districts with similar outcomes in each, Republicans would win 100 percent of the seats with only 60 percent of the votes, and the 40 percent of the votes from Democrats would not elect any candidate. Most voters would not consider an outcome where 60 percent of the voters elect 100 percent of ten representatives as fair.[2]

Various electoral systems can be designed to encourage proportional representation (PR). The single transferable vote (STV) is one of these. STV allows more votes to become effective. There are two types of transfers for STV, unlike RCV/IRV. The first is the transfer of surplus votes for those candidates who surpass the quota with extra votes to spare. The second is the transfer of votes from those candidates who are eliminated because they have the fewest votes.[3] Although electoral laws on the transfer procedures vary, transfers of surplus votes precede the transfers from eliminated candidates. In a party-based electoral environment, it is reasonable to expect many of these votes would transfer to another party nominee, and this adds to the proportionality. For now, let's sidestep the issues of how to compute a quota and how to transfer surplus ballots, although these may be critical legal definitions for a close race.

There certainly may be other standards or goals to be achieved by an election system, but majoritarianism and PR are two common objectives, both at the heart of various RCV systems. Other criteria may be important when selecting an electoral system as well. For example, an electoral system may set aside a number of legislative seats for a minority or ethnic group. Elections are also costly in terms of time, effort, and money. If a group of friends is going to lunch, for instance, an elaborate system requiring all the hungry decision-makers to evaluate all possible restaurants seems unnecessary. But a core notion of free and fair elections is that the outcome should be reflective of the collective preferences of the voters. Whether that outcome is expressed as a majority or some other quota, or whether broadly representative of voters overall, are central questions setting the context of decisions about an election.

A Taxonomy of Election Systems

Before focusing on features of RCV, it is useful to see where various forms of RCV fit into a broader set of electoral systems. Political scientist William Riker (1982), in his classic book on decision-making methods, *Liberalism against Populism*, divides decision-making systems into three broad types: majoritarian, positional, and utilitarian. For majoritarian methods of selection, as discussed above, alternatives can be compared effectively in pairs, or two alternatives at a time. If there are more than three alternatives, majoritarian methods search for a Condorcet winner, defined as an alternative that bests every other in pairwise comparisons. A "round robin" tournament is a search for a Condorcet winner. Positional methods comprise most political elections, including plurality and ranked choice systems. Utilitarian decision-making requires an assignment of value or utility to each alternative. Utilitarian methods are at the core of the economic system; any good or service can be assigned a price, a measure of cardinal utility. A consumer who chooses to select an item—or "vote" for the item—in the economic market decides that the value (in utility, minus the price) is greater than other items and makes a purchase. But utilitarian methods do not work well in the political setting.[4]

Each of these systems assumes that a voter could rank order all alternatives in terms of personal preferences in some fashion—which alternative is the best, the second best, and so forth down to the worst. Plurality elections are simple because a voter, theoretically, only needs to decide which option is the best.[5] To evaluate an electoral procedure, a necessary assumption is that voters could rank all candidates and order the preferences into a list or profile. This helped the eighteenth-century intellectual the Marquis de Condorcet to develop the notion of which alternative should win: the one that a majority of voters prefer in each pairwise comparison of every other alternative.

Most political elections are positional in orientation. Plurality elections only require a voter to identify their most preferred outcome, the top preference. RCV presumes voters rank more than the top outcome, identifying their second, third, and other choices as well. At the time Condorcet considered how to construct social choices, so did another French intellectual, Jean-Charles de Borda. He was unpersuaded by Condorcet's method, believing it would seldom lead to practical choices. Yet, Borda believed that rank orderings were an effective way to make social decisions. However, rather than making pairwise comparisons or transferring ballots, Borda assigned points to each ranking, points inversely related to the ranking from first to last.[6] The alternative with the largest sum of points is the winner. This method is now frequently called the Borda count. Thus, the general notion of ranking preferences has a long history. Borda and Condorcet disagreed about who proposed the better method, a quarrel they never fully resolved.[7] But many other observers have discussed the relative merits of differing electoral systems.

Classification of electoral systems has become a cottage industry. Scholars have categorized methods of national parliamentary elections, though it is somewhat difficult to generalize the variety of electoral systems used around the globe. Nearly every electoral constituency makes subtle, and sometimes not so subtle, variations of its own to a broad electoral system type. These differences can be meaningful. Scholars who try to classify electoral systems based on their characteristics are not unlike early researchers in the life sciences who sorted plants and animals into useful categories. Those early intellectuals might be thought of as lumpers or splitters, depending on their tendency to generalize or distinguish.[8] Election scholars may establish broad categories to explain general patterns and develop theoretical expectations (lumpers). Others may want to distinguish applications within an election type and show how this variation in electoral law may influence outcomes (splitters). This chapter starts by lumping election types to establish broad categories of electoral systems; subsequent chapters split among RCV applications to distinguish detailed but important effects of preferential voting systems.

Democracies use many methods to elect representatives to their national parliaments. Electoral system classifications include plurality/majority, PR, mixed majority methods, and other miscellaneous methods. Table 2.1 outlines these broad categories as well as some subcategories and examples of countries that utilize these electoral systems. The table reports data for 199 nations in 2004 (Reynolds, Reilly, and Ellis 2005). Several of these countries have altered their electoral systems since 2004. Much of the world is divided between plurality elections and PR, though many other systems are used cross-nationally. The literature on electoral systems is vast. Some excellent, representative works on cross-national elections and their implications include Rae (1967), Lakeman (1970), Taagepera and Shugart (1989), Lijphart (1990, 1999), Farrell (2001), Norris (2004), Herron, Pekkanen, and Shugart (2018), and Passarelli (2020).

The most common form of electoral system for the world's democratic countries is plurality/majority, though the most frequently used subsystem is list PR. Moreover, a majority of the population living under a democracy uses single-member district plurality (SMDP)/first-past-the-post (FPTP) to select its leaders, but this is deceptive as some of the world's most populous

Table 2.1 Electoral system taxonomy national parliaments

Electoral System Category	Electoral System Type	Country Examples	Brief Description
Plurality/Majority 24%, 43.5%	Single-member district, plurality/first-past-the-post	Canada India United States United Kingdom	Candidate with the most votes win
	Two-round system	France Iran Mali	If no candidate obtains a majority or quota, a second round about the top vote-getters
	RCV/AV	Australia Papua New Guinea	Ranked choice voting, one vote, one candidate elected
	Block Vote	Lebanon Tuvalu	Multiple candidates elected, as many votes as officials elected
	Party Block Vote	Cameroon Singapore	Block vote with votes for a party rather than a candidate
Mixed 15%, 21.7%	Mixed-member proportional (MMP)	Germany Italy Mexico	Two ballots, one for SMDP and one for party list for proportionality
	Parallel	Japan Russia	Two ballots, one for PR and one for other systems
Proportional Representation 36%, 24%	List PR	Brazil Indonesia Spain (Congreso) Turkey	One vote for a political party, candidate selected from a party list
	Single transferable vote (STV)	Ireland Malta	Ranked choice voting, one vote, multiple candidates elected
Other 3%, 0.7%	Single nontransferable vote	Japan (1948–1993) Jordan	One vote, multiple candidates elected
	Limited vote	Gibraltar Spain (Senado)	Multiple votes, but more candidates elected than votes
	Borda count	Nauru	Points are assigned based on rank ordering of candidates

Electoral System Category	Electoral System Type	Country Examples	Brief Description
	Approval voting	None	Voters distinguish candidates which they approve (and do not approve)

Percentages are the number of countries (out of 199) using electoral system, percentage of total population (of all countries). Data are for 2004.
Adapted from Reynolds, Reilly, and Ellis (2005).

democracies such as India and the United States use plurality voting to select members of their national legislatures.[9] Newer democracies tend to adopt some form of list PR. In a list proportional system, voters choose among political parties rather than individual candidates. Each party provides a list of candidates to be selected. List PR has attracted little attention as an electoral system for use in North America.[10]

Mixed-member proportional (MMP) systems typically have components of both plurality/majority election as well as PR. For instance, German voters cast a ballot in a plurality contest within their electoral constituency (Wahlkreis) and a second ballot for a party list of candidates in their state (Land). This system offers both a single member of the Bundestag who represents the district as well as some PR for the state. In addition, the size of the Bundestag may be increased to allow greater proportionality among parties. However, the effects of mixed systems are difficult to generalize (Shugart and Wattenberg 2001, Moser and Scheiner 2012).

Preferential or ranked choice systems fall within three types.[11] First, the alternative vote (AV), or the instant runoff version of RCV, is used for parliamentary elections for the Australian House of Representatives and Papua New Guinea parliament. Second, the STV, the multimember version of RCV, is the electoral system in Ireland and Malta. Third, hybrid systems of preferential voting are used to elect members of the Australian Senate and for members of the Parliament of Nauru. Table A.1 in Appendix A summarizes several important characteristics among common preferential voting systems. In addition, there are other related electoral systems that do not involve transfers of ballots based on preference but that operate under similar goals. These include cumulative voting and approval voting. However, since these voting procedures are used (currently) for subnational systems, a fuller description will appear in Chapter 3.

For many nations, the method of election is uniform across the country. However, if there are multimember districts, the number elected from each district may vary from one region to another. Even for countries with PR, multimember districts are often created. Israel and the Netherlands are rare instances of nations in which the electoral district encompasses the entire country, making proportionality more easily attainable. For list PR systems, key definitional questions involve the threshold or quota, the minimum share of votes needed to guarantee a party's representation. There are several mathematical or legal definitions for determining the quota, as there is no universally accepted standard.

The United States is somewhat unusual from other countries in that the methods used to elect members of the federal Congress are at the discretion of the states, rather than defined by national law, at least so long as they fit within broad constitutional bounds.[12] The American system permits state variations in electoral law, even for members of the US Congress. This allows electoral experimentation, such as those found in Maine and Alaska, Louisiana and Georgia, Washington and California, and so forth. Most democracies, even other federal countries, regulate parliamentary elections at the national level. Many countries implement different electoral systems from the national pattern for regional or state representative bodies.[13]

The discussion above is focused on legislative, or multimember, elections. National executives are selected through a variety of electoral methods as well, although the range is narrower. Not all democracies have an elected president or similar executive. However, among those that do, nearly all national executives are chosen through some form of plurality/majority election. Most are elected in simple plurality elections, although quite a few are elected through a runoff or two-round system. Only two national executives are selected through preferential voting. The president of Ireland is elected through traditional RCV/AV. The chief executive of Sri Lanka is chosen through a modification of RCV sometimes called the contingent vote or, more appropriately, the supplementary vote. Rather than eliminating candidates one at a time from the bottom, only the top two candidates go to an instant runoff. However, the runoff has never been used since all elected presidents received a majority on the first ballot.

Elections in Nauru, a small island nation in the South Pacific, involve a modified Borda count. Using a ballot like that for the Australian House of Representatives, a Nauruan voter must give a unique rank to each and every candidate; otherwise, the ballot is invalid. However, unlike traditional RCV, which involves transfers of ballots from one candidate to another, points are assigned to each candidate based on the preference ordering, the reciprocal of the ranking. A candidate receives one point for each first-place rank, one-half point for second place, one-third point for third place, and so on. Points for each candidate are summed over all voters. Depending on the number of candidates to be elected—two, three, or four from Nauruan districts—the candidates with the most points win. Table 2.2 displays the points accumulated for a Borda and modified Borda ballot. This modified Borda system is named for Desmond Dowdall, the Irish immigrant who became Nauru's justice minister and devised the election method.[14] State legislators in Oklahoma devised a similar system in 1925. Other modified Borda systems were used for seats set aside for ethnic Hungarians and Italians in the parliament of the European nation of Slovenia and are used to narrow the field of candidates for presidential elections in the Pacific islands state of Kiribati.

Although the number of political elections using the Borda count is few, the method is commonly used for other rankings, such as identifying top sports teams and players. For example, American college football team rankings of both the Associated Press Poll (sports writers and broadcasters) and the College Football Coaches Poll use a modified Borda count. Each of the approximately sixty "voters" provides their perceived ordered ranking for the top twenty-five teams or "candidates." For each ballot, twenty-five points are assigned for the top team, twenty-four points for the second-place team,

Table 2.2 Example of a Borda count

Rank (R)	Candidate	Traditional Borda Count	Dowdall Modified Borda
1	A	7	1 = 1.000
2	B	6	1/2 = 0.500
3	C	5	1/3 = 0.333
4	D	4	1/4 = 0.250
5	E	3	1/5 = 0.200
6	F	2	1/6 = 0.167
7	G	1	1/7 = 0.143
All candidates ranked.		Each candidate receives (7+1)-R or (8-R) points	Each candidate receives (1/R) points

and so forth, down to one point for the twenty-fifth-ranked team. The points are accumulated to produce that week's overall ranking. Similarly, the Ballon d'Or, the award sponsored by the magazine *France Football* for the best men's (or women's) footballer or soccer player, also uses a modified Borda count. One hundred journalists in as many countries rank the top five from a shortlist of thirty professional players. Points are assigned in the reverse order (although first place receives six, rather than five points) and accumulated to determine the winner. These are modified Borda systems, however, as all alternatives (sports teams or players) are not fully ranked.

Another social choice method developed by Edward J. Nanson combines both elements of the Borda count and the transfer method of RCV. Nanson, an Australian mathematician, created a procedure that first uses elements from the Borda count. A set of alternatives, the top half, is then reconsidered to find a majority winner. One key advantage is that Nanson's rule satisfies the Condorcet winner criterion: an alternative that beats every other will be selected. As shown above, RCV does not satisfy this fundamental criterion of decision-making.[15] Although Borda methods are excluded from our typology of ranked choice systems, some political practitioners count them among preferential voting. However, there are no vote transfers for Borda or modified Borda methods.

Ranked Voting for National Parliaments

Both primary forms of preferential voting are found in national parliamentary elections. The instant runoff version to elect public officials from single-member districts has been used in Australia and Papua New Guinea since the 2007 election. Fiji also implemented RCV from 1999 to 2006. The prototype for RCV/IRV, or the AV as it is known to comparative election scholars, is the system of election for the House of Representatives in Australia. Each Australian voter marks a paper ballot to create an ordered list among all candidates in their constituency. The election produces one winning candidate who represents that electoral constituency. Papua New Guinea and Fiji (temporarily) adopted the AV from the Australian model.

Single transferable voting is used to select multiple legislative representatives from a single constituency. The Irish electoral system is the archetype for STV. Voters from each electoral district select three, four, or five representatives for the Dáil Éireann, the lower chamber of the Oireachtas, the parliament of Ireland.[16] An Irish voter, however, only has a single vote to cast in the election. Again, the ballot allows an Irish voter to give a rank to every candidate, although that is not required. Since multiple representatives are elected, political parties tend to nominate multiple candidates in each district. After one party candidate is elected, surplus votes can be transferred to another party candidate. A major national party is likely to run the number of candidates equal to the number of members of the Dáil elected from the district. Members of the upper chamber, the Seanad Éireann, are not directly elected.

As each voter casts only one vote and ballots are accumulated and transferred primarily on the basis of party, the STV system is known within Ireland, as well as in the electoral system classification discussed above, as PR. However, unlike in list PR, the election is candidate-centric; that is, voters rank order candidates, though identified by party identification, not political parties directly. As a result, Irish elections are not quite proportional in terms of their outcomes.[17] Certainly, STV allows more proportionality than plurality or majority preferences, as smaller parties may be able to attain representation.

Malta also uses STV as a system of PR. The application of STV is similar to that used in Ireland. Candidates on the ballot are identified with their political party. A voter ranks preferences consecutively on the ballot, and the voter may identify as many or as few ranks as preferred. Five members to the House of Representatives, the Kamra tad-Deputati, are elected from each of the thirteen electoral districts. The Maltese electoral environment is unusual because it is a two-party system. Independents and minor parties compete, but they attract comparatively few votes.[18] Ireland, by contrast, has a multiparty system with several holding seats in the Dáil, although two parties, Fianna Fáil and Fine Gael, predominate. Estonia used STV in the election of 1990 while on the verge of independence, but political leaders did not give the electoral system time to establish roots and switched to a list proportional system.[19]

Australia serves as a model for the discussion of ranked choice elections as each major system is utilized for one chamber of parliament. In Australia, modern voters in an RCV/AV election for the House of Representatives are expected to complete a full ranking of all candidates in sequential order. So, for instance, if there are eight candidates running for a single seat in the Australian House of Representatives, a voter must give each and every candidate a unique number from one to eight. Filling out a complete ballot ordering candidates from one to last would count as a "formal vote" and would be counted in the election. Failing to mark a ballot correctly gives the voter an "informal vote" and the voter's ballot would not be counted.[20] Figure 2.1 gives an example ballot for an Australian preferential election for the House of Representatives. By contrast, in Papua New Guinea, unlike Australia, voters are limited to only their top three rankings.

Elections for the Australian Senate are conducted through STV. In general elections, six senators are elected from each Australian state and two from each territory. For the Senate, the ballot is divided into two sections: an upper section listing political parties and a lower section listing individual candidates by party affiliation. A line divides the upper and lower sections. A voter must choose to complete either the upper, party-based section or the lower, candidate-based section, but not both. Australians refer to this as voting above the line (party) or below the line (candidates). A voter in each state may not need to mark a full ranking. Rather, a ballot must show either six rankings (1 to 6) above the line or twelve rankings (1 to 12) below the line. Figure 2.2 provides an example of a preferential ballot for an Australian Senate election. Ballots for the House of Representatives are printed on green paper; ballots for the Senate are printed on white paper.[21]

Philosophical Origins of RCV

Most nations using RCV to elect members of their parliament adopted a version of RCV following independence from Great Britain: Australia in 1901, Ireland in 1920, and Malta in 1921. Indeed, the notion of preferential voting as a method of electing political representatives from the mass public is British in origin. For Australia, the RCV movement was a reform, but for Ireland and Malta, the method of election was a British import.

The STV emerged in the United Kingdom in the mid-1800s in response to concerns that plurality elections from single-member districts do not produce proportionality and can deny representation for political minorities. In 1859, English barrister Thomas Hare first proposed the electoral scheme in a publication titled *Treatise on Election of Representatives*. Soon thereafter, political philosopher John Stuart Mill, in his influential work *Considerations on Representative Government*, commented on the "perfect feasibility of the scheme." Mill believed that "Mr. Hare's plan [is] among the very greatest improvements yet made in the theory and practice of government," adding that it was "approaching to ideal perfection" for remedying the problems that Mill saw with the electoral system used in Britain. Mill's concern was

RANKED CHOICE VOTING IN THE FAMILY OF ELECTORAL SYSTEMS   37

Figure 2.1 Ballot for Australian House of Representatives.

House of Representatives Ballot for New South Wales (Banks), 2022. To cast a formal ballot, a voter must rank all candidates from 1 to 6. Reproduced from Australian Election Commission.

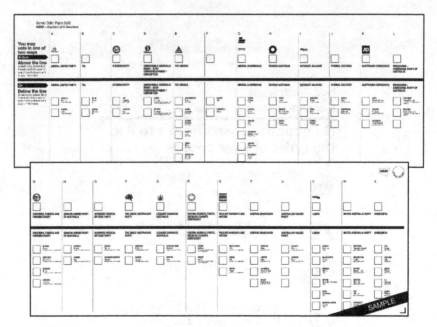

Figure 2.2 Ballot for Australian Senate.

Senate Ballot for New South Wales, 2022. To cast a formal ballot, a voter must complete the ballot either *above the line* (at least six parties in order) or *below the line* (at least twelve candidates in order), but not both. Reproduced from Australian Election Commission.

that political minorities should have a voice in legislative politics and that neither plurality elections nor other reform proposals, such as multimember districts with cumulative voting, could guarantee this. Hare's scheme, on the other hand, had the advantage of giving voters in a broader geographic area "the power of combining with one another to return a representative" even if they found themselves in the minority in the local area (Mill 1862).[22] From Mill's description of Hare's proposal as a method to eliminate geographic divisions, however, the impression is given that all candidates for the entire British parliament would be up for a national election on a single ballot. That idea of an election with thousands of candidates and hundreds elected seems impractical and unrealistic. However, the general idea of multiple MPs elected from larger districts took hold as a platform for political reformers.[23]

Similar electoral systems were proposed in the nineteenth century. Hare's Danish contemporary, Carl Andrae, proposed a similar system. Andrae's method preceded Hare's and was used earlier to elect members of Denmark's parliament after 1855.[24] Although Andrae seems to have invested more time in developing implementation procedures for STV, less attention has been given to Andrae's contribution in the English-speaking world.

Popularized by Mill's writings, the idea of transferable voting took hold in Australia. Among those who borrowed the ideas from Mill and Hare and applied them to smaller constituencies was political reformer Catherine Helen Spence (1861). Spence's proposals were more reasonable than Mill's and were ultimately adopted. Her efforts coincided with those of Tasmanian Attorney General Andrew Inglis Clark and other reformers to introduce PR, first in Tasmania, then in other states, and eventually for preferential voting in Australian federal elections. "Spence's and Clark's work has been the major instance of idealism prevailing in the introduction of an electoral system in Australia," according to Bennett and Lundie (2007, 2). "The more usual motivation for election system change has been political calculation—which could be motivated by a desire to protect or boost one's own position, or to inflict damage upon one's opponents."

The use of the Hare system was proposed for Ireland in the late 1800s when Irish members of the British parliament were pushing for Irish Home Rule. Many saw PR as a way to assure the various factions in Ireland, including the Protestant minority, of a place in a new government. Indeed, Arthur Griffith, founder of the Sinn Féin ("ourselves alone") movement (and later the president of the Free State Government during the Irish Civil War), was an early member of the Proportional Representation Society of Ireland. But it was not until 1919 that Ireland first used the STV for local elections in Sligo. This was followed a year later by its use in local elections throughout Ireland (Sinnott 1996).

Ireland has been using PR for its parliamentary elections since the creation of the constitution of the Irish Free State (Saorstát Éireann) in 1922. The structure of that constitution was subject to the approval of the British government under the terms of the Anglo-Irish Treaty of 1921, and many provisions in the document created a decidedly British-style state (Gallagher 1996). But the requirement for PR met with the approval of both the Irish, who had already begun using the STV as a form of PR, and the British, who sought a way to guarantee a voice for the Protestant minority under the rule of the Irish Free State (Sinnott 1996).

In 1937, when the Irish national leader Eamon de Valera presented a new constitution to Ireland for a vote, it specified that the STV would be the form of PR to be used in all elections for the Dáil (house) and Seanad (senate) of the Oireachtas (parliament). But the system has not been without controversy, and it has been reconsidered twice since then. In 1959, while preparing to step down as Taoiseach (prime minister), de Valera led his party to propose a change to the constitution to abolish the STV in favor of a plurality system, apparently out of the belief that it would be better for his Fianna Fáil political party. The amendment was defeated in a plebiscite by a margin of 48 percent to 52 percent. In 1968, the Fianna Fáil party once again presented the amendment to the electorate, but this time lost by a resounding 39 percent to 61 percent (Sinnott 1996).

The system continues to have its critics. In 1999, a Fianna Fáil member of Dáil proposed that Ireland switch to a dual-ballot electoral system like Germany's, where voters in single-member districts vote for both a party and a local candidate (Coghlan 1999). Although a committee of the Oireachtas held closed meetings on the issue (FitzGerald 2000), several Fianna Fáil backbenchers publicly indicated their opposition to a change (Donohoe 2000). In early 2012, the government cabinet voted to establish a constitutional convention to review certain aspects of the country's 1937 constitution.[25] The convention consisted of thirty-three elected members of the Dáil and Senad, chosen by the parties, plus sixty-six members selected by a polling organization to reflect a cross-section of the Irish public.[26] The convention addressed the topic of the STV system in May 2013 and asked for public input on the convention's website.[27] After considering other possible electoral systems, including the MMP system, the convention voted 79 to 20 in favor of retaining STV.[28] The Irish electorate seems satisfied with STV as a method of election, and it produces both inter- and intra-party competition.

Public opinion in Malta also seems to accept STV as a cultural status quo. Malta has a high level of voter turnout, much higher than Ireland's. The Irish experience of multiparty election fits theoretical expectations of what should happen under STV, while Malta's strong two-party environment is inconsistent with expectations. Australia's more complicated system of preferential voting produces high rates of voter turnout, but Australia also implements compulsory voting. Mandatory voting was introduced in Australia shortly after preferential voting, in 1911 for federal elections and earlier for some Australian states. Papua New Guinea, however, also has high turnout without compulsory voting. In national electorates with preferential voting, the demand did not rise from the public. Thus, there seems to be no natural institutional companion to the adoption of STV. As Homeshaw (2001, 96) summarizes after a review of the origins of ranked voting in Australia, Ireland, and Malta, "STV was an idea that emerged not from the people, but from liberals squeezed between conservative elites and the enfranchised masses."

Mathematical Problems with RCV

Before we proceed to movements for RCV in the United States, it is worth noting that some theoretical problems with instant runoff and the STV may hinder their acceptability by some. Of course, neither plurality voting nor RCV resolves the problem of Condorcet cycling, when one alternative is beaten by another. As in the example of three candidates, Jane, Kate, and Luke, where J>K>L>J ..., all social choice mechanisms fail to select a satisfactory alternative. This situation is somewhat analogous to a three-way tie; no single alternative is perceived better by a majority of voters than some other. No electoral system will resolve this situation.[29]

Ranked choice elections, however, can produce worse social outcomes. Consider five friends who make a collective decision about what healthy vegetable to serve for the evening meal. As shown in Table 2.3, their possible choices are Asparagus, Broccoli, or Cauliflower. Like voters in an election, we will preserve the friends' anonymity by assigning them numbers for identification. The friends' preferences for the three vegetables are shown in the table. No single alternative receives a majority vote, though both Broccoli and Cauliflower receive two votes each. For our instant runoff, friend 3 is decisive. Her vote is transferred from her first choice, Asparagus (which is dropped after the first round of voting), to her second choice, Broccoli. By

Table 2.3 Vegetable choice among five friends

Person	1st	2nd	3rd
1	Broccoli	Asparagus	Cauliflower
2	Cauliflower	Asparagus	Broccoli
3	Asparagus	Broccoli	Cauliflower
4	Broccoli	Asparagus	Cauliflower
5	Cauliflower	Asparagus	Broccoli

First round, Asparagus 1, Broccoli 2, Cauliflower 2: Asparagus is dropped.
Second round: Broccoli 3, Cauliflower 2: Cauliflower dropped; *Broccoli wins.*

a 3–2 vote in the second round, Broccoli becomes the socially approved vegetable. However, Asparagus is the Condorcet winner. Asparagus beats Broccoli, the RCV winner, by a 3–2 vote as well as beating Cauliflower by a 3–2 vote. Asparagus, universally the first or second choice of all the hungry voters, is eliminated early. If the friends' meal was culinarily divisive, Asparagus would seem the better option. Generally, the majority winner from RCV may be artificially produced by the order of instant runoffs—the order candidates are eliminated—and not simply by the preferences of the voters. On the other hand, RCV/IRV cannot select a Condorcet loser—that is, an alternative that loses to every alternative—as it would lose in the final round.[30]

This simple example, however, also shows that RCV is not immune to strategic or tactical voting.[31] If voters express their ranked preferences tactically, they may be able to find a different, perhaps even better (for them) outcome. In the five-friends example, a particularly Broccoli-loathing voter #5 could change the outcome by marking her ballot as A>C>B rather than C>A> B. In doing so, her favorite veggie, Cauliflower, loses in the first round. However, the otherwise likely winner Broccoli would be paired with Asparagus in the second round, and Asparagus would win 3–2.[32] In this example, tactical or strategic voting leads to the consensus (Condorcet) winner; however, strategic voting could also cause a consensus candidate to lose in an early round.

Sometimes RCV is promoted because the requirement for a majority can eliminate a highly divisive individual who has a sizeable following, but not enough support to constitute a majority. This is certainly possible. However, RCV can also produce the opposite effect. In fact, it can prevent the election of a widely accepted second choice (such as Asparagus in the example above) in an otherwise fractured political environment (imagine if Cauliflower and Broccoli were seen as polarizing extremes).

Numerous social scientists have also identified other various flaws of RCV. Doron (1979b) has observed that it fails the reduction principle. That is, the elimination of a *losing* candidate who is Pareto-dominated, or universally preferred, by a winning candidate can turn the winning candidate's victory into a loss. Doron and Kronick (1977) label the STV "perverse" because it allows a candidate to lose by acquiring *more* votes; this is possible because acquiring more votes can change the order in which candidates are eliminated. Ranked choice systems violate monotonicity; that is, candidates can lose an election when voters place them *higher* on their order of preferences, or vice versa (Doron 1979a, Riker 1982, Miller 2017). A monotonic relationship seems like an appropriate standard here. As an alternative receives more support, the alternative should perform the same or progressively better, not worse. Plurality election is clearly monotonic; attracting a greater share of the votes will not cause a candidate to do worse. Potthoff (2023) identifies several associated issues with ranked choice decision-making.

A simple example shows how RCV may violate monotonicity when only one candidate is selected from a field of three candidates: Collier, Mendenhall, and Williams. The preference orderings of seventeen voters are provided in Tables 2.4a and 2.4b. In the first count, Williams garners six votes, Mendenhall six, and Collier five votes. Candidate Collier is eliminated because he has the fewest votes. The ballots of those who most preferred Collier are now transferred to their second choice, adding three votes for Williams and two for Mendenhall. Thus, candidate Williams wins on the second count with a 9–8 vote, and Williams is elected.

However, consider the revised scenario if two of the voters who most prefer Mendenhall decide to throw their support for the presumed winner, Williams. These two voters switch their rankings from Mendenhall > Williams > Collier to Williams > Mendenhall > Collier, so Williams has even more first-place votes than in the initial scenario. Although these two voters increased the margin for the former winner, their actions caused Williams to lose the election. In the revised first count, Williams receives eight votes, but less than the quota, the required majority of nine. Collier retains five votes, but Mendenhall has only four. In this revised set of ballots, Mendenhall is eliminated after the first round. Candidate Mendenhall's votes are transferred to Collier, however, giving him a total of nine votes. So, increasing the relative support for Williams, the previous winner, causes Williams to lose and Collier to get elected.

There is some debate among scholars about the likelihood of a nonmonotonic outcome in a "real-world" situation. Some observers, such as Douglas Amy (2000) and RCV advocates, believe the likelihood of nonmonotonicity in actual elections is small. Indeed, Plassman and Tideman (2014) and Graham-Squire and Zayatz (2020) suggest that only about 1 percent of elections are subject to the monotonicity problem, although these empirical calculations also include noncompetitive elections. However, political scientist Joseph Ornstein and mathematician Robert Norman (2014) created a model

Table 2.4a Violation of monotonicity three alternatives, seventeen voters: Original initial preferences of all voters

	Preference		
Voter	1st	2nd	3rd
1	Williams	Mendenhall	Collier
2	Williams	Mendenhall	Collier
3	Williams	Mendenhall	Collier
4	Williams	Collier	Mendenhall
5	Williams	Collier	Mendenhall
6	Williams	Collier	Mendenhall
7	Mendenhall	Williams	Collier
8	Mendenhall	Williams	Collier
9	Mendenhall	Collier	Williams
10	Mendenhall	Collier	Williams
11	Mendenhall	Collier	Williams
12	Mendenhall	Collier	Williams
13	Collier	Williams	Mendenhall
14	Collier	Williams	Mendenhall
15	Collier	Williams	Mendenhall
16	Collier	Mendenhall	Williams
17	Collier	Mendenhall	Williams

First count: Williams 6, Mendenhall 6, Collier 5 → Collier dropped.
Second count: Williams 9, Mendenhall 8 → Mendenhall dropped, *Williams wins.*

of a three-person election and concluded that nonmonotonicity would likely occur in at least 15 percent of such elections. Political scientist Nicholas Miller (2017) also examined three-candidate races and determined that the likelihood of monotonicity failure ranges from "quite common" to "very substantial" in close contests. Of course, the rationale for RCV exists fully for close elections; plurality elections—and other systems—likewise work fine in lopsided election outcomes.[33]

This logical inconsistency of nonmonotonicity is not simply theoretical. For example, the 2009 election for mayor of Burlington, Vermont, included five candidates on the ballot. Three candidates each received over 20 percent of the votes in the election, and no candidate received a majority. Republican Kurt Wright led the field on the first ballot with almost 33 percent of the vote. Second place went to Vermont Progressive Party candidate and incumbent Mayor Bob Kiss with 29 percent, followed by Democrat Andy Montroll with 23 percent and independent Dan Smith with 14.5 percent. Kiss was the

Table 2.4b Violation of monotonicity three alternatives, seventeen voters: Revised two preference reversals, voters 7 and 8

	Preference		
Voter	1st	2nd	3rd
1	Williams	Mendenhall	Collier
2	Williams	Mendenhall	Collier
3	Williams	Mendenhall	Collier
4	Williams	Collier	Mendenhall
5	Williams	Collier	Mendenhall
6	Williams	Collier	Mendenhall
7	*Williams*	*Mendenhall*	*Collier*
8	*Williams*	*Mendenhall*	*Collier*
9	Mendenhall	Collier	Williams
10	Mendenhall	Collier	Williams
11	Mendenhall	Collier	Williams
12	Mendenhall	Collier	Williams
13	Collier	Williams	Mendenhall
14	Collier	Williams	Mendenhall
15	Collier	Williams	Mendenhall
16	Collier	Mendenhall	Williams
17	Collier	Mendenhall	Williams

First count: Williams 8, Collier 5, Mendenhall 4 → Mendenhall dropped.
Second count: Collier 9, Williams 8 → Williams dropped, *Collier wins*.

incumbent mayor, and both Wright and Montroll were city councilors, so all seemed reasonably well known by municipal voters. Wright would have been elected under a plurality vote. In the instant runoff, as RCV was called at the time, two rounds of vote transfers were made (see Table 2.5 for the RCV outcome). First, ballots of voters who preferred Smith and a scattering of others were transferred to second choices. No candidate received a majority, so votes for Montroll were transferred to either Wright or Kiss. Following this second round of transfers, that is, in the third round of balloting, Kiss received a narrow margin over Wright, 51.5 percent to 48.5 percent, and was elected mayor.

Examination of the voters' actual ballots, however, reveals that Kiss only received a majority among ballots remaining in the final round, not of citizens casting votes overall. He received a majority of the remaining 8,374 votes when paired with Wright; however, he did *not* receive a majority of the original 8,976 votes expressing a first preference. Wright, if no voters

Table 2.5 Mayoral election in Burlington, Vermont, 2009

Candidate	Round 1	Round 2	Round 3
Kurt Wright (Republican)	2,951	3,294	4,061
Bob Kiss (Progressive)	2,585	3,294	4,313 ✓
Andy Montroll (Democrat)	2,063	2,554	
Dan Smith (Independent)	1,306		
James Simpson (Green)	35		
Write-ins	36		

changed their behavior, should presumably have lost to Kiss in a typical runoff election. But this example shows that the objective of majoritarian winners has a somewhat arbitrary definition. RCV may produce a majority winner only for the final round, after some voters' ballots are dropped in the transfer process, omitting those voters from the decision process. However, the 2009 Burlington mayoral election is also an example of three conditions for fair decision-making: first, failure to select a Condorcet winner, that is, a universally preferred alternative; second, violation of the monotonicity criterion; and third, a paradox raising questions of the method generally.[34]

First, analysis of ballots cast raised questions about whether this election outcome truly represented the will of Burlington voters. Assuming voters represent their preferences sincerely, an analysis of ballots suggests that neither Wright nor Kiss, the two leading candidates, had a majority of support among the three leading candidates. Instead, the candidate who came in third, Montroll, bested both Wright and Kiss in pairwise comparisons. Montroll was the Condorcet winner, preferred by voters over each and every candidate, but lost the RCV election. This outcome results from dropping Montroll in the third round due to fewer first-place rankings than the other two candidates. Voters frequently ranked Montroll second, or in between Kiss and Wright, and that order caused him to lose the election. Wright would win a plurality election, Kiss would win a runoff and the RCV election, and Montroll would win almost any other type of electoral system (Laatu and Smith 2009).

Second, small shifts in recorded preferences could alter the RCV outcome. Ornstein and Norman (2014) showed that if Republican voters who ranked the Progressive candidate second actually marked their ballots for the Progressive first, the Democrat would win. An upward shift of support for the winner by 750 voters (out of approximately 9,000) in this contest would have caused the winner to lose. They demonstrate that this possibility is reasonable given the evidence from marked ballots, although Burlington voters were not required to rank all candidates.[35] Ornstein and Norman, like Miller (2017), find that the likelihood of a violation of monotonicity increases substantially as the competition among the top three candidates increases.

Third, the Burlington election is an example of the no-show paradox. The supporters of the Republican Wright, who ranked the Democrat Montroll second, would have been more satisfied with the outcome if they had not voted at all. Because of the circumstances discussed above, Montroll would have defeated Kiss in a pairwise or head-to-head contest. If 900 or so fewer Wright voters turned out to vote, then Kiss and Montroll would meet in the final round, causing Kiss to lose. Thus, supporters of Wright would be more satisfied with the outcome if they had not voted, contrary to the expectation that citizens are better off participating in the election.[36]

RCV has some inherent difficulties in application, though, to be clear, so do plurality elections, runoffs, and PR. The key for political leaders is to make trade-offs to best reflect voter preferences. Australia, Ireland, and Malta have discovered a system that works well for those polities. But there also have been decades of relative stability and support for those electoral systems. There is also a lengthy history of RCV in North America, which, like the Burlington, Vermont, case study, reflects more volatility.

3
Local Elections and Ranked Choice

A number of communities in North America have adopted or considered preferential voting systems in recent years. Abandoning the traditional labels of election scholars, single transferable vote (STV) or alternative vote (AV), the proposed electoral systems carry the names of proportional representation (PR), instant runoff voting (IRV), or ranked choice voting (RCV). There have been several waves of electoral system reform involving some form of preferential voting. The first coincided with the Progressive movement near the beginning of the twentieth century. These early reforms typically involved the STV or something closer to PR. This Progressive wave also washed across Canadian municipalities and provinces, as some adopted a form of the AV and some STV. For most cities, support for preferential voting ebbed after a few elections, but other cities implemented STV/PR through the late 1940s. One town adopting STV in this wave, Cambridge, Massachusetts, continues to use STV for local elections.

More recently, pressure to adopt "instant runoff voting" or IRV returned at the beginning of the twenty-first century. This electoral reform movement was revitalized when San Francisco adopted preferential voting for mayor and other elected city officials in 2002 (holding its first election in 2004). Oakland and a few other cities in California and elsewhere followed. A few municipalities abandoned preferential voting after one or two elections. The electoral reform movement was revitalized under a new label, "ranked choice voting" or RCV, although this was more a repackaging of IRV rather than a real change. Minneapolis, followed by its sister city St. Paul, adopted RCV for mayor and city council seats. Minneapolis also began using something akin to STV for its election of park and recreation commissioners and members of the Board of Estimate and Taxation. Portland, Maine, and other municipalities in Colorado, Maryland, and other states have used RCV. Many of the early adopters were municipalities with home rule, so cities chose to begin preferential elections under their own charter. A more recent trend is for states to approve RCV for localities, giving cities the option to adopt the electoral system.

Ranked Choice Voting. James W. Endersby and Michael J. Towle, Oxford University Press.
© Oxford University Press (2025). DOI: 10.1093/9780197798959.003.0004

Most of these municipal RCV elections are nonpartisan. Cities may have factions or socioeconomic groups that influence outcomes, but most of the candidates for these RCV elections have no party label on the ballot. State or provincial elections with RCV (considered in Chapter 4) have been uniformly partisan.[1]

Proportional Representation and Preferential Voting in the Twentieth Century

The Progressive movement swept across the United States and Canada in the late nineteenth and early twentieth centuries, bringing in numerous political reforms. The Hare system was a small part of that movement, although it was generally called PR. The particular variations implemented were versions of the STV. These efforts at ranking preferences were one component of a broader platform of governmental reforms, including an emphasis on municipal home rule, ballot propositions to increase citizen control of local government, and general efforts to reduce the power and growth of political machines (see Santucci 2022 for an extensive discussion). In addition, academics and practitioners created the Proportional Representation League (the Proportional Representation Society in Canada) to provide information and lobby for political reform and, in particular, municipal adoption of the Hare system (Hoag and Hallett 1926). From the onset, both scholars and practitioners were divided on the goals of PR. For some, PR was a means to produce a voice for minority groups—ethnic, religious, ideological, and so forth. Broader representation of interests would weaken political machines and improve local governance (Moley 1918). For others, the goals of PR were unrealistic as people (both politicians and the general public) hold preferences that are recognizably multidimensional. Moreover, STV/PR would lead to choices based on personality and charisma rather than competence, contrary to the goals of the broader movement (James 1916).

A similar electoral system was also introduced by Attorney James W. Bucklin. Following progressive electoral success, Colorado voters approved a constitutional amendment allowing municipalities to create home rule charters.[2] Bucklin's charter proposal for commission government in Grand Junction, adopted in 1909, included elections that allowed voters to register first and second (and other) preferences on the ballot.[3] A candidate receiving a majority of the first preferences would be elected on the first count. However, if no candidate received a majority, then second preferences marked on the ballot would be added to the original to determine the winner. A subsequent round could continue with marked preferences lower than second if no candidate received a majority of valid votes. Bucklin voting can be and was used for single-member and multimember elections.

The key difference between RCV and Bucklin voting is whether ballot preferences are transferred (from sequential, losing candidates, RCV) or accumulated (as lower rankings are added, Bucklin). From an election administration perspective, computation of winners is easier under Bucklin than RCV as it involves total votes, not recalculation from individual ballots. It is worth noting that Bucklin's original Grand Junction plan did involve dropping the lowest candidate in the first round if no candidate received a majority, and the lowest again after the second round. Thus, the method is nearer to RCV than most modern commentators recognize. The list of purported advantages resembles those claimed for RCV today (Bucklin 1911: 90–91). Although voters record a preference order on the ballot, Bucklin voting is not ranked choice. However, then as now, election observers often muddle Bucklin voting and RCV, as both require voters to rank preferences among candidates on the ballot, and second (and subsequent) preferences can be taken into account when there is no immediate majority winner.

The Bucklin method was first used for municipal elections in Grand Junction, Colorado, in 1909. Since the Bucklin or Grand Junction method involves both recording of voter preferences and an instant runoff, Bucklin voting became a popular alternative in many cities for a brief time. Over sixty municipalities in Colorado, New Jersey, Ohio, Washington, Oregon, and elsewhere adopted this electoral system.[4] Generally, state courts upheld the Bucklin method, although the Minnesota Supreme Court declared preferential (Bucklin) voting as used in Duluth to be in conflict with the state constitution.[5] Bucklin voting ultimately failed to meet most standards of reformists. There was no proportional element, and it did not break urban political machines. The number of votes cast, in elections with no majority winner, often exceeds the number of ballots cast, creating confusion.[6] Moreover, many voters soon realized that the aggregation of second (and subsequent) preferences essentially canceled out their first preference in close races, as their votes might count for both first- and second-place candidates.[7]

Bucklin voting is still used in the United States today. In 1913, the nation's central banking system, the Federal Reserve System, was created during the period when Bucklin voting was a popular political reform. Directors for each of the twelve Federal Reserve Banks are elected through Bucklin voting, although the Federal Reserve Act of 1913 refers to this method simply as a "preferential ballot." This selection method remains unchanged.[8]

Is the Bucklin method preferential voting? Certainly, it was described as such, but Bucklin does not fall strictly within the taxonomy of RCV. Electoral scholars generally do not consider the method within the RCV family, as ballot preferences are aggregated rather than transferred.[9] However, from an individual voter's perspective, the ballot looks similar to ranked choice, nearly identical when compared to the supplementary vote and to the context of RCV applied in the contemporary setting of many American cities. As noted earlier, the real difference in the electoral systems is not about casting of ballots but in the post-election counting of votes. Even informed political observers have difficulty distinguishing between Bucklin and RCV/IRV.[10] For instance, an Oregon constitutional amendment adopted in 1908 permitted "equal proportion representation" for multimember elections allowing voter "expression of his first, second or additional choices among the candidates for any office." In Portland, Oregon, and other communities, the implementation was Bucklin voting, not the RCV/STV version of PR.[11] However, the Bucklin experience served as an important historical transition between plurality district voting and STV–PR for many communities.

The first American city to implement the STV version of PR was Ashtabula, Ohio, in 1915 (Hatton 1916, Boynton 1917, Harris 1930). From there, other municipalities, also flexing their independence with home rule, experimented with a form of RCV to elect city councils with the goal of achieving PR. Next came Boulder, Colorado; Kalamazoo, Michigan; West Hartford, Connecticut; Sacramento, California; and a number of cities in Ohio, including Cleveland, Cincinnati, and Toledo. Table 3.1 provides a list of some known early RCV reform adopters.[12]

Cincinnati proved a model as the "best-governed city" in the United States, based on its adoption of STV/PR. Characterized from the 1890s as corrupt and inefficient under the control of the Cox-Hynicka political machine, the 1924 adoption of a new charter with electoral reform transformed the city. The subsequent election led to a bipartisan council supporting and instituting reforms extending from the new charter. Charles P. Taft, who had not particularly favored the electoral system at the time of its adoption, took the view that "proportional representation is the most important single element in the success of good government in the city and must

Table 3.1 Municipalities in the United States with preferential voting systems

Municipality	Adoption (Elections)	Reason Ended
Ashtabula, OH	1915–1929 (8)	Charter amendment
Boulder, CO	1917–1947	Referendum
Cambridge, MA	1940–present	
Cincinnati, OH	1924–1956 (16)	Referendum
Cleveland, OH	1921–1931 (5)	Charter referendum*
Coos Bay, OR	1946 (1)	Referendum
Duluth, MN	1915 (1)	State court decision and subsequent legislative statute (Bucklin)
Hamilton, OH	1926–1960 (4+)	Referendum
Hopkins, MN	1948–1961	Referendum
Kalamazoo, MI	1918–1919 (2)	State courts ruled unconstitutional
Long Beach, NY	1943–1947 (2)	Referendum
Lowell, MA	1941–1957	Referendum
Marquette, MI	1922?–1932?	(Nanson Method)
Marshfield, OR	1944 (?)	Referendum
Medford, MA	1950–1952	Referendum
New York, NY	1936–1941, 1949	Referendum (Limited Vote)
Norris, TN	1936–1947 (?)	Referendum
Oak Ridge, TN	1948–1957	Referendum
Quincy, MA	1950–1952	Referendum
Revere, MA	1947–1951	Referendum
Sacramento, CA	1920–1921 (1)	Legislative statute prohibited
Saugus, MA	1947–1951	Referendum
Toledo, OH	1934–1949 (8)	Referendum
Wakefield, MI	1924–1926 (?)	(Nanson Method)
West Hartford, CT	1921–1922 (1)	State courts ruled unconstitutional
Wheeling, WV	1935–1951	Referendum
Worcester, MA	1950–1960	Referendum
Yonkers, NY	1939–1948	Referendum

*A subsequent county referendum in Cuyahoga County was judged unconstitutional by the Ohio courts on technical grounds.

Sources: Hoag and Hallett (1926), Hallett and Hoag (1940), Kneier (1947), Weaver (1986), Santucci (2017) original information. The table excludes approximately sixty cities using the Bucklin method and several cities using cumulative voting.

be preserved at all costs."[13] Generally, it is less clear whether the electoral system or simply political activism from a majority of voters was responsible for reform success.[14] However, Cincinnati served as a paragon for other municipalities.

The city with the largest population to use STV/PR in this early phase was Cleveland, then the nation's fifth-largest city. Cleveland's STV elections, however, were not at-large or citywide. For STV to produce outcomes akin to proportional, the entire electorate should be in a single constituency with a large number of representatives selected at large. Cincinnati worked this way, electing nine council members. However, in Cleveland, twenty-five members of the city council were elected through four districts of five, six, or seven members. The small community of West Hartford likewise elected fifteen members from four districts. Boulder had a council of nine but only elected three members for six-year terms in each election.[15] If PR is a primary goal, then division into districts undercuts the ability to achieve success. Moreover, the focus on civic welfare across the entire constituency, rather than divisions over local interests, may be an important factor of representation and reform.[16] Cleveland's experience with STV/PR was less successful at curbing corruption. At the time of its demise in 1931, advocates of charter repeal argued that PR in Cleveland actually contributed to the development of political bosses, cronyism, and the loss of voter representation in city government.[17]

There were roughly as many municipalities in the United States that considered adopting some form of STV or PR and rejected it.[18] Moreover, most adopting cities experimented with the new system of election and abandoned STV after a few election cycles. Cincinnati's implementation seemed successful at countering machine politics and boss rule, but other cities were less successful in the implementation. For instance, in Ashtabula, the Ohio city first to adopt its version of PR, a majority of voters rejected the electoral reform at a subsequent charter amendment election. Some state courts rejected STV as an unconstitutional reach of home rule.[19] Some state courts rejected STV/PR as violating state constitutions, and others sustained it.[20] The Michigan courts judged STV/PR elections in Kalamazoo as a violation of the constitutional right for a voter to select all officers elected from a geographical district.[21] In other states, legislatures prohibited local government adoption of STV, as in California.

Evaluations of municipal experience with STV/PR in the early twentieth century were enthusiastic but mixed in terms of achievements of objectives.

First, it was difficult to disentangle the influence of electoral system change along with other factors embedded within the Progressive Era reforms such as home rule, city manager government, and an emphasis on improved municipal administration. The effects of STV/PR on voter turnout, in particular, were difficult to ascertain. Although voter participation increased in many initial elections, turnout fluctuated over time. In some locations, such as Toledo, turnout consistently declined.[22] Likewise, this era saw a number of reforms related to registration and ballot design; these changes arguably affected rates of voter participation.[23] While diversity among elected officials generally increased, particularly in terms of representation of women and large ethnic minorities, proportionality in group representation was generally not attained. The number of candidates contesting an election did not increase as expected.[24] A common complaint was the large number of spoiled ballots.[25] Other criticisms were that a substantial number of candidates were elected without reaching the assigned quota and that a number of voters' ballots were nontransferable.[26] On the other hand, fewer voters could claim a wasted vote, as more ballots counted toward ultimate winners. However, which candidate received a vote from a particular voter was opaque.[27] Columbia University Professor Raymond Moley (1923: 669), an electoral reform proponent, concluded that the STV/PR electoral experience in Cleveland reveals "the need of a careful revision of the too extravagant claims of its supporters."

Electoral reform went beyond traditional STV. Two cities in the upper peninsula of Michigan, Marquette and Wakefield, implemented a version of Nanson's method.[28] This electoral system, devised by Australian scholar E.J. Nanson, involves a combination of methods devised by Borda and Hare, an intersection of Bucklin and traditional RCV.[29] If no candidate receives a majority, Nanson's method, as applied in Michigan, involves elimination of candidates, though not in the same manner as RCV. Candidates eliminated are those who could not obtain a majority, that is, Condorcet losers. However, rather than a strict transfer, preferences below the first are weighted and aggregated. A voter's recorded second preference is weighted as one-half vote. If the decision goes to a third round, the third preference is weighted as one-third of a vote. If no majority winner can be found, the alternative with the highest number of weighted votes is selected.[30]

The movement for political reform hit western Canada as well. As noted by Harris (1930: 30), preferential voting in some form was "adopted by practically all of the cities in the western provinces of Canada." The Progressive movement was associated with farmers' political activity and included PR as a component of an overall platform for change.[31] As shown in Table 3.2, municipalities adopting STV ranged from rural towns to urban areas such as Vancouver, Edmonton, and Regina. For most communities, the experiment with RCV lasted for only a few elections, and the cities returned to plurality or block voting[32] by the end of the decade of the 1920s. This is similar to the experience of municipalities in the United States. However, a couple of large cities maintained the method into the early 1970s, only then returning to the more traditional plurality election. In Calgary, Alberta, the entire city was one district, and city councilors were chosen through STV. This system lasted until 1961, when single-member districts were drawn and city council members were elected using IRV/AV through 1971. Civic leaders in Winnipeg, Manitoba, also turned to STV as a method to resolve labor unrest

Table 3.2 Municipalities in western Canada with preferential voting systems

Province	Municipality	Elections
Alberta	Calgary	1917–1971
	Edmonton	1923–1927 (5)
	Lethbridge	1928
British Columbia	Mission City	(1917–1921)
	Nelson	1918
	New Westminster	1918
	Port Coquitlam	(1917–1919)
	South Vancouver	1918–1928
	Vancouver	1921–1923 (3)
	Victoria	1921
	West Vancouver	1918–1930
Manitoba	St. Boniface	none?
	St. James	1923–
	Winnipeg	1920–1970
Ontario	London	2018
Saskatchewan	Moose Jaw	1921–1924
	North Battleford	1921–1924
	Regina	1921–1925
	Saskatoon	1921–1926

Sources: Hoag and Hallett (1926), Pilon (1996), Johnston and Koene (2000), original information.

and class conflict (see Johnston and Koene 2000 for an excellent history of regional adoption and repeal of STV).

Cambridge: The Single Single Transferable Vote City

For one city, the adoption of ranked choice elections extended well beyond the decades of the early twentieth century. In 1938, the Massachusetts legislature allowed municipalities to elect town councils and school committees through at-large elections with PR or other public officials through preferential voting.[33] Cambridge, across the Charles River from Boston, proposed adoption of this "Plan E" method of municipal governance: a city manager form of government with the STV for its municipal elections. However, the initial proposition was defeated by voters that November. A new ballot question appeared on the ballot in 1940, and this time Cantabrigians voted in favor of passage. The first STV municipal election in Cambridge occurred in 1941. Elections for nine seats on the city council and six seats on the school committee have been held in November of each odd-numbered year since. Voters subsequently rejected proposed repeals of STV in at least five elections.

The Cambridge form of STV has become a municipal prototype of this electoral system. Municipal elections in Cambridge are nonpartisan, unlike national STV elections in Ireland and Malta. However, the nonpartisan nature of elections does not prevent the development of factions or slates in city politics. Many candidates coalesce around a slate, although the cleavages are more fluid over time. Nevertheless, this distinguishes the Cambridge experience from that of the Irish and the Maltese; it is unclear whether results are proportional and what is represented by election outcomes. Certainly, elected officials in Cambridge have traditionally reflected greater diversity than in surrounding communities, but it is less clear whether that is due to the city's unique culture or produced by the electoral system.

The reallocation of ballots in Cambridge, or in any STV system electing multiple candidates, is complex. In the traditional single-winner IRV election, candidates with the lowest number of votes are dropped sequentially, and ballots for each losing candidate are reassigned to the next remaining candidate in the voter's preference order. That process (setting aside, for now, difficulties voters may have in completing a ballot accurately) is relatively straightforward. However, for a multimember election, such as in

Cambridge, excess votes are also transferred from winning candidates who attracted more voters than needed for an election. The number of these excess or surplus votes is the difference between the quota, the predetermined minimum necessary for election, and the number of votes a candidate holds during the round the candidate exceeds the quota.[34] In Cambridge, the quota is determined by taking the total votes cast and dividing by one more than the number of officials elected: ten for the city council (9 + 1) and seven for the school committee (6 + 1), then adding one vote.[35]

The complication is *which* surplus votes to transfer. Since voters may rank candidates any way they like, transferring surplus ballots through different methods may influence the ultimate outcome. Of course, a core element in fair elections is that voter preferences should determine election winners, not different ways of tabulating (transferring) ballots. Transferring a surplus from the top or bottom of the pile, for instance, presumably transfers ballots that differ systematically in terms of the next preferences of voters. Thus, different winners could result. With modern computing technology, it might be possible to transfer fractional ballots in a consistent manner. However, even that process becomes additionally complicated as multiple winners are determined through subsequent rounds and surplus ballots are transferred multiple times.[36] Most voters seem unaware or confused about the transfer process, particularly of surplus votes.

The city of Cambridge is constrained to a transfer method authorized by Massachusetts law. Massachusetts statutes restrict municipal elections to PR methods that were used in a US city on January 1, 1938.[37] Cambridge opted for the transfer procedure generally known as the "Cincinnati method" as it was used in that Ohio city.[38] Ballots are numbered sequentially, and a skip number is computed based on the number of votes for the winning candidate and the surplus voters.[39] A systematic random sample of ballots is transferred from the winning candidate to the next ranked, viable candidate. For example, if the skip number is 6, then the 12th, the 18th, the 24th, and so forth, ballots are chosen to transfer excess votes to the next preference for a viable candidate on that ballot. Cambridge conducts a random draw of precincts prior to the election in order to facilitate the transfer of surplus votes. During each round of the counting process, surplus votes from winning candidates are transferred to other candidates still in the running. After that, each ballot for the candidate with the fewest votes in that round is transferred to the voter's next viable preference on the ballot.[40] This order repeats (surplus votes from winners first, then dropping the bottom candidate if there are no surplus votes) until winners for all seats on the multimember commission are determined. It is possible that a candidate could be elected without reaching the quota if no additional candidates can be dropped without leaving vacant seats.[41] The idea, from the Progressive Era forward, is that a more representative group of politicians would lead the city after the election.

Although the discussion here has focused on municipalities, other local governments also use STV to elect representatives. As a result of a 1969 New York legislative decentralization plan, a Board of Education and thirty-two community school boards were established with control of New York City public schools. The community school boards, each with nine elected members, held authority over elementary and middle schools. The nine members of each school board were elected for three-year terms using STV. A 2003 reorganization plan eliminated the elected community school boards, thus the PR elections. The STV elections were characterized by low voter turnout, due in part to difficult demands on voters to evaluate and rank a long list of candidates. The tabulation process of counting and transferring votes was difficult. Moreover, there is some evidence that the community school boards were often captured by organizations seeking control of school decisions. Nevertheless, the elections led to a greater breadth of interests represented in school governance. The representation of women and ethnic minorities was enhanced (Weaver and Baum 1992).

The Twenty-First Century RCV Adoption Rollercoaster for Local Elections

The next RCV wave hit American cities in the early twenty-first century. The twentieth-century wave emphasized PR and government reform through the STV. This second surge emphasized majority winners in single district elections with the AV or, as initially packaged by reformers, the IRV. This contemporary movement is distinct from its predecessor. It is worth noting that advocates of PR in the last century explicitly rejected this more modern form of RCV. Clarence Hoag, secretary of the American Proportional Representation League, lumped Bucklin and IRV/AV together as undesirable electoral systems. Hoag's rationale was that both methods were "defective" as each "may drop out a candidate preferred by a majority of the voters to any other one of the candidates taken out singly."[42] Part of the original motivation for election reform was PR (Richie and Hill 1999), and that continued with reforms such as for New York public school elections.[43] However, by the end of the twentieth century, the focus of the reform movement was on creating majorities in single-member districts rather than PR.[44]

This second IRV wave flowed into more liberal, or progressive in the modern sense, cities and spread to other localities. San Francisco, California, was the first to adopt preferential voting for the mayor, council, and other elected public officials in 2002. Public dissatisfaction with the city government led many San Francisco residents to feel that politics as usual was ripe for change (Gallagher 2000, McDaniel 2016). Burlington, Vermont, in the case study described earlier, followed in 2006. The North Carolina legislature established an opportunity for cities to experiment with RCV in 2007. Takoma Park, Maryland, headquarters of the preferential voting advocacy group FairVote, also adopted IRV. Communities in central Colorado followed. Pierce County, Washington, the Tacoma area, experimented with RCV in 2009. Minneapolis, Minnesota, adopted RCV elections by 2009 for both single-winner elections (mayor, city council seats) and multimember contests (for tax and park boards). Other California cities in the Bay Area, including Oakland, Berkeley, and San Leandro, held RCV elections in 2010. St. Paul, Minnesota, and Portland, Maine, followed with RCV elections in 2011. Other cities already have or plan to join the RCV bandwagon. An empirical analysis of these cities' experiences with RCV follows in Chapter 6.

The growth in public interest in RCV is explained in part by grassroots and traditional lobbying by national interests. Just as the Proportional Representation League, under the leadership of Clarence Hoag and George Hallett, and other organizations coordinated national efforts favoring STV, similar groups provided political energy in support of RCV. The Center for Voting and Democracy (CVD), later rechristened FairVote, was established as a nonprofit association in 1992 by cofounders Robert Richie and Steven Hill. CVD, or FairVote, focused on electoral reform and describes itself as "the driving force behind advancing ranked choice voting."[45] Rob Richie remained as executive director/CEO of FairVote. Although he retained his status as a senior advisor, Steven Hill left FairVote and became political reform director of the New America Foundation.[46] FairVote's annual income in 2011 and 2012 was only $300,000, modest by the standards of many effective policy think tanks. In more recent years, FairVote has received numerous grants, including $4 million from the Laura and John Arnold Foundation and $2 million from the William and Flora Hewlett Foundation. FairVote's growth and ability to attract major donors perhaps is indicative of mounting dissatisfaction with American elections and an interest in finding alternatives. For instance, FairVote's 2019 Form 990 shows nearly $4.3 million in receipts and about $3 million in total expenditures, including over $1.5 million in employee compensation. The organization engages in direct and indirect lobbying.[47] FairVote coordinates with local organizations, providing education and strategic support. An early priority of CVD/FairVote was proportional or "full representation," but as the public has found the RCV/IRV form more attractive, the priority has shifted toward that method.[48]

Electoral system changes within recent decades often followed a circuitous path. Adoption and repeal of RCV elections today, just as a century ago, evolve from political malaise more often than spontaneous eruptions of public demand for change. Interest groups—national and local—can be important influencers of electoral system change. Local conditions, however, must be ripe. Most communities adopted RCV elections through voter approval of a municipal ballot proposition, and most of these continue to hold RCV elections. But some cities try RCV and then reject it.

During the resurgence of support for IRV in the decade of the 2000s, Burlington, Vermont, adopted the electoral system. As noted in the case study above, its municipal elections are partisan, and Burlington had three factions: Democrats, Republicans, and Progressives. Indeed, the rise of a viable third alternative for elections in Burlington, as well as Vermont generally, both preceded and followed RCV. For example, future US congressman, senator, and presidential candidate Bernie Sanders was first elected as mayor of Burlington in 1981 with less than 44 percent of the vote. Although endorsed by the Citizens Party, Sanders ran (then and later) as an independent.[49] Burlington elected Peter Clavelle, a member of the Vermont Progressive Party, as mayor from 1989 through 2006. The mood in Burlington was that with three viable factions, IRV provided an alternative to choosing between the lesser of two evils. Ranking candidates would allow the expression of true, rather than strategic, choices.

But the Progressives lacked a candidate in 2006, so Bob Kiss, a member of the Vermont House, jumped into the mayoral contest late. Four other candidates were in the race, including nominees from the two major parties. It was surprising to most observers that Kiss led after the first round with

39 percent of the vote, while the Democrat had 32 percent and the Republican 27 percent. Following transfers from trailing candidates, Kiss bested the Democrat, 54 percent –46 percent.[50] Kiss ran for a second term in 2009, winning again narrowly, as discussed in the case study in Chapter 4 about monotonicity and Condorcet losers.

However, after 2009, financial problems mired the Kiss administration. The municipally owned service provider, Burlington Telecom, could not fulfill its mandate to service all of Burlington, and its state charter required this before it could expand service to lucrative suburbs. The mayor and his administration were accused of moving money around in the city budget to cover up the financial difficulties. According to veteran Vermont journalist Aki Soga, the financial improprieties became "the crowbar to open up the opposition for IRV." General dissatisfaction with municipal affairs got voters to think, "Hey, we ended up with this guy because of IRV. We don't think it's a good idea." A coalition of Democrats and Republicans collected signatures on an initiative to repeal IRV. The initiative passed narrowly on March 2, 2010.[51] After two mayoral elections with IRV in 2006 and 2009, the city of Burlington, Vermont, abandoned preferential voting and adopted a traditional runoff if the leading candidate did not attract at least 40 percent of the vote.

If electoral systems can change once, they can change again. Burlington voters, on March 2, 2021, approved a charter amendment authorizing RCV for city councilor elections. The measure passed by a wide margin, 64 percent –36 percent. However, RCV will not be used for mayoral elections. The city council initially passed (6–5) a proposal to use RCV for elections for mayor, council, and school commissioner, but Mayor Miro Weinberger vetoed that proposal. The city council modified the proposal to refer to councilor elections only, and Weinberger signed it. The Vermont General Assembly approved the charter amendment in May 2022, and the Burlington City Council authorized the return of RCV for the March 2024 elections.[52]

Some RCV municipal elections began under a pilot program. The North Carolina legislature allowed several cities to experiment with RCV. In 2007, two cities agreed to implement the trial program: Cary and Hendersonville. The election in Cary followed the standard RCV/IRV format. Voters cast ranked ballots for mayor and three council members (one at-large). The sole council seat with no first-round majority winner occurred in District B. Political newcomer Don Frantz received 38.1 percent of the votes in a three-person contest, leading the second-place candidate by ninety-six votes and beating the incumbent who placed third. For the second round, election software was unavailable, so ballots had to be hand-counted. Staff originally had difficulty reaching a consistent result. After a lengthy delay for the calculation of transfers, Frantz was elected by forty-eight votes, receiving 50.9 percent of the remaining ballots (only 46.4 percent of all valid ballots). Frantz notes that voters in low-turnout municipal elections are "pretty informed voters. They know what's going on for the most part." Yet he also heard about a lot of confusion on the part of voters, despite a significant local election campaign. Although the North Carolina pilot program lasted through 2009, Cary opted to forgo RCV and return to the plurality–runoff system that local voters found more familiar. The pushback was "just from people being confused." Given the additional cost of the election to the city, voters felt of RCV, "it's just not worth it."

Hendersonville accepted the pilot program in both 2007 and 2009. However, all elective city offices were filled after the first round of vote tabulation, so the experiment was never fully tested. That may be fortuitous, however. For the two council seats, Hendersonville neither divided the electorate into single-member districts nor did they apply STV methods. Instead, Hendersonville gave voters a pick-two, rank-three style ballot, a preferential version of block voting, which we refer to as multiwinner ranked voting (MRV).[53] To elect two public officials, block voting allows each citizen to cast a vote for two candidates, and STV gives each citizen one vote with ranked preferences among all candidates to elect two. In the Hendersonville scenario, each citizen has two first-place votes and then three additional ranked preferences. However, the quota for election was set at 25 percent.[54] The standard Droop quota in this case was just over one-third. All quotas were passed in the first round. Local opinion surveys reported voter satisfaction with choice voting; however, since no second round was required, it is difficult to know how to interpret these findings.[55]

The city of Aspen, Colorado, introduced a similar system in 2009. Two council members were elected at-large in each election. Aspen officials hoped to copy the San Francisco model and eliminate runoffs, which were costly in terms of money and time. However, with no districts, Aspen struggled to develop a plan to use a transferable vote perspective for the election of only two council members. The feeling was that since two were elected, each voter should cast two votes. This perspective fits neither the IRV mold to select one majority winner in each race nor the STV rationale for a voter to have one vote and an electorally proportional outcome. The final MRV proposal, drafted by then-special counsel for the city Jim True, first added the first and second preferences and narrowed the field to four candidates. Trying to develop an equitable method with ranked choices to elect two representatives with two votes was, according to True, "a little bit of a challenge, figuring out the best way to do that."[56] Nine candidates competed for council and five for mayor, an unusually large number for this small city. The election of the mayor followed the traditional IRV path. For the city council, after first and second preferences were added, four leaders advanced to the instant runoff. The bottom candidate was eliminated, and those ballots were transferred to the next preference. After one candidate received a majority, the process began anew among the three remaining candidates, again with first and second preferences and omitting the first winner. Following a single election in 2009, voters in Aspen narrowly defeated an advisory ballot proposition referred to voters regarding RCV, 801–808.[57] Voters repealed RCV in 2010, 1726–918.[58]

State legislatures may grant localities the option for RCV. In New Mexico, municipalities were responsible for conducting their own elections. However, in 2018, the New Mexico legislature passed an act allowing municipalities to permit counties to conduct elections.[59] As part of that transfer of responsibility, cities could also adopt new election systems—either a top-two runoff or a ranked choice system. The two cities, Santa Fe and Las Cruces, opted for RCV elections beginning in the next election.

The Utah Legislature created a pilot program for four cities to implement RCV in 2018. Only two communities, Vineyard and Payson, accepted the challenge and held RCV elections in 2019. The Clerk of Utah County, home to both cities, conducted a survey on voters' attitudes regarding RCV. A substantial majority, 86 percent, found the election method easy to use, and 82.5 percent wanted to use RCV in future elections.[60] Following this early success, Utah expanded its Municipal Alternative Voting Methods Pilot Project, and twenty-one new municipalities joined the group with their first ranked choice elections in 2021.

However, the implementation in the first two Utah cities is neither the IRV nor the STV variety. Instead, these communities use a third variant, a multiwinner or block-vote instant runoff. This MRV method is similar to the Aspen method. Transfers are made from first preferences until a first majority winner is determined. Then, all voter ballots are reconsidered with the first elected candidate omitted. Then transfers are made as necessary for all ballots until a second candidate attains a majority.

The city of Portland, Maine, initially adopted RCV/IRV only for mayoral elections in 2011. Preferential voting was chosen for a newly created political office. Prior to this, the mayor was the presiding officer for the city council and was selected internally. The new position was an elective office. There was no elective incumbent and no history of elections for a city executive. Elections in Portland were also nonpartisan and politically left of center. The first mayoral election drew a field of fifteen candidates, with the leading candidate earning only 26.6 percent of first-place ballots.[61] Subsequent elections, however, attracted only three to four candidates per election. Implementing RCV for this new office, however, did not change the existing electoral system for council elections. Similar circumstances produced RCV for another American city. Voters in Boulder, Colorado, approved a ballot proposition for RCV in mayoral elections in 2020. The mayor was not previously an elected position.

As Portlanders became comfortable with the new election method for mayor, a call for expanding RCV to other municipal offices followed. Portland expanded RCV to city council and school board elections with passage of a March 2020 public referendum. The proposition received overwhelming support, 81 percent –19 percent. However, the city also used a runoff form of RCV to elect a charter commission in a special election on June 8, 2021. Five members were elected from districts, but four members were elected at-large. Traditional STV was not applied, although multiple at-large winners were selected. Instead, a MRV procedure was implemented. An IRV runoff was conducted in which one commissioner was chosen at a time. Voter turnout in the election was low (14.4 percent), although this is not unusual for a special municipal election. A progressive slate captured six of the nine elected seats.[62]

Some community adoptions of RCV are more in form than in actual application. Early adopters in Colorado include the towns of Basalt and Carbondale. Basalt required RCV for the election of the mayor (only) in 2002. However, the 2020 election was the first time that three candidates competed in the mayoral election. Despite provisions allowing RCV, Carbondale has not experienced an election with three-candidate competition. By contrast, following its adoption in 2008, Telluride used RCV in its next three elections for mayor.

The city of Sunnyvale, California, is often listed among cities that instituted IRV. In 2009, the method was used to select the mayor, but this position was a two-year position as presiding officer. The mayor was selected by the seven city council members, the only individuals who could vote on the measure. So, the instant runoff was for small-group decision-making, not a mass electorate. Moreover, the practice was changed in 2010 after a single use due to perceptions that it was too confusing to break ties for transfers (a likely scenario considering only seven voters and the application depends on no one getting a majority of four votes).[63]

Two adoptions of RCV came from legal settlements. In both cases, the intent was to create more diverse outcomes from the municipal elections.

Eastpointe, Michigan, adopted STV to settle litigation regarding African American voter participation. The first use of STV in this Michigan town occurred in 2019 to elect two members of the city council. Ironically, the first Black mayor of the municipality, Monique Owens, was elected in 2019, but *not* through ranked choice methods. The mayoral election was held simultaneously under simple plurality. Owens was elected with 32.5 percent of valid votes cast, only nineteen votes more than her closest rival. Previously, she was the first Black council member elected in a plurality election. Both council members elected through STV in 2019 were White, although in a 2020 special election, Eastpointe voters selected a second Black woman to the city council. This was a special election to fill a vacancy for one seat, so IRV was used in 2020. Two incumbents were reelected in 2021.

Palm Desert, California, also adopted RCV through a legal settlement following a dispute over the municipality's at-large election of city council members. The settlement created a downtown district represented by one council member and a larger surrounding district represented by four council members. It also calls for RCV in elections, but this part of the agreement was postponed in 2020 "due to financial and logistical difficulties related to COVID-19."[64]

Disagreement over how to refer to these methods of preferential voting has occurred from the beginning. During the early adoption in American municipalities in the 1910s and the 1920s, the term PR was used to describe the STV and aligned methods. Today, the method of elections in Cambridge as well as the national electoral system in Ireland are often referred to as PR or proportional representation. Early commentators such as Harris (1930: 48) noted that these terms are neither accurate descriptions nor clear to voters.[65] Likewise, the terms RCV and IRV are used interchangeably, although RCV may refer to all forms of ranked preferences, including STV, MRV, and even other electoral methods. Other applications, like those examples outlined above, are called RCV when they may not fit the mold of popular, ranked choice elections.

Cities with Related Electoral Systems

In efforts to approach PR through other voting schemes, some municipalities adopted the *limited vote*. This system for multimember elections gives each citizen fewer votes than there are candidates to be elected (but more than one vote, which is given to each voter under STV). For example, an 1873 charter revision in New York City created seven districts, with three aldermen elected from each district, and an at-large election for seven aldermen. A voter was allowed only two votes to cast for the district election of three aldermen and only four votes in the at-large election of seven aldermen. Boston, Massachusetts, in 1893, implemented an at-large election for twelve aldermen, but voters were limited to casting votes for only seven candidates.[66] The purposes behind the limited vote were similar to STV: to represent minority groups, dismantle political machines, and provide some level of PR. State courts were mixed in their assessments of the limited vote.[67] More recently, in response to 1988–1989 court settlements, twenty-one Alabama towns adopted limited voting (Still 1992). Other communities and counties have utilized limited voting in Pennsylvania and Connecticut (Zimmerman 1994).

Another system to represent minority voting blocs, but with less emphasis on proportionality, is cumulative voting. Under cumulative voting, each voter is granted a number of votes equal to the number of candidates elected in a multimember district. However, voters may accumulate their votes for one or more candidates. If there are three candidates elected from a district, for example, a voter has three options: casting one vote for each of three candidates, casting two votes for one candidate and another for a second candidate, or casting all three votes for a third candidate.[68] In a way, this method allows a voter to cast something analogous to cardinal or utilitarian voting, showing how much a candidate is preferred.

Several cities adopted cumulative voting, including boroughs throughout Pennsylvania, Rockford, Illinois, and Wilmington, North Carolina. Cumulative voting was also introduced to many cities in the early twentieth century. Early state court decisions were mixed in their interpretations of cumulative voting.[69] Recent adoption of cumulative voting is often a response to judicial decisions on block voting or at-large elections generally. As these election systems typically represent majority groups only, ethnic minorities may gain representation through a system more proportional in effects.[70] Three Alabama towns, along with the Chilton County Commission and the School Board, adopted cumulative voting as a response to 1980s litigation. Other cumulative voting elections have ranged from the city of Alamogordo, New Mexico, to the village of Port Chester, New York, to Missouri's Ferguson-Florissant School District. Academic research on cumulative and limited voting suggests that both exhibit some success in promoting the representation of minorities. Both involve relatively straightforward election administration. However, these systems, cumulative voting in particular, may be costly in terms of information demands on the part of voters, as they must know more in order to vote effectively.[71]

Yet another electoral system used by some municipalities is approval voting. This election method, also applied to either single-winner or multiwinner contests, was developed by political scientist Steven Brams and mathematician Peter Fishburn (Brams and Fishburn 1978, 2007). For approval voting, individual preferences are not ranked on the ballot. Candidates are simply divided into two camps, those that are approved or acceptable to the voter and those that are not.[72] Tabulation of the winner is straightforward, election officials count the number of approvals for each alternative. The option(s) with the most votes is(are) selected. Since preferences are not ranked, approval voting is not an RCV system, however, there are some common characteristics. Both ranked and approval voting methods aim to increase the likelihood that a voter expresses full and true preferences on the ballot. Both methods aim to select winners mutually preferred among the electorate. Approval voting, however, does not focus on majoritarianism. There is no need to attract over half of the ballots for election. Multiple alternatives could receive a majority, or none could. The emphasis is on relative magnitude, and on more positive assessments. An advantage of approval voting is that neither ballots nor tabulation software needs substantial modification for implementation. Pure approval voting is similar to block voting but with no limit on the number of valid votes that a citizen may cast.

Approval voting has been adopted by some constituencies. The method has been incorporated by a number of scientific and technical societies for the selection of board members.[73] Just as FairVote supports efforts for RCV, the Center for Election Science, a nonprofit organization with substantial funding, lobbies for the adoption of approval voting.[74] Two cities adopted modifications of approval voting. Fargo, North Dakota, approved the system for the election of city council members through a ballot initiative in November 2018. Fargo residents chose two city commissioners (of four) in the first election, held on June 19, 2020. The two winners received a majority of approval votes out of the field of seven.[75]

Later in 2020, voters in the city of St. Louis, Missouri, adopted a ballot referendum for a form of approval voting in a variety of municipal elections, including mayor and the board of aldermen. The first election was the March 2021 nonpartisan primary, a new experience for St. Louis voters. The top-two candidates, regardless of the proportion of votes received, advanced to the April 2021 general election. Four candidates ran in the nonpartisan mayoral election (three were Democrats and one a Republican). Two candidates competed for aldermanic seats in six wards, three candidates in another six wards, and six candidates in the twenty-first ward. Candidates for comptroller and three wards were unopposed. In all but two races for alderman (the fourth and twelfth wards), a single candidate received a majority of approval votes in the primary; nevertheless, the top two advanced to the general election. In the April general election, leading candidates in four wards, including two with an outright majority in March, lost. Just as in a traditional runoff, the group of voters participating in the primary and general election may differ. However, voter behavior in the 2021 St. Louis municipal elections was puzzling.[76] St. Louis voters were more reluctant to cast multiple approval votes, it appears. Voters in the mayoral contest approved of 1.6 candidates on average, while in the Fargo commission race, voters approved of 2.3. Other American localities are considering proposals for approval voting in municipal elections as well.

From the voter's perspective, these voting systems produce ballots that look quite similar. To a voter, the distinction between ranking and approving preferences may seem subtle. For example, Table 3.3 provides a comparison of different electoral systems on a generalized ballot. The scenarios include those for a single winner (plurality, RCV/IRV, approval, Bucklin) and for a multiwinner contest for selection of three representatives (block, RCV/STV, cumulative, limited). The voter prefers, in order, candidates April, May, June, Sunny, and Luna, and finds the first three acceptable (important for Bucklin and approval voting). For each scenario, the voter expresses sincere preferences among five candidates.

Table 3.3 Ballot examples for the voter preferential and associated voting systems

	One Candidate Elected			
Alternative	Plurality	RCV/IRV	Approval	Bucklin
April	X	1	X	1
June		3	X	other
Luna		5		
May		2	X	2
Sunny		4		

	Three Candidates Elected					
Alternative	Block Vote	RCV/STV	Cumulative* A	B	C	Limited**
April	X	1	3	2	1	X
June	X	3			1	
Luna		5				
May	X	2		1	1	X
Sunny		4				

For this example, the voter orders the candidates: April, May, June, Sunny, and Luna. However, the voter does not really approve of the two alternatives ranked lowest. Sincere voting is assumed for all electoral systems.
*All three possibilities exist for the voter depending on the magnitude of the voter's preferences, although *only one* of these three options could be cast for a given election.
**Since three alternatives are selected, two votes are assumed for the limited vote (if three votes are allowed, it would be block voting, and if one vote is allowed, it would be a single nontransferable vote).

From the voter's view, plurality is simplest and easiest to complete without error—just select the one you want. Moreover, from a voter's view, both RCV systems are identical; only the ballot counting process and the number of candidates elected differ. Although not repeated for Table 3.3, this equivalence holds for approval and Bucklin voting, single- and multiwinner ballots appear the same. Cumulative voting provides a voter with a broader range of potential votes to cast. For this case of three candidates, there are three possible ways to vote depending on the magnitude of preference. Plurality, limited, block, and approval voting only require a voter to express some level of acceptability, constrained only by the maximum number of selections (for this example, 1, 2, 3, or 5, respectively). All other methods require a voter to express an ordering of preferences.

Voter options, of course, include marking fewer than the maximum number allowed. One option is abstention, implicitly recording that no candidate meets standards of acceptability.[77] Another option is bullet voting, also known as plumping or plunking, explicitly identifying only one preference even when more alternatives are available. Recording fewer preferences in a multiwinner context is much like a voter's self-expressed limited, approval, and/or cumulative vote. Another reasonable explanation, however, is that a voter may not fully understand the process of voting. Marking a single preference is easier. Indeed, in an election of nine council members with twenty candidates, a voter may simply be unable to give an accurate ordering from first to twentieth preference. Identifying only a few preferences may seem more rational than electing an unfamiliar candidate through arbitrary rankings.[78]

The contemporary wave of RCV has been limited largely to the United States. Only one municipality in Canada, the city of London, Ontario, used RCV, for a single election in 2018. The Ontario Provincial Assembly passed the Municipal Elections Modernization Act of 2016, permitting municipalities to conduct a "ranked ballot election." London opted for RCV in 2017. The mayor and fourteen councillors representing wards were elected on October 22, 2018.[79] Subsequently, the Ontario Assembly, citing the extra cost for the London election, rescinded its authorization for RCV in local elections in 2020.[80]

In the United Kingdom, Northern Ireland, since 1998, and Scotland, since 2007, have been using STV in local elections. The city of London (England) has used the supplementary vote, a variation of RCV, for the election of mayor since 2000. London voters mark their ballot with their top two preferences. If no candidate receives a majority after the first round, then the two leading candidates (only) advance to an instant runoff. Ballots initially cast for an eliminated candidate switch to their second preference. These second preferences, if for one of the two runoff candidates, are reallocated. The candidate with the majority of remaining votes wins. The supplementary vote tends to reward larger parties or candidates with broad support, and it also promotes compromise through the second preference. The supplementary vote is also used to elect the twenty-five members of the London Assembly, directly elected mayors throughout England (since 2015), and forty-one police and crime commissioners in England and Wales. All these elections are partisan. The supplementary vote shares characteristics with RCV, but it is comparatively narrow.

The 2021 New York Mayoral Election

The most populous municipality in North America utilizing RCV is New York. On November 5, 2019, New York City voters approved a change to their city charter, establishing RCV for primaries and special elections beginning in 2021. The campaign for approval was supported in part by a $500,000 gift to the Committee for Ranked Choice Voting NYC from billionaire John Arnold. The measure passed by an overwhelming margin, 73.6 percent–26.4 percent. Previously, elections were decided by a plurality, or by a runoff for citywide races if no candidate received at least 40 percent of the vote.

The voters' decision was not universally welcomed. In December 2020, seven months before the city's primary for mayor, several community leaders, led by city council member Adrienne Adams, brought suit for an injunction, arguing that the city failed to properly educate the public about the upcoming change and that the system would be unfavorable to communities of color. Council member Eric Adams (the leading candidate for mayor who later won the nomination) agreed with the assessment. The petition for injunction was denied.

The primaries were held on June 22, 2021, with twelve candidates in the Democratic Party mayoral race. The system for New York City allows voters to rank five candidates on the ballot. Since the winner of the Democratic mayoral primary would be the likely winner in the November general election, and since there were only two candidates in the Republican primary, the Democratic mayoral race garnered the most attention.

Some could point to the primary as evidence that RCV reduces campaign acrimony and promotes fewer extreme candidates. Candidates Andrew Yang and Kathryn Garcia campaigned together in the final weekend of the campaign, even distributing campaign material with both of their names and photographs. Yang specifically asked voters to rank him first and Garcia second (though she chose not to do the same). The leading candidates were all political moderates who eschewed some of the more controversial positions of the progressive wing of the Democratic Party; Eric Adams, for example, is a former police captain who emphasizes law and order and opposed calls to "defund" the police.

At the same time, the alliance between Garcia and Yang aroused allegations and denials of racial motivations. Adams, the ultimate winner in the primary, accused Yang and Garcia of forming an alliance to undermine Black and Latino voters. There was considerable acrimony between

Yang and Adams, with Adams calling Yang a "liar" and Yang stating that Adams "cuts corners and breaks rules." Adams called the alliance a "back room deal." Adams' assertion was supported by Ashley Sharpton, the daughter of civil rights leader Rev. Al Sharpton. But others disagreed. Candidate and civil rights attorney Maya Wiley and the NYC public advocate Jumaane Williams, both of whom are African American, criticized Adams for making the claim. After the election, *The Washington Post* published an op-ed from Wiley, titled "I lost the NYC mayoral race, but women and minorities win with ranked-choice voting." She suggested that RCV will encourage "a new pipeline of diverse candidates who are not beholden to powerful interests."[81]

The experience in New York City can be used by advocates and opponents of RCV and offers a clear example of the importance of election administration. The administration of the election was inept. Even prior to the 2020 general election, a *New York Times* article began a description of the Bureau of Elections this way:

> The official who oversees voter registration in New York City is the 80-year-old mother of a former congressman. The director of Election Day operations is a close friend of Manhattan's Republican chairwoman. The head of ballot management is the son of a former Brooklyn Democratic district leader. And the administrative manager is the wife of a City Council member.

The article goes on to discuss the poor work culture in the office, noting that New York State is the only state in the county where election board jobs are primarily given as patronage by the political parties.[82]

Against this backdrop, the Board of Elections took several actions that drew considerable criticism. On Election Night, the Board released preliminary results showing Adams ahead by over 88,000 votes, despite over 120,000 uncounted absentee ballots. Then the Board did not release any more results for several days. Steven Hill, describing himself in the *New York Daily News* as "main architect of the ranked-choice voting system used in San Francisco, Oakland and other cities," argued that transparency is needed in the release of results. He criticized the Board of Elections for taking too long; he asserted that results are best released on a regular schedule so the public can see what is happening.

But the bigger problem occurred on June 22. In a move described as "head scratching" in *Politico* and "lunacy" in Maya Wiley's *Washington Post* op-ed, the Board of Elections released results showing what second-round results could look like, despite having nearly 125,000 uncounted ballots. Even worse, these results then needed to be removed a few hours after being posted when it was discovered that they included 135,000 test ballots from preliminary runs of the election software.[83] The final results were released in early July. The outcome showed that Eric Adams, the early leader, beat Kathryn Garcia, 50.5 percent by 49.5 percent in the eighth round of tabulation. Adams' 403,333 votes constituted 43 percent of the 937,699 votes cast.

Although many municipalities hold nonpartisan elections, some, like New York and Minneapolis, have candidate affiliations with political parties. Most state elections are partisan. Chapter 4 investigates RCV and related systems in partisan and state elections. An empirical analysis of municipal RCV elections follows in Chapter 6.

4
RCV in Partisan and State Elections

The Progressive movement reached beyond the political institutions of municipal government, and it was broader than the crusade for nonpartisan elections. The reformers also aimed for government efficiency, transparency, and democratic decision-making. This demanded efforts to clean up the political parties as well. Candidates for elective office in some cities, such as New York, compete first for party nomination, then for public office in a general election. Partisan elections are the norm for state and federal electoral offices as well. Only one state, Nebraska, holds nonpartisan elections for state office, and only for the unicameral, the Senate. Other elections are awash in party politics.

Since many local elections were either nonpartisan or so removed from national and state politics that party affiliation was not a salient factor for voters, multimember elections were problematic. Because of the tendency for plurality elections to produce two-party competition, the need for preferential voting is slight. However, primary elections, institutions in which party identifiers in the mass public select their party nominees, are vulnerable to problems associated with the participation of more than two candidates. Primary elections are another prime target for multiparty competition.

Moreover, in many locations, particularly those with one dominant political party, the competition for office is effectively decided in party primaries. So, political reformers also turn their attention to party nomination contests. The introduction of ranked choice voting (RCV) into partisan elections in the United States and Canada is not new. In fact, the notion of party primaries, for which partisans in the mass electorate can select party nominees, is part of the same progressive wave that brought in preferential voting and proportional representation. Just as RCV is used to determine the outcomes in state and national elections in other countries, it can be applied to partisan competition in the United States.

This chapter considers the American experience with partisan preferential elections. Chapter 5 returns to city elections with the beginning of an extensive analysis of recent RCV elections in US municipalities.

RCV in State Party Primaries

Although modern reformers may point to several states that currently allow RCV for decision-making in partisan elections, preferential voting in the United States was evident over a century ago. The movement for popular elections combined with a majoritarian impulse produced both runoff elections and preferential voting. At least nineteen states have had second primaries—closed or open—at one time or another. Often, the desire for a runoff or RCV follows an unsatisfactory experience with a prominent public official elected by a minority of voters (see Bullock and Johnson 1992). American primary elections themselves date from the late nineteenth century, and most states did not establish primaries until the early twentieth century. Political party labels typically restrict the range and number of candidates in the general election. There is no such limitation for the range of competition in party nomination contests, so the number of competitive candidates has the potential to be much larger, and the margin for the winner has the potential to be much smaller. The push for primaries came from Southern states, where one-party Democratic dominance for a century after the Civil War made winning a party nomination tantamount to election.

It is important to note that early party primaries were initially considered to be different from general elections. With regard to RCV and related electoral systems, state courts tended to interpret decision rules pertaining to primaries loosely, as state constitutional protections typically did not apply as strictly to party nominating contests. This gave some states more flexibility with electoral system reform for party primaries. The US Supreme Court, in a decision involving voting rights for Black citizens, effectively extended federal constitutional protections for general elections to party primaries in 1944.[1]

Charles Merriam and Louis Overacker (1928: 83–84) conducted the first extensive study of primary elections through the mid-1920s. They found that eleven states used preferential voting in primaries at one time or another. Legislatures repealed RCV primaries in seven states: Idaho (1909–1919), Indiana (1913–1917), Louisiana (1916–1922), Minnesota

(1912–1915), North Dakota (1911–1913), Washington (1907–1917), and Wisconsin (1911–1915). In Oklahoma, the state Supreme Court ruled the state law unconstitutional. At the time of their study, three states continued to use some form of RCV in primary elections: Alabama, Florida, and Maryland. At that time, only six states had legislative provisions for a runoff, so RCV was used in half. By the mid-1930s, only Maryland used RCV.[2] The strongest argument in favor of preferential voting in party primary elections in the early twentieth century was the savings from the cost of administering a second (runoff) primary.[3]

Only the laws in Minnesota and Maryland matched the standard RCV/instant runoff voting (IRV) procedures. Voters ranked first and second preferences among candidates for each race on the party ballot. If no party candidate received a majority of votes, then the candidate with the lowest votes was dropped, and ballots were redistributed to the second choice. The process continued "until some one candidate had a majority or only two candidates remained, in which case the highest was declared the nominee."[4] However, the Maryland primary was indirect. Votes were cast and accumulated by counties, but delegates to a state convention were bound in their votes using a Hare-like system.[5]

The Florida primary should be characterized as the supplementary vote. Voters in Florida rank their first and second preferences for candidates in races with three or more alternatives. If no candidate receives a majority of votes in the initial round, then the two candidates receiving the most votes would be paired in an instant runoff. Votes would be tabulated for either candidate ranked higher on the ballot in the instant runoff. Alabama primaries utilized Bucklin voting, where all the first and all the second ranks were counted for each of the top two candidates. The candidate with more votes became the party nominee.

A selection system similar to that of the modified Borda count was planned for use in the Oklahoma primary. A law adopted in 1925 would have implemented a system in which voters ranked their preferences among candidates in order. If no candidate received a majority of votes, then second-place ranks would be added as one-half point each. If no candidate still received a majority of the original vote, then third-place rankings would be added at one-third point each.[6] The Oklahoma Supreme Court, however, ruled this system as unconstitutional, not because of the transfer method, but because the electoral law required a voter to rank multiple candidates. According to the Court, requiring voters to express preferences for more than one candidate violated the state constitution's guarantee that "No power, civil or military, shall ever interfere to prevent the free exercise of the right of suffrage."[7]

So why were these early attempts at preferential voting repealed? The Oklahoma case was unusual because the decision involved the interpretation of voting rights under the state constitution. For the others, repeal resulted from dissatisfaction with the observed application in primaries. Benjamin Williams (1923: 113) observed that many "close students of [RCV] have seen it as a satisfactory solution to the problem of minority nominations. But when put to the test of actual experience it has been found to be unworkable." He provided three key reasons. First, voters demonstrated confusion at the more complicated ballot, and most did not mark a second preference. In the Indiana primaries of 1916, for example, only 23 percent of voters expressed a second choice when given over 660,000 opportunities to do so. Second, winning candidates still did not receive a majority of votes cast for that office. In Louisiana, not a single candidate obtained a majority (of all votes cast) through an instant runoff. Third, the leading candidate in the first round was simply elected without change in the second round. In short, considerable effort produced no tangible effect on election outcomes.[8] Texas political scientist Douglas Weeks placed the blame almost exclusively on the failure of most voters to mark a second preference on the ballot. With too few voters registering a second choice, states opted to either establish a traditional primary runoff, with higher rates of and better-informed voter participation, or to simply return to a plurality election, as the leading candidates tended to be selected as nominees anyway.[9] "The elimination of preferential voting...," according to Merriam and Overacker, "indicates a strong feeling that it is either unnecessary or useless."[10]

Recent political developments have brought back the idea of RCV for party primaries. Utah, following its pilot program for RCV in several cities, also implemented RCV for state party conventions in 2020. The coronavirus pandemic may have influenced this decision in 2020. However, the Republican Party, traditionally the dominant party in the state, used RCV methods at its state convention on several occasions and used RCV for the nomination of candidates for special elections to the Utah legislature. Despite this experience, a 2020 poll of likely Republican primary voters found reluctance to changing the selection system to RCV. In a poll conducted for the *Salt Lake Tribune*, only 29 percent of respondents favored RCV, while 64 percent favored maintaining the current system of voting. A poll of delegates to the Republican state convention, however, revealed that they favored RCV over a series of sequential votes, 72 percent–21 percent.[11] Nevertheless, Utah politicians seem to be leaning toward further adoption of RCV in the state. Political parties in other states, such as Virginia, have tried or are also considering alternative election procedures. In 2020, Virginia Republicans chose the state party chair using RCV, and, at the 2021 state party convention, chose their statewide nominees using RCV. The 2021 convention was held via satellite locations due to Covid-19 restrictions. The governor's race took six rounds, the lieutenant governor five rounds, and the attorney general three rounds. In all cases, the leader in the first round was elected, and the rank order of the candidates in each round never changed. Glenn Youngkin, the gubernatorial nominee, went from 33 percent in the first round to 55 percent in the final round; the lieutenant governor and attorney general nominees rose from 32 percent to 54 percent and 37 percent to 52 percent, respectively.[12]

As noted in the discussion of municipal elections, other divergent yet similar electoral systems also appear in American political history.[13] Cumulative voting was used for over a century to elect legislators in Illinois. Illinois voters elected three legislators from a district. Each voter marked three votes on the ballot. All three votes could be cast for one candidate, one vote could be cast for each of three candidates, one and a half votes could be cast for each of two candidates, or two votes could be marked for one candidate and the third for a second candidate. In order to combat north–south sectional divides and regional party dominance, delegates at the 1869–1870 Illinois Constitutional Convention developed this electoral mechanism to incentivize minority representation. Cumulative voting was retained for Illinois House of Representatives elections through 1980. The voluminous scholarly literature surrounding cumulative voting in Illinois suggests that the electoral system was effective at producing intraparty competition and modestly successful at representing the minority party.[14]

For state primaries, a fundamental incentive for RCV is the elimination of a costly second primary, particularly for races with a large number of candidates. For Illinois and its experience with cumulative voting, an independent primary system to nominate candidates could be eliminated altogether. Cumulative voting, like multiwinner ranked voting (MRV) and single transferable vote (STV), allows competition among and within political parties. A key argument in favor of cumulative voting is the tendency for representation of a substantial, homogeneous minority group.[15]

Other Elections for Preferential Voting

Most state elections involve candidates with party labels on the ballot. However, there are other nonpartisan elections where RCV could be applied. There are state and regional boards and commissions for a variety of policies from education to water conservation. If majoritarianism and/or minority representation are important, it may be reasonable to apply preferential voting for these electoral contests. On the other hand, relatively few of these nonpartisan state and regional boards involve significant electoral competition—some even occur with no candidates at all—so the demand for RCV is less clear. However, to the extent that elections for these public offices may be controversial, RCV may be a reasonable solution.

Another potential state application is in the area of state judicial elections. At least some judges are elected in every American state except Delaware. Some judges compete in partisan races, some in nonpartisan races, and some in judicial retention elections. The use of RCV in partisan elections was considered above, and RCV does not apply for retention elections because voters have only two options.[16] However, for nonpartisan judicial elections, like nonpartisan contests for the election of local public officials, RCV may have potential if majoritarian outcomes are important for judicial legitimacy.[17]

North Carolina tried preferential elections for certain judicial offices in 2010.[18] At that time, the state's judicial elections were nonpartisan but subject to a runoff if there were more than two candidates. If three or more candidates competed, the initial election would be held during the state's party primary election, and the top two runoff would occur at the general election. If a vacancy opened between the primary and the runoff, voters could mark their top three preferences, and an instant runoff (through RCV) would determine the winner if no judicial candidate received a majority of the vote. The motivation for this law was a previous election for the state Supreme Court in 2004. In that race, Paul Martin Newby won the election with only 22.6 percent of the total vote; the second-place finisher, James Wynn, received 19.7 percent. Four elections met the criteria for a ranked choice election on November 2, 2010. Since only the top two candidates with the most votes advanced to the runoff, the election was a supplementary election as discussed earlier.

One of these elections was for the state Court of Appeals. A seat opened in 2010 when Judge Wynn resigned his seat on the NC Court of Appeals to accept a federal judgeship. Governor Beverly Perdue appointed North Carolina Superior Court Judge Cressie H. Thigpen, Jr., the first African American president of the North Carolina State Bar Association, to fill the vacancy on the Court of Appeals. This August appointment was made after the May 4 primary election, so it triggered an election with an instant runoff. For the 2010 North Carolina general election, thirteen candidates contested this race for the Court of Appeals. Voters were allowed to mark up to three preferences among the thirteen candidates. Thigpen led the field but received only 20.3 percent of first-place votes, still 100,000 votes more than his nearest rival, former Court of Appeals Judge Doug McCullough, with 15.2 percent.[19] Table 4.1 provides the votes in the judicial election. Rather than traditional IRV with sequential elimination from the bottom, North Carolina law limited the number of candidates in the runoff to two. In other words, this procedure was the supplementary vote, discussed earlier. Ballots cast for other candidates were reallocated according to the voter's second or third preference. So, Thigpen and McCullough faced each other.

This runoff that followed, however, was not what most observers would call "instant." The final count after transferring second and third preferences of voters did not begin until the official results were available near the end of November. Following the transfers, the result was particularly close, about 50.3 percent–49.7 percent, with McCullough taking over the lead. With such a narrow margin, Thigpen requested a mandatory statewide recount. The final results from the November 3 election, which some referred to as the third round, were unavailable until shortly before Christmas.[20] Although there were minor changes in counting from the recount, McCullough retained his winning margin and took his seat on the Court of Appeals. North Carolinians' appeal for IRV seemed to fade, and the legislature eliminated the option in 2013.

The outcome of the North Carolina 2010 judicial elections was fruitful for further evaluation of RCV. From one perspective, the Court of Appeals election was a success in terms of achieving the goals of preferential voting. Moreover, three other elections for county judges—the Superior Court races in Buncombe, Cumberland, and Ronan counties—had three candidates competing, and instant runoff outcomes were determined with little controversy. In two of the races, one candidate received a majority of first-place votes to win. In the third race for Superior Court, an instant runoff was held, and the leading candidate lost to the initial second-place finisher.[21]

Table 4.1 North Carolina Court of Appeals, 2010

Candidate	Round 1 Votes	Round 1 Percent
Cressie Thigpen	395,220	20.3%
Doug McCullough	295,619	15.2%
Chris Dillon	201,870	10.4%
Anne Middleton	174,556	9.0%
Daniel E. Garner	153,971	7.9%
Jewel Ann Farlow	151,747	7.8%
Harry E. Payne, Jr.	99,257	5.1%
Stan Hammer	96,451	5.0%
Mark E. Klass	90,526	4.7%
Pamela M. Vesper	90,116	4.6%
John F. Bloss	78,857	4.1%
John Sullivan	69,971	3.6%
J. Wesley Casteen	45,610	2.4%
Total Votes	1,943,771	100.0%

	Round 2	Recount	Percent/ Pct. of Total
Cressie Thigpen	537,445	537,325	49.7% [27.6%]
Doug McCullough	544,023	543,980	50.3% ✓ [28.0%]
Nontransferable	[862,303]	[862,466]	[44.4%]
Total votes	1,081,468	1,081,305	
Percentage of total	55.6%	55.6%	

On the other hand, judicial elections are often low information contests. If voters have difficulty identifying a clear first choice, ranking a second and third or further candidate may add levels of difficulty for less informed voters. Less than a third of North Carolina voters who gave a different first choice had ballots that actually were transferred to one of the two candidates in the runoff. Of voters who gave a first preference among the thirteen candidates, only 55.6 percent had a ballot applied in the instant runoff. While McCullough received over half of the valid votes on the final tally, this accounted for only 28 percent of the ballots recording a first choice. That allowed more voters to give their preference between the top two candidates, but the declaration of a "majority" winner seems artificial.

For one segment of the voting public, eliminating the need to cast a ballot for a runoff—either a second primary or a general election runoff—could enhance voting rights. Since runoffs often occur within a few weeks of the initial election, those potential voters who are absent from the constituency during this time have difficulty voting quickly. For instance, military and other governmental personnel serving overseas may have time constraints in terms of securing a second ballot and returning it in a timely manner. For presidential primaries in particular, some candidates may even drop out before the election. The ability of Americans overseas to cast a rank ordered ballot may assist with the ability to cast a ballot at all.

The federal Uniformed and Overseas Citizens Absentee Voting Act of 1986 (UOCAVA) guarantees the rights of citizens residing outside the United States to be able to register and vote in federal elections.[22] Election officials are required to provide absentee ballots to overseas voters 45 days before an election, a difficult timeline to meet for states with traditional runoffs. Alabama, Arkansas, Louisiana, Mississippi, and South Carolina are early adopters of provisions that allow RCV for these overseas voters. Regardless of the merits of RCV for elections generally, providing an opportunity for voters who may not otherwise be able to cast a vote in a runoff seems an appropriate use of RCV. Of course, this—like other applications of voting with transfers—does add a level of complexity for election administrators to determine official election outcomes.

Preferential Voting in Canadian Provinces

Canadian elections are often characterized as first-past-the-post (FPTP) or single-member district plurality (SMDP) elections. This is the electoral system applied at the federal level for the House of Commons and, currently, for the unicameral legislative assemblies in all ten provinces and three territories. The Canadian party system traditionally has two major parties (currently the federal Liberal and Conservative parties) but with additional parties representing regional or ideological interests.[23]

However, Canadian provincial election systems historically had considerable diversity. Only Quebec, where British electoral practices were imposed on the French Canadian population, and Newfoundland and Labrador, not entering as a province until 1949, consistently had FPTP/SMDP electoral systems for provincial elections. Eastern provinces, briefly including Ontario constituencies in Toronto and Ottawa, tended to create multi-member electoral systems. Political parties, according to this tradition, represented diverse groups in society (Catholic and Protestant, English and French). The system in Prince Edward Island included two races or ballots within a single constituency. Western provinces, however, tended to adopt preferential voting or ranked choice systems in the early twentieth century.

The Progressive Era wave of governmental reform swept across western Canada as it did in the western United States. The trend by which western municipalities adopted electoral reform in western Canadian cities also influenced the method of election of provincial legislative assemblies. Table 4.2 summarizes the electoral innovation, including RCV, adopted for western provincial legislative elections. The first stage to encourage representation was the creation of multimember districts in urban centers. Multimember districts were found in the maritime provinces from confederation, but the West established these later. Block voting tended to elect a single party without minority representation. The second stage, for Alberta and Manitoba, was the application of preferential voting. The alternative vote (AV), that is RCV/IRV, was used for rural ridings (Canadian election districts), and a version of STV was used to elect members of the legislative assembly from urban districts. British Columbia lagged but adopted preferential voting as a response to third-party growth in the 1950s. However, the system in British Columbia was only used for two provincial elections. Of the western provinces, only Saskatchewan passed on RCV for elections of members of the Legislative Assembly, although the province did adopt RCV in some municipalities.

Adoption of RCV in early twentieth-century Canada, however, was not successful in achieving many of its goals. Electoral system change appears to have influenced party systems little, with a possible exception of the rise of the Social Credit Party in British Columbia.[24] Jansen (2004) examines IRV/AV in the western provinces and finds that voter turnout did not increase (or decrease) compared to plurality election, nor did

Table 4.2 Electoral systems in western Canadian provinces

Province	SMDP	Multimember District	RCV/Alternative Vote	STV
Alberta	1905–1921 (5) 1956-date	1909–1921 (3) Calgary, Edmonton, Medicine Hat	1926–1955 (8) rural	1926–1955 (8) Calgary, Edmonton 5–6; Medicine Hat 2
British Columbia	1871–1949 1956-1986 1991-date	1871–1949 Vancouver, Victoria, others 1956–1986 Vancouver, Victoria, others	1952–1953 (2)	
Manitoba	1903–1915 (5) 1920–1922 (2) 1941–1953 (4) 1955-date	1914–1915 (2) Winnipeg	1927–1936 (3)	1920–1945 (7) Winnipeg 10 1949–1953 (2) Winnipeg 3@4, St. Boniface 2
Saskatchewan	1905–1917 1921-1964 1967–date	1921–1964 Saskatoon, Regina, Moose Jaw		

The table excludes military representation (at–large, dedicated seats).

proportionality or representation of small parties in legislative assemblies. However, he finds more smaller parties did compete for elections (even if they did not win seats) and, unfortunately, that the number of rejected ballots increased. Overall, his conclusions are that RCV elections were not substantially different from SMDP elections that preceded and followed them. Over five elections in Alberta from 1940 to 1955, Qualter (1970) observes that out of 237 candidates elected under preferential voting in rural Alberta, most (168 or 71 percent) were elected with an absolute majority on the first count. Many others involved leading candidates who were subsequently selected on a second ballot. Only a few, seven or 3 percent, involved one candidate usurping the initial leader. In the urban areas of Calgary and Edmonton, the circumstances under STV diverge. More candidates trailing on the first ballot were elected following transfers, fourteen of fifty-six or 25 percent.[25] STV, providing something akin to proportional representation, produces change in representation. AV/IRV typically produces the same outcomes as the plurality method, assuming all voters are casting ballots sincerely, that is, not strategically.

Selecting Canadian Party Leaders through RCV

Canada's largest federal political parties select their leaders through a modification of RCV. The Canadian executive is not selected through popular election, at least not directly. The prime minister is the head of government and represents the party with the most seats in the House of Commons. The British monarch is the titular head of state, although the governor general, appointed on recommendation from the prime minister, acts on behalf of the monarch for Canadian public affairs. Under the Constitution Act of 1867 (the British North America Act), the governor general appoints the prime minister officially, but in practice, the party leader of the largest party in the Commons forms the government.[26]

In the past, the party leader was elected at a national party convention of a few thousand party delegates. Convention members could vote sequentially until one candidate received a majority of votes. This system is similar to the selection of presidential nominees at party conventions in the United States, although party nomination in the American system has been decided on the first ballot since the Republican Convention of 1952.[27] Sequential balloting, like runoffs for mass electorates, allows candidate maneuvering and strategic endorsements. Moreover, the selection of party leadership remains in the hands of party elites, rather than the rank-and-file party members. In Canada, a movement for popular selection of party leaders led to the application of a One Member, One Vote (OMOV) method of voting combined with a form of RCV.

The leaders of the two largest parties, the Liberals and the Conservatives, are elected by party members through a weighted form of preferential voting. The notion of OMOV was used earlier by some provincial parties. The federal Conservative Party of Canada has selected its leaders through this method since 2003.[28] The Liberal Party of Canada first employed this method of party leadership selection in 2013. Under this method, the leadership election was opened to all party members throughout Canada who could cast a ranked ballot for declared candidates remotely. To represent the population generally, a party member votes within each riding or electoral district that is assigned 100 points. Each ballot is weighted inversely to the number of votes in the electoral constituency. A party member could be anyone who signed up and paid party dues.[29]

For instance, the Conservatives used OMOV and RCV in the election of their party leader in 2017. In this leadership election, around 259,000 Conservative supporters were eligible to vote. Approximately 141,000 of these party members cast ballots in the leadership election. This number falls far short of the many millions of Conservative voters in Canada, but it is also far larger than the several thousand delegates that would be likely to attend a national leadership convention. In 2017, some of the leading candidates for the leadership position dropped out before the election. The ranked choice ballot listed twelve candidates for party leader, and polls suggested no clear consensus among voters.

No candidate received a majority of points on the first ballot. The leader, Maxime Bernier, led the field, but he received less than 30 percent of first-place ballots. Former House of Commons Speaker Andrew Scheer came in second, followed by Erin O'Toole. As each candidate with the lowest number of votes was dropped and ballots were reassigned to the next preference remaining in the pool, Bernier's lead narrowed as Scheer gained ground. Figure 4.1 shows the series of votes graphically. Bernier maintained the lead position until the 13th and final ballot. On the last ballot, Scheer overtook first place 51 percent–49 percent. However, it is less clear that Scheer's win constituted a majority. The number of ballots that ranked neither of the two candidates was three times the size of the winning margin. Moreover, there were claims of irregularities about members receiving ballots in time for postal voting and allegations about invalid registrations. Because ballots must be weighted in order to represent a cross-section of members across Canada, the tabulation seemed, to some, to lack transparency. Nevertheless, Scheer became the Conservative party leader.[30]

Of course, not all leadership RCV elections are decided by a narrow margin. Conservative Leader Stephen Harper won with over 56 percent of the points on the first ballot in 2004; Liberal Leader Justin Trudeau won with 80 percent of first ballot points in 2013. Likewise, delegates in leadership conventions also produced narrow and controversial outcomes. For instance, in the Liberal convention of 2006, Stéphane Dion moved from third place on delegates' first ballot to defeat the leading candidate Michael Ignatieff on the fourth ballot.

For the first Liberal Party election in 2013, about 300,000 Canadians were registered as Liberal Party members, far short of the population of Liberal voters but far greater than the small number of convention delegates. Many leading candidates aspired to become the next party leader, but most dropped out of the race before balloting. Not all members voted, but over 130,000 members cast votes online or by phone. Six candidates remained on the ballot. One of those, Justin Trudeau, the son of former Prime Minister

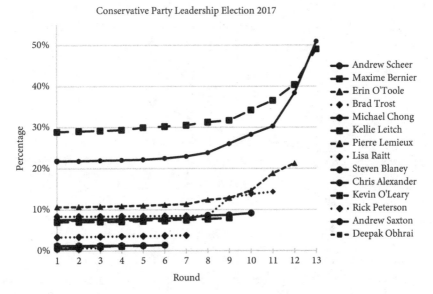

Figure 4.1 Conservative Party of Canada Leadership Election, 2017.

Pierre Trudeau, received almost 79 percent of the votes and over 80 percent of the points, and the lop-sided victory eliminated the necessity of ballot transfers.

The 2017 Conservative leadership vote, where a candidate in second place, Andrew Scheer, ultimately triumphed, is not unusual. The next election, held in 2020 after Scheer resigned the leadership position, included four candidates, none receiving a majority of points on the first ballot. This race is depicted in Figure 4.2. Former Progressive Conservative party leader Peter MacKay was slightly ahead of Erin O'Toole on the first ballot. However, on the second ballot, O'Toole outpolled MacKay and won by a large margin on the final ballot. Leslyn Lewis had more votes than either O'Toole or MacKay on the second ballot, but she was eliminated as she had fewer weighted points.[31] These leadership elections presumably are highly salient contests among well-informed voters.

In 2022, vote transfers were unnecessary for the Conservative Party. Pierre Poilievre won handily on the first ballot over a field that included Jean Charest and Lewis. He received 68 percent of the points and 71 percent of the votes in the leadership election.

The use of RCV for party leadership elections seems worthy of consideration for other contests. The Social Democratic Party of Germany

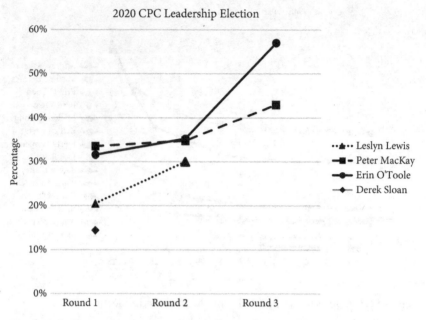

Figure 4.2 Conservative Party of Canada Leadership Election, 2020.

considered it briefly for leadership elections in 2019 as rank-and-file membership was involved directly for the first time. However, the party opted for a two-round election with a runoff instead. Just as preferential voting may work well in nonpartisan contests, such as those typically found in municipal elections, RCV has potential for intraparty election outcomes. Internal competition among similarly aligned political candidates may lend itself more to other decision-making methods such as RCV or approval voting. Likewise, for the selection of offices or award winners within organizations, preferential voting may have some advantages. However, like the examples discussed above, RCV decisions may not necessarily lead to satisfaction for the full membership or the pool of voters making the decisions. Selection of methods for voting and decision-making involves trade-offs among goals and priorities.

5
RCV in State and Federal Elections

Several state legislatures approved preferential voting for local elections or within-party primary elections. Similarly, western Canadian provinces used both single- and multiwinner versions of ranked choice voting (RCV) in the past, although the electoral system is unused for provinces today. The use of RCV for state and federal elections within the United States is quite limited. The first two states adopting RCV provide valuable lessons to reformers as well as to supporters of the status quo. Maine uses RCV in federal (since 2018) and primary (since 2020) elections, although not for general elections for state offices. Alaska adopted RCV for all state and federal elections beginning in 2022.

Maine

In November 2016, voters in the state of Maine approved, by a margin of 52 percent–48 percent, an initiative to adopt RCV for elections to "U.S. Senate, Congress, Governor, State Senate, and State Representative." Maine's penchant for political independence seems to be a factor in its adoption of RCV. In particular, the margins for gubernatorial elections may have contributed to voter concern, as five governors were elected between 1974 and 2018 with less than 40 percent of the vote, and four others with less than 50 percent. Only three governors during this time span received an electoral majority. Maine elections frequently involved a progressive or green faction in addition to the two traditional parties. Multicandidate competition preceded electoral system change. Although circumstances were ripe for restructuring elections, significant organizational efforts were necessary in order to facilitate statewide political reform.

Before the initiative, several organizations were involved in efforts to promote RCV and related activities to improve the political process. Around 2008–2009, the state League of Women Voters embarked on a process to evaluate various potential reforms and to decide which deserved additional

Ranked Choice Voting. James W. Endersby and Michael J. Towle, Oxford University Press.
© Oxford University Press (2025). DOI: 10.1093/9780197798959.003.0006

support. Maine Representative Joanne Twomey of Biddeford had sponsored a bill in 2001 that would provide RCV for all state and federal elections in Maine.[1] The bill died in committee, and it did not influence the League's agenda directly. But the notion of RCV as an improvement to the electoral process was percolating among left-of-center activists in Maine. Within a couple of years, the League endorsed the general idea of RCV.[2] The Maine Citizens for Clean Elections (MCCE) was formed in 1995 to promote an initiative petition for the Maine Clean Elections Act, a program for a public funding option for election campaigns. This grassroots organization expanded its involvement to other reform measures, consistent with its mission to disentangle wealthy interests from the election of political representatives.

The 2010 election of Republican Paul LePage as governor provided the catalyst for change. LePage received only 38 percent of votes (which rose to 48 percent in a three-way race in 2014). As governor, LePage was combative and controversial. During his two terms in office, he vetoed 652 bills, more than the number of gubernatorial vetoes in Maine over the previous century. His tenure in office, for many Mainers, instilled a sense that a different electoral method was needed.

Support for RCV resonated with members of both the Maine League and the MCCE. Eventually, the two organizations developed a cooperative venture, Democracy Maine, in order to pursue joint priorities such as RCV, the preservation of same-day voter registration, and the public financing of campaigns.[3] Around this time, Harvard-trained economist and former state Representative and Senator Dick Woodbury and others created the Committee for Ranked Choice Voting.[4] Woodbury was a political independent and, in the Maine tradition, promoted the interests of unaligned voters and candidates. Around this time, the organizations settled on a strategy of pursuing a ballot initiative for RCV in state and federal elections. Part of the motivation to act quickly was the sense that national funders—FairVote and its sponsors such as the Laura and John Arnold Foundation—expected timely action and results.[5] There was an underlying competitive tension between those working for FairVote and for the Committee for Ranked Choice Voting. The national organization, FairVote, provided education and support, but the state organizations did the groundwork to keep the initiative going.

Communication among the various partners was critical. The national organizations needed to signal that funding would be made available if the state organizations prioritized RCV and maintained progress. The local groups needed the perception that their efforts would not be wasted due to a lack of resources when they were needed. As Anna Kellar, executive director of Democracy Maine, noted, "the League was all volunteer during this whole period, and the MCCE went between three and five staff depending on how grant funding was going," and most staff members focused on the Initiative for Clean Elections. Moreover, Kellar notes that for some within the organizations, particularly with regard to Republicans and other board members for the MCCE, it was important to persuade members that focusing on RCV would not dilute efforts on other common issue priorities such as campaign financing.

Moreover, following a successful ballot proposition, it would be left to the local organizations, the League and the MCCE, to oversee the implementation of RCV. Both were well positioned to interact with the Maine legislature and with the secretary of state. Passing the citizens' initiative would be difficult enough. Seeing reforms implemented would require significant work by advocacy troops after any ballot victory. The Maine organizations had experience with this following the initiative for the Maine Clean Elections Act, and a struggle would follow the RCV ballot proposition as well.

One item discussed in the planning stage was whether a ballot proposition was the best direction to go. The League's legal consultant John Brautigam raised questions about state constitutional provisions that required a plurality vote for state elected officials. Brautigam asked, "how serious is this problem? Is there some way we can take an incremental approach that gets around the problem? Should we just seek a constitutional amendment?" The legal issues were deemed significant enough to create "a moot court where we pretended that we were litigating these questions. We got some jurists in there, and we wrote briefs. We really hashed it out, and it was quite a great process." The conclusion, Brautigam recalls, "is that there were plausible non-frivolous arguments on the other side that [the RCV initiative language] should be constitutional." Of course, this kind of issue is seldom a subject of debate among the general public, but it would influence the legality of RCV implementation. After a year's work collecting signatures, the initiative petition was delivered to the Secretary of State's office by October 2015. The ballot question was scheduled for the November 2016 ballot.

The narrow approval of Maine's 2016 RCV voter initiative faced immediate opposition. State Republicans, under the leadership of controversial Governor Paul LePage, asked the state's Supreme Judicial Court for an advisory opinion. The Court unanimously advised that RCV violated the Maine Constitution's plurality requirement for general elections for state offices, though it remained silent on the issue of federal elections and on party primaries. The state Constitution, as the Court observed, specifically included the phrase "by a plurality" of votes regarding elections of members of the state House and Senate and of the Governor.[6] The legislature's response failed to produce a consensus for repeal of the law or for starting a constitutional amendment process. So, in October 2017, the Maine Legislature voted to delay implementation of RCV until approval of an amendment to Maine's constitution, indefinitely, if necessary.[7]

However, the state Constitution has a provision allowing citizens to repeal legislation through the initiative and referendum process.[8] This constitutional provision allows Mainers to exert a "people's veto" to repeal an act of the legislature. The organizations and their allies again began a process of collecting signatures on petitions for the people's veto on provisions pertaining to federal elections and all primary elections. A sufficient number of signatures were gathered, and the Elections Division of the Secretary of State's office confirmed the petition and placed the question on the statewide ballot on June 12, 2018. Fifty-four percent of voters favored the people's veto initiative to repeal parts of the delay.[9] RCV was scheduled to be introduced for the June 2018 primary and the November 2018 general election.

Maine's RCV odyssey, however, was not yet over. Legislative staff raised issues about whether the people's veto conflicted with existing statutes. State law regarding primary elections also specified that nominees were selected with "a plurality of votes."[10] Both proponents and opponents of RCV took legal action. Within several weeks, restraining orders were filed by the Committee for Ranked Choice Voting to speed up the process and by Republican Senate President Michael Thibodeau and other members of the Maine Senate to slow down the process. Eventually, Democratic Secretary of State Matthew Dunlap announced plans to proceed with RCV for the 2020 primary and general elections. The legal cases were combined and moved to the Maine Supreme Judicial Court. The Court released its decision on April 17, 2018, effectively reversing the silence from its own advisory opinion. The Court ruled, "ranked-choice voting is the law of Maine with regard to the primary elections on June 12, 2018."[11]

Maine's first statewide ranked choice election was the 2018 primary election. No Republican candidate failed to reach a majority in the primary. The Republican gubernatorial nominee, Shawn Moody, campaigned for first-place votes only. Two Democratic contests, for governor and US Congress, District 2, had no majority winner, so ballots were transferred to determine the party nominees Janet Mills and Jared Golden.

In November, Maine became the first state to use RCV for a federal general election on November 6, 2018. Elections for the US Senate and for the US Representative, District 1, produced majority winners. However, in Maine's second congressional district, as discussed in the Introduction (see Table 0.1), the results of the first round of counting were 46.3 percent for Republican incumbent Bruce Poliquin and 45.6 percent for his Democratic opponent Jared Golden. The two trailing candidates captured the remainder, and their votes were transferred, if possible, to Poliquin or Golden. In the last round of tabulation, finalized twenty days after the election, Golden was declared the winner with 50.6 percent.

Prior to the second round of tabulations, however, Poliquin filed a motion in the US District Court to stop the Secretary of State's count, arguing that the US Constitution should be understood to only require a plurality. Judge Lance Walker denied an initial request for immediate relief two days later. Since the election was particularly close, Poliquin requested a hand recount.[12] As the recount proceeded, Judge Walker issued a ruling rejecting Poliquin's claim on December 13.[13] The following day, Poliquin terminated the recount. Although he appealed to the First Circuit of the US Court of Appeals to stop certification, the Court initially denied his request. On Christmas Eve, Poliquin withdrew his appeal. Jared Golden was elected to the US Congress. On December 28, Governor Paul LePage signed the official certification for the 2nd District election but wrote "stolen election" on the document next to his signature. (See Figure 5.1.)

Following the 2018 election, the Committee and the other advocacy groups sought to expand RCV to more Maine elections. In the next session, a bill was introduced to extend RCV to presidential primary and general elections.[14] The bill was approved by both chambers in the Maine Legislature in August 2019. Governor Janet Mills refused to sign the bill, but it became law without her signature on January 12, 2020. However, the enactment occurred too late to be effective for the presidential primary election on March 3.[15] A challenge was made to US District Court that RCV violates rights under the US Constitution. The parties in the lawsuit protested that they should not be required or encouraged to rank—thus vote for—candidates they do not want to be elected. That is, similar to the Oklahoma primary law, they should not be subject to compelled speech. Another

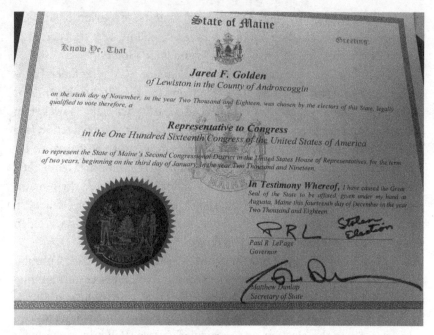

Figure 5.1 Maine Certification of 2018 Election for 2nd congressional district.

Maine Governor Paul LePage wrote "Stolen Election" on the election certification for the first congressional election decided by transferred ballots under RCV.

Source: LePage, Paul R. Twitter Post, December 28, 2018. https://twitter.com/Governor_LePage/status/1078726890746191872/photo/1

claim in the lawsuit was that RCV was burdensome; that is, the information demands for ranking multiple choices were too strong, particularly for older and less educated voters. Judge Lance Walker, however, dismissed the case on August 19, with a decision that echoed his earlier ruling.[16] The Court refused to intervene in the election. Thus, RCV appeared on the ballot for the presidential race on November 3, 2020, making Maine the first state to apply preferential voting for the presidency in a general election.

The experience of Maine is perhaps cautionary. Since plurality elections have been the norm for US elections, the transition to a system where the first-round plurality winner is defeated can result in allegations of unfairness. In Maine, supporters of Bruce Poliquin realized that they would have won the 2018 election under the plurality rule. Unfortunately, this left some in Maine's 2nd congressional district with a feeling that Jared Golden's election was somehow illegitimate. Golden received 50.2 percent in the final round paired with Poliquin, but he also received only 49.2 percent among all first-choice ballots—less than a majority. Republicans could legitimately cry foul in that the RCV outcome was not, in fact, a majority. Golden's election could reasonably be seen as decided by those who did not rank either candidate first. Of course, another caution should be made against comparisons to hypothetical elections. If the election were indeed a plurality election, candidates and voters may have changed their behavior by campaigning differently or engaging in strategic voting.

During his campaign, Poliquin urged his supporters to mark their ballots for a single first-place vote. Golden, on the other hand, encouraged third-party voters to rank him as another, intermediate preference. This strategy may have simply been a tactical error on the part of the Poliquin campaign. In an RCV election, a candidate definitely wants their supporters to mark a first-place rank on the ballot in order to win outright or to avoid elimination. However, a candidate who discourages voters from marking a second- or lower-place rank puts the candidate at a disadvantage in a transfer round.

Although Governor LePage and Republicans were most vociferous in their attack on the implementation of RCV, Democrats had suspicions as well. Many of the leaders behind the RCV initiative supported independent, unaligned candidates such as Eliot Cutler, who ran for governor against LePage, and former state Treasurer Terry Hayes, a former Democrat who left the party to run as an independent. To some, then, the RCV movement was simply an attack on both major parties. So, it is important to note that there was not a shift to nonpartisan elections; instead, the focus was on representing the voting population more fully. In addition, Maine RCV would be used within primary elections as well. The broader effort was to represent Mainer voices at all levels of elections. Although displacing the major political parties was not the fundamental reason for lobbying for preferential voting, certainly, a motivation for ranked choice elections was to broaden the scope of political discourse beyond traditional two-party polarization. That motivation also applied within the second state to adopt RCV.

Alaska

Like Maine, Alaska also has a streak of political independence. For example, of the twelve gubernatorial elections from 1974 to 2014, eight winners captured less than a majority of voters. Two of those received less than 40 percent. Moreover, political partisanship seems to be less important to many Alaskans. Wally Hickel, former Republican governor and Secretary of the Interior, was elected as governor again in 1990 under a minor party label; Hickel previously came in second as a write-in candidate in 1978. Incumbent Senator Lisa Murkowski lost the Republican primary election in 2010, but she won the general election after mounting a write-in campaign. Several members of the Alaska Legislature are politically independent or nonaffiliated. Like Mainers, Alaskans are willing to go beyond the traditional two major party organizations.

In November 2020, Alaskans, by a narrow margin of 50.5 percent–49.5 percent, approved a ballot proposition to incorporate RCV in state elections.[17] The election reform proposal went further than adopting RCV. There were three components to the Top-Four Ranked-Choice Voting and Campaign Finance Laws Initiative, all planned to interact to give Alaskan voters more electoral clout. First, traditional primaries are replaced by an open primary from which the top four plurality vote-getters proceed to the general election. This top four primary applies to all state executive, legislative, and congressional elections. Second, general elections will use RCV. This includes both elections from the top four primary winners as well as the presidential election. Third, the original sources of campaign contributions over $2000 must be disclosed. This measure intends to shine light on the contributors of so-called dark money, or efforts to conceal the original persons or institutions making second-hand donations through an intermediary organization.

The motivation behind the initiative was the feeling that the system of primary elections in particular, as well as plurality general elections, is a broken system. Influential leaders in the major parties are able to manipulate the outcomes to elect extremist candidates. Scott Kendall, campaign coordinator for Senator Lisa Murkowski's reelection campaign in 2016 and chief of staff for Governor Bill Walker from 2016 to 2018, developed the ideas behind the initiative. Kendall first landed on the idea of "an open primary with real choices.[18] But what we had to avoid was extremist politicians winning with, you know, 28% of the vote, which is what a plurality system leaves you with." Top two primaries, like those in California and Washington, did not seem attractive as most state legislative districts would result in general elections with either two Democrats or two Republicans. Particularly for a state with a substantial population of independent voters, that is effectively disenfranchising the population. Moreover, limiting the number of candidates constrains the issues discussed during the campaign. That led Kendall to thoughts of an open primary with the top three or four taken to a general election.

With three or more candidates, of course, there is no guarantee of a consensus or majoritarian election winner. That recognition led Kendall to the idea of combining a top four primary with RCV. Kendall notes, "We were trying to get a system, a basically un-hackable system. What system will give people real choices, but won't distort outcomes due to trickery?" RCV seemed a solution to potential problems with an open primary. He continues:

> What I worried about in the top four world is that you have three moderates and one crazy person. The crazy person manages to pull off 29% of the voter, and the other three split the vote. You literally end up with someone who's aberrant, and that 71% of the state, for example, would have preferred any one of the other three. Ranked choice voting cures that problem.

Neither the range of issues discussed nor the type of candidates competing are problematic. The problem with plurality voting in a multicandidate environment is election by accident. So, Kendall backed into RCV with the credo, "if we give this many choices...first do no harm."

After coming up with the plan, Kendall drew others around him. The reform movement was largely a volunteer operation.[19] Coalitions were formed to support and oppose the ballot proposition. The association formed in favor of the initiative, Alaskans for Better Elections (ABE) Yes on 2, tried to involve independents, Republicans, and Democrats.[20] Opponents to the measure established the association Defend Alaska Elections. Campaign spending on the initiative exceeded $7 million, spent mostly by the camp favoring the proposition.

For supporters, the combination of top four open primaries and RCV constitutes a unified reform package. The transparency that comes from campaign finance disclosure of sources was likewise an important part of the package for election reform advocates. The establishment challenge to the initiative focused on this element. In August 2019, Alaska Attorney General Kevin Clarkson claimed that the initiative was unconstitutional because it violated the state's single-subject rule. Lieutenant Governor Kevin Meyer, based on the Attorney General's recommendation, ordered the Division of Elections to block the gathering of signatures to get the proposition on the ballot.[21] Under the single-subject rule, confining legislative bills as well as voter initiatives, a proposed initiative can involve only one proposed subject or change.[22] The Better Elections committee challenged the decision in Superior Court. Judge Yvonne Lamoureux sided with ABE and directed that signatures should be collected. The case was appealed to the Alaska Supreme Court. Justice Daniel Winfree's unanimous opinion affirmed the constitutionality of the ABE initiative.[23] The single subject of the referendum was election reform.

Once the ballot proposition was scheduled for the November 2020 election, advocates for reform began a statewide campaign for the initiative. One important constituency was Alaskan Native stakeholders. Although composed of many different tribes or bands, the Alaskan Native population makes up about 15 percent of the state's population, and some rural communities have concentrated populations. This group is often underrepresented, and the opportunity for enhanced political representation under RCV appealed to some members of the Alaska Native community. An early endorsement from Bryce Edgmon, then Speaker of the House and the first Native Alaskan to attain that position, was helpful in this community.[24] Many prominent political leaders, including former Senator Mark Begich and Governor Mark Dunleavy, opposed the initiative.

The critical event, perhaps a tipping point for the success of the ballot proposition, was the 2020 primary election. Incumbent state Senator John Coghill lost in the Republican primary for District B. Coghill had served in the Senate since 2009. Previously, he served in the House from 1999 to 2009 and had been majority leader in both chambers. However, the Alaska governor and pro-Trump forces targeted several legislative incumbents in the 2020 primaries. The election for Coghill's seat was close. Results from a recount after the election showed that Robert Myers defeated Coghill by only 14 votes out of 3,464 valid votes cast. Turnout in the primary was only 22.3 percent. The surprising outcome may have persuaded some voters statewide to support the ballot proposition on political reform in the general election.[25]

With voter approval of the ballot question in 2020, the path to enactment of RCV in Alaska seemed straightforward. The opportunities to block implementation of an initiative are fewer in Alaska. As Scott Kendall says proudly, "we have the best constitution in the country, hands down. I'll take that argument from anyone in any state. It has a very strong democracy, direct democracy component." The Alaska Constitution has a provision that an initiative measure cannot be vetoed and may not be repealed by the legislature for two years from its effective date.[26] That guaranteed at least one election cycle with the top four primary, ranked choice general election should occur, barring intervention by the courts. A postelection legal challenge claimed that the election reform package violates constitutional rights as political parties are unable to select their own nominees. Although the two major parties opposed the initiative, neither signed on as a party to the lawsuit.[27] On January 19, 2022, the Alaska Supreme Court affirmed a lower state court decision that the ballot proposition was constitutionally sound.[28]

Preferential voting among up to four candidates in the general election encourages more candidate competition, a broader discussion of political issues, higher voter turnout in both primary and general elections, and greater citizen satisfaction with their political choices. At least, those are the goals of the Alaska plan. The first application of Alaska's plan began with the June 11, 2022, special (open) primary election. A vacancy opened in the US House of Representatives with the death of Don Young, who held the seat for almost five decades. Forty-eight candidates, including sixteen Republicans and six Democrats, filed for the seat in the special primary election. No candidates won a clear majority, so four candidates—Republicans Sarah Palin (former governor and vice presidential candidate) and Nick Begich (the third generation of a prominent political family), independent Al Gross (orthopedic surgeon), and Democrat Mary Peltola advanced to the special general election of August 16, 2022.[29] Gross withdrew from the general election.[30]

Neither Palin's nor Begich's campaign encouraged supporters to rank the other second, even though both were Republicans. In the special general election, Peltola, the Democrat, led with 40.2 percent of the first-round votes, and Palin came in second (31.3 percent). Begich ranked third (28.5 percent) and was the first to be eliminated. Although many Begich supporters ranked Palin second, some transferred their votes to the Democrat and others ranked no candidate second.[31] In the final tally, Peltola bested Palin to win the election, 51.5 percent–48.5 percent. Mary Peltola became the first Aboriginal woman to serve in the US Congress. It is notable, however, that Peltola did not win a majority of all votes cast, only a majority in the final round.[32] Like Poliquin's experience in the first RCV congressional election in Maine, discouraging voters from marking anything beyond a first rank may be a poor campaign tactic. The leading candidate in the first round of the election was defeated because not enough votes were transferred from the candidates with fewer early round votes.

Arguably, the Alaska system was successful in achieving its objective of electing moderate candidates, or at least those with a broad range of support. In the 2022 general election for the US House, Peltola again faced Palin and Begich along with Libertarian Party candidate Chris Bye, who ranked a distant fourth, selected from a field of twenty-two names on the primary ballot. This time, however, Peltola received nearly 49 percent of the vote in the first round, trailed by Palin (26 percent) and Begich (24 percent). If voters on the right had ranked the three candidates fully and consistently, Palin might have won. By the November general election, more Alaska voters ranked more candidates on the ballot. However, enough supporters of Begich and Bye ranked Peltola above Palin. The incumbent Mary Peltola was reelected in the final round by a comfortable margin, 55.0 percent–45.0 percent. In the US Senate contest held simultaneously, incumbent Lisa Murkowski maintained a slim, 2,000-vote lead over her conservative Republican challenger Kelly Tshibaka, 43.4 percent–42.60 percent. After vote transfers from right-wing Republican candidate Buzz Kelley and Democrat Patricia Chesbro, Murkowski was selected over Tshibaka in the final round, 53.7 percent–46.3 percent. Although other factors in the Alaska model may also influence the outcomes, these races at the top of the ticket appear more in line with the preferences of moderate Alaska voters.[33]

As with the implementation of preferential voting in Maine, it may take some time to evaluate the success of the Alaska model. A key difference in the electoral system in Alaska is the single-vote open primary with an RCV runoff among the top four. In previous Alaska state elections, it was unusual for there to be four or more candidates running for most seats, so the RCV component may be a critical factor to encourage intraparty competition and representation of a broader range of candidates, perhaps with the representation of more moderate candidates. However, for RCV and other political reforms, it is important to remember that in the American federal system, states are laboratories of democracy. One or two states, like Maine and Alaska, may experiment with policy innovation so other states can learn if the model works well for them.[34] Alaska voters may reconsider its RCV system; an initiative petition to repeal RCV reached the ballot in 2024, but it lost by a narrow margin. Hawaii recently adopted RCV for federal special elections.[35] Nevada voters initially approved a ballot question to switch to a system like Alaska's for state and federal races: an open primary with a top five RCV general election. However, Nevada requires a majority in two succeeding general elections for a state constitutional amendment by initiative. Voters rejected RCV in 2024.[36]

Why did RCV begin at the statewide level in these two states? Both have substantial groups of voters and political elites who claim to be politically unaffiliated. Both states have active competition among more than the two major political parties. Thus, both are arenas where preferential voting may suit the political environment, particularly for those resisting an urge to vote strategically. But these two states also have a political culture that is somewhat unique from the rest of the country. As pressure mounts in other states to modify electoral systems, lessons from these two states may guide policy decisions. But those lessons are yet unprepared. It is notable that the partisan orientation of each state differs—Maine trends Democrat and Alaska Republican—so their experiences may tell us more together than separately.

Presidential Elections

The United States has a lengthy and complicated process of nominating and electing its chief executive. The processes themselves are subjects of frequent criticism and regular calls for reform. Could RCV change the presidential selection process? There are two stages to the presidential selection process—the nomination phase and the general election phase. Each brings different challenges and possibilities for RCV reformers.[37]

In the nomination phase, a state may utilize either a primary election or a party caucus to select delegates to the national nominating convention. For the two major parties, the process now involves potential presidential candidates campaigning from January through June, from state to state, through a series of primaries and caucuses. The outcomes of the primaries and caucuses influence how many delegates each candidate is awarded from those states to the national nominating conventions held late in the summer. Over the course of the primary and caucus season, candidates who fail to accrue a sufficient number of delegates typically drop out of the race, thus narrowing each party's field of candidates.[38]

From the electorate's perspective, voters cast a ballot for their preference among presidential candidates. State and party rules vary on whether and under what circumstances delegates are bound to vote for the candidate at the convention. In order to win the nomination, a successful candidate must receive the vote of a majority of delegates at the national convention. The political parties control the process of nominating candidates to run for president (within parameters set by state and federal law). Although each party always worries about a brokered convention with no candidate receiving a majority, since 1952 both parties have nominated a candidate on the first ballot.

Delegate selection rules for the US political parties are rather complex. The Democrats have a more uniform set of complicated rules that apply throughout the country. The Republicans allow the states and territories greater leeway in developing their own rules. Thus, there is considerable variation in the delegate selection process. In some states, the Republican rules are fairly straightforward, but in others, their rules closely mirror the Democrats.

Since 1972, the Democratic Party's rules have required that the bulk of its delegates to the presidential nominating conventions be chosen in each state according to the proportion of the vote for the presidential candidates in the primaries and caucuses.[39] Roughly three-quarters of each state's delegates are chosen by votes in the congressional districts, and another quarter is chosen at-large according to the statewide total. But there is a catch: candidates must pass a threshold of 15 percent of the vote in order to be eligible for delegates.[40]

In some states, the Republicans use proportional allocation of delegates in a manner similar to the Democrats, although the thresholds vary. The Republican rules allow states to use winner-take-all rules for the selection of delegates, but only for those states that delay their primaries. For example, in 2020, states could only use winner-take-all rules if they delayed their primaries until after March 15. In some states, the Republican primaries are proportional unless the lead candidate achieves a certain percentage, in which case the decision method switches to winner-take-all. In some states, Republican delegate selection is not strictly winner-take-all, but a hybrid system allocates more delegates to the winner.

The method of delegate assignments would influence the outcome. For winner-take-all states, the application of RCV/instant runoff voting (IRV) would be straightforward. Transfer of ranked ballots from preferences of lower ranked candidates could be conducted until a majority winner is determined. Delegate selection with proportional assignment would require some form of single transferable vote (STV). However, proportionality is typically defined in terms of first choices, and current rules already meet that standard. Further, as noted earlier, STV is often classified as a PR system, but the relative proportionality varies considerably based on the rules to transfer votes into delegates. There is no single form or species of STV (Tideman 1995, Farrell and McAllister 2006) and evidence from national elections in other countries suggests the particular variety of STV influences the proportionality of party representation (Farrell and Katz 2014). It is rather difficult to predict the result of using STV in a multistage selection system, and little would be gained over the current first-choice proportional rules.

The party establishment usually wants to narrow the field of candidates relatively soon. However, it is unclear whether RCV would either help or detract from that intention. In fact, it could probably go either way. Table 5.1 uses 2020 presidential contenders to provide several, admittedly oversimplified, scenarios. The first preference is the same for all cases, and the second, transferable preference differs across each scenario. In this example, the leading candidate receives 35 percent of the vote, with the following two candidates receiving 20 percent and 17 percent. Sixteen delegates are selected from the state. Under current PR rules with a 15 percent threshold, the leading candidate, Biden, receives eight delegates, while the two trailing candidates, Harris and Klobuchar, receive four each. Table 5.1 examines what would happen based on different combinations of second choices. This proportional allocation would be the same if the distribution of second choices followed the pattern of first choices. Depending on how the next

Table 5.1 Hypothetical presidential primary: Sixteen delegates assigned according to PR with threshold and RCV with next preference assigned

Candidate	Vote %	15% Threshold	2nd Choice Biden	2nd Choice Harris	2nd Choice Klobuchar	2nd Choice Equally
Biden	35	8	10	5	6	7
Harris	20	4	3	8	3	5
Klobuchar	17	4	3	3	7	4
O'Rourke	12	0	0	0	0	0
Booker	8	0	0	0	0	0
Gillibrand	5	0	0	0	0	0
Warren	3	0	0	0	0	0

For 15 percent threshold, delegates are proportioned among the candidates above the threshold. This is equivalent to assuming all transferable ballots among the candidates above the threshold are distributed in the same relative percentages as the first preference for each candidate. Equal distribution means all candidates receive one-third of outstanding ballots.

transferable choice occurs in this example, the range of votes for the leading candidate Biden spans from five to ten, with two scenarios—either Harris or Klobuchar as the common second choice—changing the overall winner in the state. The example provided in Table 5.1 is for illustration only, but it does indicate the substantial changes that a preferential ballot could produce. These changes would occur across the constituencies with delegate selection, thus potentially extending the time to narrow down the field or changing the party nominee.

The second stage in presidential election encompasses the general election and the electoral college allocation that follows. Voters choose among the major parties' nominees, along with third-party or independent candidates, in the general election in November. But as is generally understood by American voters, those popular votes are used to select a state's slate of electors to the Electoral College who do the actual job of electing the president.[41] Each state receives a number of electoral votes equal to its number of Representatives in the House plus its number of members in the Senate (the latter is always two). Three electoral votes are given to the District of Columbia.

The electoral college has been the focus of reform efforts since the early days of the US Republic. Delegates at the Constitutional Convention could not agree on a method of electing the president. They ultimately designed a method that assigned each state a number of electors based on their total congressional delegation and left it to each state to determine how its electors would be chosen. Over time, each state decided to select its electors through a popular vote, with most states adopting a winner-take-all method. Two states, Maine and Nebraska, assign electoral votes in a different manner than other states. Rather than assigning votes according to a unit rule, where the plurality winner in the statewide election receives all of the state's electoral votes, under this congressional district plan, two electoral votes are assigned to the statewide winner and one electoral vote to the winner in each congressional district.[42]

State voters select which candidate they prefer for president in the general election, and the plurality winner—except in Maine and Nebraska—determines the list of electors for their state.[43] Those electors meet at their state capital in January and cast electoral votes for the president and vice president. Currently, there are 538 electors, so a majority vote of 270 is required to win. Congress, in a joint session, counts the votes and certifies the winner. If no candidate receives a majority, the House of Representatives must select a president by majority vote among the top three candidates, with each state's delegation in the House getting one vote. The Senate selects the vice president.

RCV/IRV could translate popular votes into electoral college votes under the unit rule (winner-take-all) or the congressional district plan (Maine or Nebraska). Legal scholar Edward Foley (2020: 128) suggests RCV as one of a variety of options for presidential election reform and notes that the system meets constitutional standards for the selection of electors. In either case, the popular vote for a constituency could be used and transferred votes from trailing candidates applied.[44] The state of Maine allowed preferential voting for the presidential elections in 2020 and 2024. All winners received majorities on the first ballot. The use of the term "winners" may seem strange to anyone unfamiliar with the arcane elements of presidential election.

The majoritarian impulse has the potential to alter results. In 2016, twelve states had presidential election winners attracting less than half of the votes.[45] Although more press coverage has been devoted to the outcome of the 2020 election, only four states had a presidential winner with less than a majority.[46] Certainly, the replacement of the Electoral College by a nationwide popular vote using RCV/IRV is possible through constitutional amendment, but the complications and the magnitude of effects that this systematic change would entail suggest this is neither wise nor desirable.

The American system of electing the president is not particularly effective at producing majority winners nationally. Since World War II, eight presidential elections (of twenty) produced a president elected with less than 50 percent of the popular vote. The Electoral College, however, seems effective for manufacturing majorities. These electoral vote winners often appear to be Condorcet winners. However, in the 2016 election between Donald Trump and Hillary Clinton, many American voters complained about selecting between the lesser of two evils. Clinton won the popular vote, but Trump won the electoral vote. There is some evidence from opinion surveys that, in head-to-head contests, Trump may have been the Condorcet loser, not only to Clinton but also to minor party candidates Gary Johnson (Libertarian) and Jill Stein (Green) (Potthoff and Munger 2021). This circumstance is unusual and Condorcet losers are typically the minor party candidates (Abramson et al. 1995).

Rather than weighing hypothetical advantages and disadvantages, however, a more fruitful exercise would be to examine the ranked choice experience from recent municipal elections. Chapter 6 provides an analysis of actual elections in American cities and towns.

6
Evaluation of RCV Elections

American advocates of preferential voting systems point to many potential benefits of conversion to such a system. Many of these advantages are perceived changes to the overall election environment, and macro-level improvements. For example, some believe that it will result in less polarized and rancorous campaigning, as candidates will need to be careful not to offend voters who might rank them second (Slaughter, Fukuyama, and Diamond 2019). Others believe that it might increase the number and variety of candidates or parties willing to run in an election since leading the pack in the first round is not necessarily decisive (Mercer 2016, Hill and Richie 2004). The potential variety of candidates leads still others to suggest that RCV might increase the willingness of voters to turn out. Advocates also point to the reduction in wasted votes; this is particularly true in the single transferable vote (STV) form, as more voters could have ballots that contribute to the election of a candidate (Grigg 1981, Garland and Terry 2017). For the instant runoff voting (IRV) /alternative vote (AV) form of preferential voting, one of the most noteworthy aspects is its requirement for a majority outcome. The chief advantage of requiring a majority is greater voter satisfaction with the election outcome, as well as a stronger mandate for the elected official. Further, in a situation where there is a winning plurality for a particularly divisive candidate, the ability to change the outcome to a consensus candidate has a particularly strong appeal.

Not surprisingly, academic interest in RCV has grown along with public interest. Many scholars have begun to examine the extent to which RCV voting systems meet the expectations of advocates and reformers. Kimball and Anthony (2016, 2017), for example, examine the use of RCV and voter turnout. By analyzing groups of comparable cities wherein some of the cities have adopted RCV and some have not, they determine that there is very little increase in voter turnout before and after the adoption of RCV. An exception to this occurs when comparing cities that used a separate primary and/or runoff election, in which case the authors observe that the number of votes used in the second round of AV is substantially higher than in a runoff.

Ranked Choice Voting. James W. Endersby and Michael J. Towle, Oxford University Press.
© Oxford University Press (2025). DOI: 10.1093/9780197798959.003.0007

Endersby and Towle (2014) observe that voter turnout for STV elections is lower in Irish parliamentary districts when it should be high (with more candidates elected) and higher when turnout should be low (with fewer candidates elected).

Some research has focused more directly on the effects of the voting and counting process itself. Neely and Cook (2008), for example, have examined whether the added complexity of RCV ballots affects the incidence of undervotes or overvotes. An overvote is when a voter—perhaps mistakenly—casts a vote for more candidates than allowed in that race; an undervote is when a voter chooses to vote for fewer candidates than allowed. Often, an undervote indicates a blank ballot for a particular office. Using data from AV elections in San Francisco, they determine that RCV ballots have lower incidences of undervotes but higher incidences of overvotes. Endersby and Towle (2014), analyzing STV results for elections to Ireland's Dáil Éireann, discovered a high level of ballots that were nontransferable, especially in cases where numerous rounds of transfers were needed to complete the election.

Burnett and Kogan (2015), using data from AV elections in three municipalities in California and one county in Washington that provided digital ballot imagery (or cast vote records), analyzed different types of ballot exhaustion. Each of these elections allowed voters to rank up to three candidates. Among other findings, they determine that when looking at the elections combined, the most common reason for a ballot to become exhausted is that the voter did not opt to provide rankings of three candidates (suggesting rules allowing—but not requiring—a full ranking of the ballot may not solve the problem of exhausted ballots). The number of ballots exhausted because voters provided duplicate choices in their rankings ranged from 5 percent to 12 percent. Further, the number of voters whose ballots were exhausted because they only voted for candidates who were eliminated in early rounds ranged considerably but was over 22 percent in San Francisco, where there was a high number of candidates running. Finally, Burnett and Kogan (2015) made an observation that we will address further in this chapter. They observed that because of exhausted ballots, in none of the four elections in their study did the winning candidates have a majority of all ballots cast; instead, they only had a majority of the final round count.

If a typical election attracted only one or two candidates, there would be no need for preference rankings among voters; a simple majority would be produced naturally. The incidence of multiple candidates (three or more) per elective office is necessary for ranked preferences to be valuable. For most elections, under both single-member district plurality (SMDP) and RCV, one candidate wins an outright majority, but in the interesting and controversial cases, the first-round winner does not capture a majority of votes.

This chapter looks at four key issues pertaining to RCV elections: the number of candidates competing, the number of exhausted and wasted votes that do not count for any candidate (winning or losing), whether first-round winners are defeated by another candidate, and the winning percentage of victorious candidates. On the latter question, we look at both first-round and final-round counts. Other benefits, such as increased voter turnout and improved voter satisfaction, would be attractive features for RCV. Addressing features such as voter satisfaction and more positive campaigns requires more and different data than are available here. Contemporary data from hundreds of elections can be used to assess how well ranked choice elections achieve the goals sought by reformers.

RCV Experience and American Municipalities

The United States now has over two decades of experience with preferential voting in a cross-section of American municipalities, so there is an abundance of aggregate data that can be used to analyze five core assumptions underlying electoral reform. First, does the number of candidates competing for office increase with the adoption of RCV? One claim of supporters is an increased range of alternatives available to voters. An assumption is that more candidates will compete for office at the time of the election. However, the incentives for more candidates to participate are unclear. Second, does the number of eligible voters participating in elections increase following the adoption of RCV? Along with the prediction of more candidates, reform advocates predict increased voter turnout. Individuals who perceive greater opportunity to exert political influence should be more likely to cast a ballot than under plurality elections. Third, do more voters' ballots count toward the candidates elected? A primary justification for RCV is that more voters can impact the final outcomes because fewer ballots are wasted. Some voters' ballots with incomplete rankings may be exhausted during the transfer process.

Fourth, do RCV elections lead to majority winners? Although other benefits may follow from RCV, the primary justification for the adoption of RCV voting is the creation of majority outcomes. If majority winners are not actually produced, a main advantage of RCV may be called into question. Fifth, how often are the winners of RCV different from those of plurality voting? If the first-round winners are ultimately chosen with transferred ballots, then there is less justification for imposing a complicated electoral system on voters. The long-term rationale must be that some winners differ from those who would be selected in plurality elections. There are many potential benefits of RCV, but they may be illusory if outcomes would be the same as under (sincere) voting in plurality elections; this information may be important for areas considering RCV adoption. The assumption is that first preferences are sincere. Although voters might behave strategically in plurality elections, they would do so under the assumption that their first preference could not win. Thus, RCV preferences, by assumption, suggest the rankings reveal sincere preferences.

In order to determine the answers to these questions, data from twenty-one US municipalities holding RCV elections from 2001 through 2020 are analyzed. Data include results for the elections of 532 public officials and are summarized in Table 6.1.[1] The data include all cities that currently use RCV (IRV, multiwinner ranked vote [MRV], or STV) for at least one elected official during this time span. This includes cities that experimented with RCV, and then repealed the practice (when the data are available).[2] Excluded are a number of cities, typically smaller communities, with an ordinance for RCV, that have never held an election with more than two candidates competing.[3] This produces a bias in favor of RCV in the analyses here. For instance, one assumption is that cities with RCV should exhibit a larger number of candidates competing for office. Omitting these elections—with only one or two candidates when RCV is available—artificially raises the average number of candidates competing, a prediction favorable to RCV advocates.[4] Moreover, winners in plurality and RCV elections produce identical winners when fewer than three candidates compete. Of course, elections with only one or two candidates are included following the initial implementation of RCV. Most of the results below omit MRV or multiwinner ranked vote systems (Aspen, Hendersonville, Payson, Vineyard) because of the complications of comparing them to other ranked choice methods (IRV or STV). However, it is worth noting that all actual winners in these communities would also have been elected under traditional multiwinner block or plurality voting.

Table 6.1 Ranked choice elections in American cities: Cases in sample

Municipalities	Election Years	Elective Offices Filled*	Elective Offices (Seats)
Aspen, CO	2009	3	Mayor, Council (4)
Basalt, CO	2020	1	Mayor
Berkeley, CA	2010–2020	30	Mayor, Council (8), Auditor
Burlington, VT	2006–2009	2	Mayor
Cambridge, MA	2001–2019	144	Council (9), School Committee (6)
Cary, NC	2007	4	Mayor, Council (6)
Eastpointe, MI	2019–2020	3	Council
Hendersonville, NC	2007–2009	5	Mayor, Council
Las Cruces, NM	2019	5	Mayor, Council, Municipal Judge
Minneapolis, MN	2009–2020	76	Mayor, Council (13), Parks & Rec (7), Estimate & Taxes (4)
Oakland, CA	2010–2020	54	Mayor, Council, Auditor, School Director
Payson, UT	2019	3	Council
Portland, ME	2011–2020	6	Mayor; Council (4) & School Board (since 2020)
San Francisco, CA	2004–2020	81	Mayor, Board of Supervisors, Assessor-Recorder, City Attorney, District Attorney, Public Defender, Sheriff, Treasurer
San Leandro, CA	2010–2020	21	Mayor, Council (6)
Santa Fe, NM	2018–2019	10	Mayor, Council (4)
St. Louis Park, MN	2019	3	Mayor, Council
St. Paul, MN	2011–2019	25	Mayor, Council (7)
Takoma Park, MD	2007–2020	51	Mayor, Council (6)
Telluride, CO	2011–2019	3	Mayor
Vineyard, UT	2019	2	Council
All cities		532	

*Includes general and special elections.

Candidate Competition

Advocates of RCV believe that election reforms should enhance representation by allowing a broader range of choices available to voters. Rather than limiting elections to a small number of candidates, simply appealing to a median ideological position or common denominator, ranking preferences should encourage the emergence of a greater number and variety of candidates competing for office. This assumption is typically discussed in terms of ideological or partisan alternatives. That is, RCV might be expected to provide incentives for a greater number of third-party or ideologically distinct candidates.[5] Although most of the cities that adopted RCV in the sample are nonpartisan, the notion that more candidates should compete for office still applies. More candidates should bring a broader range of issues into campaign discourse. In any case, a key assumption is that the number of candidates should increase under preferential voting. As RCV elections establish a foothold, the average number of candidates competing for election should rise.[6]

The expected growth in candidate competition might vary across political offices. Elective offices are categorized into four types here. First, mayors are the chief executives of the municipal government; elected mayors typically wield more power and incumbents retain higher prestige than other officeholders ($n = 41$). Second, council members or the equivalent hold the legislative authority for the city. In the sample, nearly all represent geographical districts for RCV elections (243 seats filled), although some represent the entire city in STV elections (92).[7] Another smaller number (11) of city council positions are selected through MRV. Third are other citywide elective offices. Some cities, San Francisco, Berkeley, and Oakland, elect other executive officers such as City or District Attorney, Treasurer, and Sheriff (36). Fourth, members of other administrative boards and commissions are elected in several cities. These include members of the school committee in Cambridge, the board of education in Oakland, and the Park and Recreation Board and the Board of Estimate and Taxation in Minneapolis. In this final category, some officials are elected via STV (69) and others through RCV (40).[8]

Table 6.2 reports the average number of official candidates competing in municipal ranked choice elections in the sample.[9] The mean number of mayoral candidates is about seven (6.7 per election). The number of council candidates is smaller, with 3.5 candidates per IRV/AV election and 2.3

Table 6.2 Average number of candidates per seat by election and office

Election Year	Single Member (IRV/AV) #	n	Multiple Member (STV) #	n*
Mayor	6.7	41	—	
Council Member	3.5	243	2.3	11 (92)
Other Executive	1.8	36	—	
Other Board	2.6	40	2.0	15 (69)
Total	3.6	360	2.1	26 (161)

Excludes all write-in candidates.
*Number in parentheses is total number of candidates elected. Eleven MRV elections for city council averaged 3.0 candidates per seat.

per seat in STV elections. The calculation of these means is influenced by a few outliers (such as thirty-four candidates for mayor of Minneapolis in 2013 and twenty-one candidates for a single seat on the San Francisco Board of Supervisors in 2010).[10] Other executive offices and boards of commissions attract comparatively few candidates per race. The number of candidates per seat in these races with either electoral system hovers around two candidates per seat.[11]

Overall, candidate entry does not appear to increase over time. Figure 6.1 displays the average number of candidates contesting seats in each two-year election cycle. Mayoral races show greater volatility than council races because there are fewer elections that occur within a cycle. This variation is the result of a few elections with a particularly large number of candidates. The number of city council candidates competing for seats in RCV elections appears to decline over time. However, this is because elections in San Francisco, an early adopter of RCV/IRV, tend to draw more candidates in council races. So, the early, large average of nine, then five, candidates per seat in each election cycle is driven by the number of candidates running in San Francisco.

As more cities adopt RCV elections, the mean number of candidates competing for city council decreases and averages around three per seat. For more populated cities, a larger number of candidates emerges as RCV elections are initially introduced. Subsequently, the average number of competitors tends to return near an equilibrium for subsequent elections.[12] The number of candidates contesting nine council seats in Cambridge, MA, the one STV municipality in the sample, is around two per seat. There does

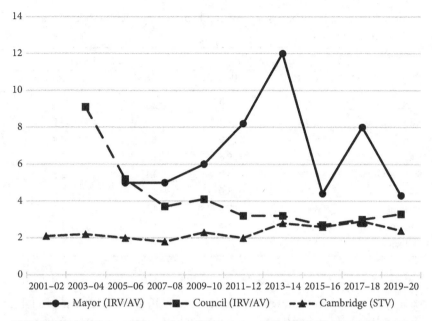

Figure 6.1 Average number of candidates competing by office.

seem to be a slight upward trend within the last several decades; however, since STV was adopted in 1940, two candidates per seat seems to be an equilibrium expectation for Cambridge city elections.

So far, the evidence concerns RCV elections only. Reformers expect the number of candidates to increase from SMDP to RCV elections. A better way to consider whether competition has increased is to compare the average number of candidates contesting an election before and after the introduction of RCV. It is important to look at several elections to account for a potential novelty effect resulting from the first RCV election. The number of candidates competing for each office for three election cycles is collected for nine American cities now holding several RCV elections.[13] Table 6.3 reports the average number of candidates listed on the ballot for several elections before and after RCV was utilized for election.

Overall, any increase in the number of candidates for municipal office in preferential elections is anecdotal rather than the result of a clear pattern. In only five of nine cities with mayoral elections is there an increase in the number of candidates competing; four have fewer candidates on average. For the cities showing an increase, one (Santa Fe) has only one RCV mayoral election and another (Telluride) has no discernible change beyond

Table 6.3 Average number of mayoral and council candidates, before and after ranked choice voting

City	Mayor Pre-RCV	Mayor Post-RCV	Council Pre-RCV	Council Post-RCV
Berkeley	4.5	6.0	2.2	3.0
Minneapolis	2.0	21.3	2.0	3.9
Oakland	6.3	12.0	3.5	4.1
San Francisco	10.3	9.6	4.7	5.7
San Leandro	6.0	4.7	3.1	2.3
Santa Fe	3.7	5.0	2.2	2.0
St. Paul	8.4	7.0	4.5	3.3
Takoma Park	2.0	1.4	1.5	1.4
Telluride	2.7	3.0	—	—

round-off error. For council elections, only half, four cities out of eight, show an increase in candidate competition; half have moderately fewer candidates competing. The results for council elections are stronger as there are multiple council elections held, increasing the level of confidence in the results. Additionally, pre-RCV elections in Minneapolis are constrained to two as, before electoral reform, the city had an open primary with the top two candidates advancing to the general municipal election.[14] On the other hand, more populated cities with a longer history of RCV show an increase in the number of candidates running for office (Oakland, Berkeley, and San Francisco for council races). However, the empirical data must leave an election analyst with the impression that the magnitude of municipal candidate competition depends less on the electoral system—plurality, majority, or RCV—and more on the contextual characteristics of the city's polity.

Voter Turnout

Advocates of RCV often herald its purported effect on increasing voter turnout. In part, this expectation is because more candidates may compete; that is, a broader range of alternatives may be offered to prospective voters. In part, this presumption results from the view that fewer eligible voters will feel that their votes are wasted under RCV; thus, they would be more likely to cast a ballot. The first expectation was considered above, and the second, more fundamental assumption will be examined below. There are other potential explanations for increased voter turnout, such as the expectation that campaigns would be more civil, but in terms of a voter's calculus of voting (or not), these explanations seem paramount.

Analyzing turnout over time involves more difficult computation than we might first expect. There are problems comparing turnout across municipalities as well as within municipalities over time. First, in the United States, turnout is a two-step process involving voter registration as well as the act of casting a ballot. Only one state has no voter registration (North Dakota), although many states allow same-day registration. This eliminates the hurdle for registration that must be overcome in most states and localities, as a voter could both register and cast a ballot at the same time. In a related fashion, some states allow or even require voting by mail and offer other reforms, all intended to increase turnout by making the process of voting easier. Stricter voter registration laws and photo identification requirements might decrease the likelihood of turnout. In short, there are many institutional components of the electoral process that may influence voter turnout beyond RCV, making it difficult to compare across localities without controlling for these factors.

Second, within the sample of RCV elections, voter participation may be affected by when an election is held. Turnout is highest for presidential elections and lower for midterm elections. Many states conduct municipal elections on a predetermined date in March, April, or May. Turnout is typically lower in these off-cycle elections (Hajnal and Lewis 2003, Martinez 2010, Endersby 2022). One simple method to increase turnout is to hold them in November on even-numbered years, concurrent with federal elections. Overall turnout is then much higher, but what draws increased voter turnout to the polls are contests for higher office, not municipal contests. The rate of roll-off, the proportion of voters who vote for offices such as president or congress but skip races further down the ballot, is large for municipal and other local offices. Some voters who cast a ballot skip the local contests. Thus, it is difficult to distinguish whether the municipal election system, RCV, really encourages more voter participation.

In the sample of RCV elections, nearly all are held in November. All but five cities, smaller communities, conduct regular elections in November, and nearly all public officials are chosen (511/532). However, two-thirds of these RCV city elections occur in November of odd-numbered years (344/511). Typically, there are fewer top-of-the-ticket races on the ballot in these odd-numbered year contests.

Third, voter turnout is a ratio of ballots cast (the numerator) to eligible voters (the denominator). An election reform positively affecting turnout, such as RCV, should encourage nonregistered but eligible voters to participate as well as registered nonvoters. However, obtaining accurate measures for the number of eligible voters is problematic. The US Census Bureau provides periodic estimates of a municipality's voting-age population. However, noncitizens and, in some states, citizens convicted of a felony are ineligible to vote, and these individuals should not be included in the denominator. Yet, the Census Bureau does not estimate these populations. The number and proportion of voters vary substantially over time and (worse for comparison) across localities (see McDonald and Popkin 2001). In a few states, municipalities may expand the base of eligible voters for city elections. For example, the municipality of Takoma Park, Maryland, reduced the voting age to sixteen and permits noncitizens to vote, although almost no members from this expanded electorate participate in elections.

Four cities are selected to demonstrate the relationship between RCV elections and voter turnout. These municipalities—San Francisco, Minneapolis, Oakland, and St. Paul—are selected because of the earlier adoption of RCV and its application for several elections.[15] This allows a comparison of several elections before and after the adoption of RCV. A polity may experience a boost in turnout, a novelty effect, following the implementation of any new election reform, and voter participation may return to normal later (Gronke, Galanes-Rosenbaum, and Miller 2007, Gronke and Miller 2012). So, it is important to look at effects over a longer term to draw stronger conclusions. Turnout is reported for citywide elections only. If RCV does increase turnout, the effect would be observed only for council districts that have elections in that year but not in others with no RCV election. This is particularly important when other, non-RCV elections for public officials are held concurrently, the typical scenario.

Elections in the four cities are in states with same-day voter registration. The Minnesota cities, as well as San Francisco for earlier years, hold elections in odd-numbered years. Although San Francisco alternates election years for council districts, citywide contests were held in odd years and are now in even years. Oakland (and the other Alameda County communities) conduct municipal elections simultaneously with state and federal elections.

Regular elections in Minneapolis are conducted every four years. Voty-by-mail elections California are conducted statewide in California, but only since 2022. Turnout figures are among registered voters, as these data are available for each of these cities. Thus, these figures overestimate the rate of turnout among eligible voters.[16]

Voter turnout for these four cities that adopted RCV is depicted in Figure 6.2. Oakland, which holds its elections concurrently with federal elections, reveals the expected pattern. Voter turnout responds to national trends; it is significantly higher in presidential elections than in midterms. The onset of RCV elections seems to have little influence on aggregate turnout in Oakland. San Francisco experienced a surge in turnout following the adoption of RCV, but voter participation subsequently fell below the norm before the electoral system changed. Turnout has since recovered to a rate approximating pre-RCV levels. In St. Paul, RCV was initiated at a time when voter turnout was uncharacteristically low, but the preferential system had no immediate effect on voter turnout. Like the experience in San

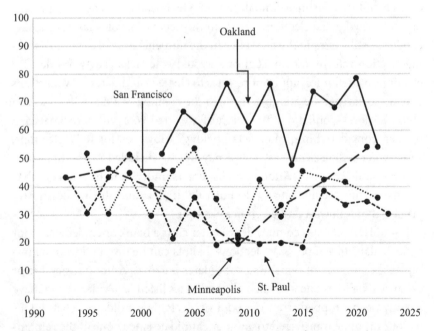

Figure 6.2 Percent turnout among registered voters in four cities adopting RCV.

Arrows denote the election year when each municipality first used RCV elections.

Francisco, turnout in St. Paul has returned to pre-RCV levels beginning with its third RCV election. If there is a citywide case for a positive effect from RCV on voter turnout, it is in Minneapolis. However, with RCV, turnout initially declined to its lowest level. Rates of voter participation have risen in each subsequent election.

Overall, the evidence that the adoption of RCV will increase participation rates among voters is weak. There is no doubt that some new or peripheral voters could be attracted to the new electoral system. Similarly, some existing voters could be deterred from participation because of the greater informational demands and complexity of the ballot. Neither seems to have a strong case according to the aggregate election returns. Other institutional factors appear to have a greater role in voter turnout than the adoption of RCV.[17]

Exhausted or Nontransferable Ballots

Another justification for RCV elections is that many ballots are wasted in plurality elections. This notion of a wasted ballot really means that a voter cast a ballot for a losing candidate, an act which leads to no direct representation following that election.[18] For plurality elections, votes cast for a losing candidate still count in the final tally. In the nomenclature of advocates seeking election reform, the concept of a wasted vote lacks clarity. While STV elections by definition apply more votes to elected candidates, IRV elections may do so early at the margins, through the creation of a majority based on vote transfers—conflating the notion of a wasted vote with a majoritarian winner, considered in greater detail below.[19] However, for RCV elections, some voter ballots with cast votes may not be included in the final tally for any candidate at all. Although most voters understand how to complete a ranked choice ballot, many do not fully understand the administrative process that follows a ranked choice election.

For SMDP, all votes count unless a voter casts a blank or voided ballot for a particular office. For RCV elections, ballots can be dropped from counting as the number of remaining candidates narrows. A nontransferable or exhausted ballot is one for which all candidates listed on a voter's ballot have already been dropped from the pool of electable candidates. That voter's ballot cannot be transferred to another candidate since none of the remaining candidates receives a ranking. These exhausted ballots are the "instant" equivalent of voters not returning to the polls for a runoff.[20] Yet voters do get an opportunity to rethink whether abstention is the right decision to make. Moreover, in electoral constituencies that limit the number of rankings to be recorded on the ballot—for instance, three rankings among six candidates—the election rules may effectively disenfranchise citizens from casting a sincere ballot among all alternatives. If a voter can and does rank all (six in this example) candidates in order from first to last, then the ballot will be counted for *some* candidate. However, if the ballot is marked for only one or any amount up to one less than the total number of candidates (five in the example), the ballot has the potential for exhaustion or nontransferability.[21] It all depends on whether preferences among any of the remaining candidates were marked by the voter.

Most RCV voters probably do not think too much about the counting and transfer process. It is somewhat difficult to generalize as there are many factors influencing a nontransferable ballot. For some RCV elections, losing candidates are eliminated one at a time for each count or round. Election regulations often allow batch elimination, dropping several candidates at once. Since several candidates may be mathematically unable to avoid elimination, particularly in the early rounds, it may take less tabulation time to remove multiple candidates simultaneously. Our impression is that the elimination process may have more to do with the tabulation software used than the codification or intent of election regulations. A related issue is whether and how write-in votes are permitted; allowing write-ins may artificially increase the number of counts or rounds. Two figures graphically depict the progression of exhausted ballots for each round. Figure 6.3 shows this for elections of a lone representative, and Figure 6.4 shows this for multimember elections. The latter case, STV elections, also has the complication that one or more winners may be elected each round as they reach and surpass the quota. The votes exceeding the quota may be reassigned to other unelected candidates.

The two figures report the percentage of nontransferable ballots for all municipal RCV elections when no candidate receives a majority of votes on the first ballot. Each graph shows the minimum, maximum, and the average number of ballots that cannot be transferred each round (not the total, as this simply increases across transfer rounds). Only one RCV/IRV election goes more than twenty rounds, so all three lines merge after twenty in Figure 6.3.[22] Despite the difficulty in displaying this process pictorially, it is evident that there are quite a few ballots that are exhausted along the road to declaring a winner. There tend to be several peaks of ballot exhaustion. The first peak covers the initial rounds as voters ranking only one (or two) losing candidates declare no subsequent preferences. Second is the point, for

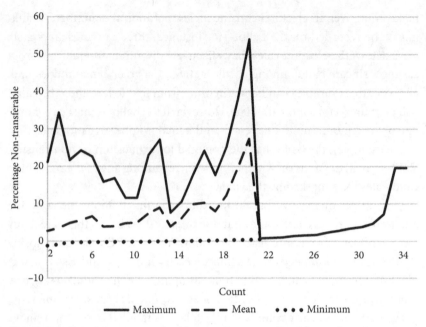

Figure 6.3 Percent nontransferable votes by count single-member election (IRV/AV).

certain constituencies, following the maximum number of rankings that are allowed.[23] Third is the final set of rounds as the candidates remaining are limited to those disapproved by many voters.

Results from American cities demonstrate that many votes are not transferred at some point during the counting, particularly as the number of rounds increases. Overall, nearly 6 percent of ballots are nontransferable on average, but this figure includes those decided in the first round with no transfers. This rate is lower for RCV/IRV elections (3.0 percent) than STV (11.5 percent).[24] If an election goes to a second round, or an election in which ranked choices matter, the average of exhausted or nontransferable ballots is 10.1 percent in AV elections and 11.7 percent in STV elections at the time winners are chosen. On average, about 1.5% of ballots are lost on the first transfer.[25] However, the mean for each transfer tends to grow as the number of rounds increases; some averages approach 10 percent in later counts. For some elections, relatively few voter ballots are exhausted, particularly for elections with a small number of candidates (three). However, it is not unusual for elections to lose many voters. Occasionally, the

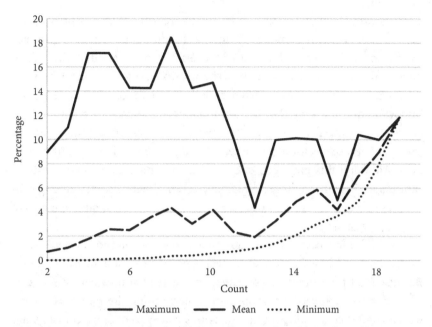

Figure 6.4 Percent nontransferable votes by count multimember election (STV).

maximum number of voters lost surpasses reasonable expectations for some elections. The number of nontransferable ballots reached 54 percent before a winner could be selected for a seat on the San Francisco Board of Supervisors in 2010. Elections with many nonviable candidates, that is, those receiving comparatively few first-round votes, may take many counts to eliminate these minor candidacies.

Write-in votes are a technical issue for all elections and complicate the clarity of the data reported here. For preferential voting, write-ins are more difficult to handle, as they complicate vote transfers. Municipalities with RCV elections handle write-in ballots differently. Some allow certified write-in candidacies; others do not allow or tabulate unofficial write-in candidates at all. Cambridge sets rankings for write-ins. In at least one case (San Francisco), votes for all first-ballot write-in candidates are reported but then discounted before tabulating RCV results. Votes for uncertified write-ins are not permitted for RCV in San Francisco, yet they are tabulated for an initial count prior to RCV. This produces a strange reporting of election results.[26] If a candidate receives a majority on the first ballot, write-ins are counted as votes cast. If any votes need to be transferred to obtain a majority winner, write-in votes are among the first to be dropped. This may produce discrepancies between tabulations of votes cast on the initial and subsequent ballots. More generally, are write-ins undervotes? Or are they valid expressions of voters on a ranked ballot of preferences? While these are important questions for election administrators, the data are analyzed here according to official election results reported by cities and counties with the caveat that these electoral constituencies may have varying reporting practices. Although this may seem a quite minor point overall, as no write-in candidate wins during these municipal elections, inconsistency among procedures to handle write-ins does seem at odds with the fundamental goal of reducing wasted votes.

STV both increases the likelihood that a voter casts a (nonwasted) ballot for a winner and also produces a greater proportion of exhausted ballots. Because multiple winners are selected, and each voter only has a ballot cast for one, more of those ballots count for some winning alternative. However, which candidate a ballot counts for is less transparent since transfers are made both from the bottom as candidates are eliminated and from the top as winning candidates who pass the quota have surpluses transferred to a lower preference. STV elections likewise lose transferable votes as more transfers are made. Voters marking less than a full profile could have their ballots exhausted, even as they voted for elected candidates who met the quota required. The reduction in wasted votes for STV comes at a loss of transparency. If a postelection IRV voter remembers their ordering of candidates on the ballot, it is possible to follow the sequence to see how their ballot was moved. For the postelection STV voter, whether the single ballot counted for a particular candidate—or any candidate at all—is unknown, as some ballots stay with a winner satisfying the quota and some are transferred as surplus votes.

How votes are applied in a plurality or majority-winner election is obvious from the final tabulation. All votes are counted and included in the total. For RCV elections, voters who do not fully rank all candidates may no longer be included in the final count. For the IRV variety, a voter may still observe from final election tabulations whether their vote elected a winner. For STV ballots, even this process of applying votes is unclear. There is a trade-off between election transparency and the secrecy of the ballot.

Changes from the Plurality Winner

One important question is whether RCV elections often produce different winners from plurality elections. The prominence of elections such as Jared Golden in the 2018 Maine congressional election or Bob Kiss for Burlington mayor is that the ultimate RCV victor is different from the initial plurality winner. While there may be many reasonable justifications for the adoption of RCV, one key reason is that RCV may produce different outcomes. A related argument is that RCV encourages sincere, that is, accurate and honest, reflection of preferences.

Table 6.4 provides information on the outcomes of first count and final round leaders. The table shows the frequency with which the plurality leader in the first count actually wins the election. The table breaks down election outcomes by the four types of elections described earlier. Elections are also divided between those electing a single candidate and the leading first-round candidates in those electing multiple candidates. Overall, over nineteen out of twenty elections select the same ultimate winner as the first-round plurality winner, 96 percent for single-candidate RCV/IRV elections and 95 percent for STV elections.

There is only a little variation among types of elections. Mayoral elections, often more salient to voters and attracting more candidates, have slightly fewer first-round leaders ultimately elected. Other executive leaders, typically with fewer candidates and less salience, show no different victors than the first-round leaders. Elections for councils and boards set the benchmark for winners, and approximately 5 percent lead to the election of non-first-round winners.

Table 6.4 First count leader(s) that win election

Public Official Elected	Single Member (IRV/AV) %	n	Multiple Member (STV) %	n
Mayor	93	41	—	
Council Member	97	243	95	92
Other Executive	100	36	—	
Other Board	95	40	96	69
Total	96	360	95	161

All eleven first-round leading multiwinner ranked votes (MRV) are elected.

Of course, these data comprise all elections, including those receiving a plurality in the initial count. Table 6.5 limits the sample to elections without a first-round winner (majority for RCV/IRV and the few cases of a candidate reaching the quota). Excluding the first-round winners lowers the percentage of first-round plurality leaders that are elected to about nine out of ten (89 percent). Again, RCV mayoral elections are somewhat less likely to elect first-round leaders (82 percent). Miscellaneous boards are somewhat less likely to elect initial leaders, but there are few cases. Since there are few first-round STV winners, the decrease in percentage for the election of first-round leaders is small and at the margin.

From the outcomes of several hundred actual elections, it does not seem that RCV would frequently select different winners from SMDP elections.[27] Of course, there are two different but reasonable perspectives on this. One is that given the complexity of RCV elections, there is little reason to change from SMDP as most elections will produce the same outcomes. If the same candidates are elected almost all the time, there is little reason to change. A second reasonable perspective, however, is that the changes in outcomes in those handful of elections are justification in themselves to change the electoral system. Those relatively small number of cases may justify change from plurality elections, just as the adoption of subsequent runoffs satisfies more feelings of legitimacy and trust of public officials and government.

Of course, it is difficult to compare results that actually occur to hypothetical results. If the number and type of candidates competing for office changed, that might be rationale enough. But, as shown earlier, that does not appear to be the case, at least not typically. Plurality elections could produce different winners if voters behave strategically.

Table 6.5 First count leader(s) that win election after more than one round

Public Official Elected	Single Member (IRV/AV) %	n	Multiple Member (STV) %	n
Mayor	82	17	—	
Council Member	90	72	93	73
Other Executive	100	4	—	
Other Board	86	14	94	50
Total	89	107	94	123

With multiple candidates, campaign activity (including financial contributions and expenditures) or voter and elite assessment of candidate viability and electability could help voters winnow out some candidates, even if they prefer them, as unlikely to win. So, we cannot be certain about comparing SMDP and RCV election outcomes. Nevertheless, the perception of major changes in outcomes seems without strong evidence.

Majoritarian Outcomes

One of the strongest arguments in support of RCV is the search for majoritarian winners. The IRV/AV form of preferential voting guarantees that the elected official has support from at least half of the voters on the final ballot, following vote transfers. The STV form should aggregate votes from a wider variety of voters. The quota (typically total votes divided by one more than the number of official candidates competing) also provides, for multiwinner elections, an analogous standard for the majority necessary in single-winner elections. Our final question considers whether outcomes are majoritarian—not in the sense of the final vote total remaining in the calculation—but in the context of the total votes cast in the first round, a more appropriate comparison than exists in much of the discussion of RCV. For example, in their early study of primary elections, Merriam and Overacker (1928) noted that primary winners often did not win a majority of those who cast first-place ballots. Benjamin Williams (1923), writing somewhat earlier, noted that most preferential primary elections did not lead to majority outcomes because voters did not mark their second-place preferences.[28]

As Burnett and Kogan (2015) observe in their analysis of RCV/IRV application in four West Coast elections, the majoritarian assumption might only apply to the number of votes in the final round of voting, and not to the total number of votes cast. RCV did not lead to a winner with a majority of all votes cast. Similarly, in the second round of counting in the ME-2 congressional district in 2018, incumbent member of Congress Bruce Poliquin lost to challenger Jared Golden after leading in the first round. A few weeks later, Poliquin filed an unsuccessful suit in federal court over what he termed a "faux majority." He noted that Golden only had a majority of the final round of counting, but that this was only 49.2 percent of the total number of votes cast in the initial round.[29] A majority winner occurs only after dropping those voters with exhausted ballots, voters who did register their preferences, but not those in the instant runoff, are excluded.[30]

Table 6.6 looks at the percentage of vote share received by leading and winning candidates under different methods of calculation. For most elections, winning percentages are fairly large and decisive. Under municipal RCV electoral systems, the leader on the first ballot averaged 63.8 percent of the total vote. A leading candidate in this instance is whichever has a plurality of voters in the first round or count.[31] Under STV elections, the leader of the first count obtained 87.9 percent of the quota.[32] The average first-round votes for the candidate that ultimately won the election, not necessarily the leader of the first round, received an average of 63.6 percent for RCV and 87.6 percent for STV. That this margin decreases suggests that margins are not always high in rounds with vote transfers.

These figures include elections that were decided in the first round with a majority of votes, a common occurrence, as noted above. Limiting cases to

Table 6.6 RCV electoral success according to several methods of calculation

	RCV/IRV (% of Total Vote)	STV (% of Quota)
Vote Share:		
Leader % on First Count*	63.8	87.9
Ultimate Winner % on First Count	63.6	87.6
Winner % of Votes After Transfers (round ≥2)	55.0	100.0**
Winner % of All Votes Cast (round ≥ 2)	49.4	99.2
Majority Winners:		
Percent Receiving an Absolute Majority (or Quota) on the First Ballot	70.0	23.6
Percent Receiving an Absolute Majority (or Quota) on Transferred Ballots (round ≥2)	43.5	91.1
Elected (round ≥2)	360 (108)	161 (123)

*Leader is the candidate with the most votes on the first ballot (IRV/AV), the plurality winner, or the top-ranked candidate who would be elected on the first ballot with no transfers (STV).
**For multimember districts using STV, only reaching the quota of ballots necessary for election matters. If seats remain open but the quota is not met, the next candidate with the highest number of transferred ballots is elected. A candidate may be elected on the first ballot without a majority, as they only need to reach the quota.

elections that did not decide the winner in the first round may seem more appropriate. For RCV/IRV elections that progressed to two or more rounds, the winning percentage was 55.0 percent for ballots in the final round of counting. This victory margin only counts among transferable ballots. However, when counting all of the votes cast in an election for the political office, including those that were nontransferable to subsequent rounds, the winning percentage averaged only 49.4 percent. In other words, on average, winners in RCV/IRV elections that advance beyond the first round do *not* receive an absolute majority of votes, just a majority of ballots that remained in the final round.

STV elections, by definition, require candidates to receive a much lower quota to be elected. Most elected candidates receive exactly 100 percent of the quota on the way to victory because excess votes are reallocated to other candidates. A few candidates in the final round receive less than the quota as nontransferable votes are lost along the way, but the last candidate elected may also receive more than the quota since the tally is halted. Thus, on average, a winning candidate receives about 100.0 percent of the quota. However, calculating the percentage among all (first-round) voters reduces the average percentage to 99.2 percent.[33]

The frequency of candidates who receive an actual majority of total votes cast, or the percentage of votes cast in the first round, is rather high for actual RCV elections. In RCV/IRV cities, seven out of ten (70.0 percent) receive a majority in the first round. Here, RCV is equivalent to SMDP because the majoritarian standard is met without any additional calculation. Of those elections without a first-round majority, the percentage winning an absolute majority of all (first-round) votes in the final round, after which the candidate is elected, is less than half (43.5 percent). For STV elections, far fewer victors are determined on the first ballot (23.6 percent).[34] Most winners under STV are determined from transferred ballots (91.1 percent).

Discussion and Conclusion

One of the oft-stated advantages of using RCV is its majoritarian design. But the experience of US cities suggests that this may not be as valid as it seems. In our analysis, preferential voting did not seem to add to the number of candidates competing for office (and thus potentially appealing to a wider percentage of the voting public). Further, these elections suggest a high percentage of ballots that are either incomplete or otherwise unable to be included in vote transfers. Most winning candidates received majority support in the first round of AV voting before needing to advance to a subsequent round. Moreover, most of the candidates who were first-round leaders in AV elections that advanced beyond the first round ultimately won the election. Of course, these candidates would have also been the plurality winners in a single-member district election. Stated differently, the plurality winner usually had a majority of support once the top choices of some voters were eliminated.

AV elections do force a majority outcome, but only because some voters are dropped from the electorate deciding the winner. STV elections also rely on a goal analogous to the majoritarian impulse; however, that impulse applies to collective representation instead of each individual representative. The goal is that voters, each armed with a single vote, achieve representation through at least one favored representative. The standard then is not reaching a majority, but a quota defined by the number of votes cast and the number of candidates seeking elected office. For the majoritarian argument in favor of preferential elections, perhaps the biggest challenge is that most elections that advanced beyond the first round did not elect a winner with a majority of all votes cast, just a majority of votes that were eligible to transfer.

The data from the elections examined here present an obvious question. Is the added complexity of RCV voting ultimately worth the administrative effort to switch to such a system? This research should give some pause to reformers. Not only is it politically divisive to change voting systems, but it also requires considerable voter education efforts, costs to shift voting tabulation methods, and added training for volunteers and staff. But the outcomes will most often be the same.

At the same time, it would be too easy to end the discussion here. We suspect that the value of such a reform is dependent on local circumstances. If a municipality is relatively free of long-ingrained disputes and tends to have at most two "camps" or political parties, there seems to be no obvious benefit to introducing such a reform. Such areas would likely mirror the data presented here, whereby the first-round winner would nearly always prevail. However, it would be a mistake to suggest that RCV should not be adopted simply because of the relatively small percentage of occasions where candidates trailing in the first round were elected. Indeed, for some locales, the discussion does not end there; it begins there. For example, in areas with a long tradition of electing controversial leaders with only a plurality, especially a plurality that falls quite short of a majority, there may be a benefit to the community of instituting a reform. Stated another way, in Table 6.6 we observe that there was no change in the outcome in 88 percent of cases that went past the first round. The question then for reformers is about the other 12 percent of cases. Is this enough of a change to make the switch to RCV worthwhile? This probably depends on local circumstances and individual points of view. Of course, changing an election system simply because of distaste for the outcome of one or two elections will certainly result in calls of "foul" by the party that could be negatively affected.

There is another somewhat intangible factor that municipalities should consider. Perhaps a significant number of voters in an area simply like the electoral system. That is, they may feel better about voting given the opportunity to rank order more than one choice. Although beyond the scope of this chapter, there has been research suggesting that voters in some areas have had a positive experience with RCV, while voters in others have not. Improvements in political efficacy, trust in government, or increased political participation might justify the electoral reform. Again, we believe that local circumstances will dictate the value of such a reform. Ultimately, however, the majoritarian argument for AV elections does not always stand on its own without other localized reasons for support.

An analysis of four key questions underlying many of the acclaimed benefits of RCV raises questions about the magnitude of the advantages. Using municipal election outcomes from hundreds of contests for public officials across the United States does not provide overwhelming evidence of the benefits of RCV. These results are consistent with findings from other scholars.[35]

More candidate competition might follow the introduction of preferential voting. However, in the aggregate, the evidence for this is weak. The average number of AV mayoral and council candidates per seat in each two-year election cycle is relatively flat. Except for a few open-seat elections, the average number of mayoral candidates for each election cycle falls within a range of about five to eight candidates on the ballot. The average number of council candidates is between two and four announced candidates. Even for STV elections, historical evidence suggests there are just over two candidates per seat. Overall, any apparent increase in the number of candidates for municipal office in preferential elections is anecdotal, typically for a vacancy for a high-profile office or for the novelty of a new electoral system. There may be modest increases in the number of candidates over a longer time frame, but future contestation seems to take on characteristics of past elections.

Other election rules may often influence the number of candidates competing, and these are not tracked for all the constituencies analyzed here. In particular, the filing fee, requirements for a number of signatures of registered voters supporting a candidate's application, or other independent factors may influence the number of candidates. In the Minnesota cities, for example, substantially increased filing fees deterred the entrance of recreational candidates on the ballot, easing the tabulation of RCV elections. Although the change in electoral law seems reasonable, it runs counter to the RCV intent of more candidates.

A second difficulty in RCV elections is getting voters to supply a full ranking necessary for effective implementation of this electoral system. Instead, quite a few voters provide only a restricted number of choices, either by a voter's incomplete ranking on the ballot or by election administration limiting the number of choices that can be made to a relatively small number. This produces a larger number of ballots that become exhausted as the election tabulation goes into the transfer process. As shown in aggregated transfer data, many ballots ultimately are not applied toward candidates in the instant runoff.

A third issue is that the final outcomes of elections under SMDP and RCV tend to produce the same winners. Looking at RCV elections, we can surmise what the plurality elections would be, assuming no strategic behavior occurs on the part of the voters (and we cannot infer RCV outcomes from plurality elections only). What this suggests is that plurality and ranked choice elections lead to the same outcomes around 90 percent of the time. Certainly, there are election outcomes that are different, and these may be quite important cases. However, the notions of outcome change appear to be more at the margins of effect rather than overhaul of the entire system.

Finally, and critically, RCV elections empirically fail to provide true majority winners. In somewhat over half of the elections with vote transfers, RCV did not produce majority winners among voters. The artificial majority created after transfers comes from dropping exhausted ballots in the transfer process, not from reaching actual majorities. This mimics the process of successive runoff elections available in some states. Information costs in RCV elections may be higher, but the costs of a second campaign and holding a second election are reduced. So, there may be a trade-off between these two options. However, it seems clear that RCV often does not fulfill its main promise.[36]

The reasons behind at least some of these problems are produced at the individual level. RCV elections place a considerable information and accuracy burden on voters that many may not be able to fulfill. Moreover, the details of the electoral law and the job of election administrators may have important effects on the determination of winners in elections. These factors produce a larger or more determinative impact in RCV elections, compared to the relative simplicity of an individual voter casting a single vote and election officials merely providing an accurate and quick count of votes cast for each candidate. Chapter 7 turns to these issues.

7
Completing and Counting Ballots

What distinguishes ranked voting from most electoral systems are the expectations for the voter to mark more information on the ballot for each race and the more elaborate and behind-the-scenes tabulation of the votes that occur after the election. Other mechanisms like approval voting and cumulative voting also permit citizens to express more than only a first-choice preference in contrast with simple plurality elections. Traditional runoff elections only ask voters to identify a first choice in the initial round and (when no majority exists) in the second stage. However, ranked choice voting (RCV) (both instant runoff voting [IRV] and single transferable vote [STV]) elections create expectations that voters have the ability to create orderings among preferences to cover "what if" possibilities. This more complex electoral environment should lead voters to spend more effort gathering information for RCV contests. However, experimental evidence suggests that they do not engage in additional information-seeking (Ntounias 2023). Some voters may easily rank candidates from first downward, but others may be less inclined to do so with clear preferences. For RCV elections, a lot of information about politics and decision-making is required of voters.

Moreover, much is also required from election administrators. Most electoral systems used in political elections involve simple counting. Tabulation for approval voting and for cumulative voting only involves counting. Following this tabulation, election authorities certify which candidates receive a sufficient number of votes. That is true of RCV elections as well, but there is the potential for multiple rounds of computations regarding which alternatives should be eliminated or elected before the next round of counting occurs, and the associated reapplication of some ballots. In the case where no candidate receives a first-round majority, reliable predictions of the outcome cannot be made until all the ballots are received and counted.

In most electoral systems, if some fraction, say 75 percent, of the votes are counted, an initial determination can be made and prognosticators can estimate the likelihood of a winner. For RCV elections, unless the winner is headed for a clear majority, 75 percent of the votes counted

Ranked Choice Voting. James W. Endersby and Michael J. Towle, Oxford University Press.
© Oxford University Press (2025). DOI: 10.1093/9780197798959.003.0008

says little about the likely outcome. Although some municipalities release computer-generated estimations of winners, the process is less predictive. Even votes for lower-ranked candidates may influence the outcome as the transfers may depend on the order of candidate elimination. Voters may need to place more trust in political institutions in order to feel that the RCV election results are tabulated correctly.[1] We feel election administrators are worthy of our trust; however, in the highly polarized political environment of the modern era, our impression is that not all voters agree with us.

RCV elections thus provide many challenges to election officials. This style of voting also provides challenges to voters' and administrators' determination of how preferential votes should be applied. This includes the style of the ballot and the accuracy and transparency of vote transfers. Here the focus is on the voter and the public official in charge of implementation of a preferential election.

Managing RCV Elections

Political constituencies with substantial resources should have no difficulty implementing RCV elections. Unfortunately, providing financial and technical resources for more complicated elections can be an impediment for many constituencies. In many states, counties, often through a county clerk's office, supervise the elections.[2] Large urban areas may be more able to handle RCV elections efficiently, simply due to economies of scale. Election administration may be more difficult in political communities small in population or in financial and technological resources, such as elections conducted by town clerks in New England, rural counties, and so forth. Staff with expertise and equipment are important for RCV elections, but they may be difficult to acquire.

One demand from RCV elections is the centralization necessary in counting ballots and determining results. Because of the reallocation of ballots through the vote transfer process, election results (except in cases of a first-round majority) cannot be determined by simply aggregating votes from precincts or other local sites. Although first-round tallies can be reported, these may not be reflective of the final outcome, nor even how a local community influences the overall election. The ballots themselves (or the electronic images) must be transferred to a central tabulating agency. For a future with statewide or presidential RCV elections, this may involve a substantial investment in tabulation procedures, staff, and equipment.

A related issue is the process in which vote counting occurs. The trend among municipalities is toward the use of computers and software for electronic tabulation of RCV elections. However, some—such as the Clerk's Office in Ramsey County, Minnesota, the home of St. Paul—still rely on hand counting of ballots as the preferred method over electronic tabulation. This method increases the transparency of the count as observers can monitor the process directly. A manual transfer of votes with observers allowed at each table where votes are sorted resembles a recount for close elections with outcomes in doubt.[3] But hand counting can be a tedious and lengthy process for RCV elections with many offices or candidates.

States typically have a certification process for voting machines, mechanical or electronic. When there is no certification for a voting machine, the tabulation must be conducted manually by election staff. The City of Minneapolis developed a manual procedure to count RCV votes before its first election in 2009. In Minnesota, there were no machines certified for RCV vote tabulation, so, like the experience in St. Paul, the tabulation first involved sorting ballots manually. In Minneapolis, this sorting was ordered by a voter's first choice, then second, then third, and so forth. The results were entered into a computer spreadsheet, within which transfers are made for each round until a winner is determined.[4] The manual process required election staff to interpret "voter intent" for ballots with incorrect or incomplete rankings. To handle these issues, election staff developed the "Minneapolis Method," a step-by-step process to determine voter intent to handle possible contingencies. Eventually, Minneapolis adopted electronic voting machines to count and transfer votes, and the Minneapolis Method was incorporated into the algorithms within the software.

When the tabulation of RCV ballots is computerized, monitoring of the transfer process is more indirect. Most larger municipalities, as well as the states of Maine and Alaska, use electronic vote tabulation for RCV elections, although hand counts may be required under certain circumstances such as a recount. The ease of electronic counting may come at some cost of transparency and the need for improved security of voting machines.[5] Advanced testing helps eliminate problems before the election. Occasionally, errors occur. In New York's first RCV election in June 2021, election officials neglected to clear counters of test ballots, leading to early reporting of inaccurate results. Around 135,000 test ballots were reported as valid votes in the mayoral race. Because New York released early and incomplete returns with the test ballots included, the press emphasized the error in its RCV reporting.[6] The state of Maine in 2022 experienced problems with the electronic transfer of ballots, although the error was caught and corrected quickly.[7] Of course, these issues occur for plurality elections as well. The debacle in the Iowa presidential caucus of 2020 shows the difficulties inherent in promoting election technology that is not effectively vetted. The magnitude of the problem, however, may be larger for RCV elections with no first-round majority winner.

The RCV tabulation process is made easier with electronic cast vote records (CVRs). A CVR is a digital ballot image for each voter. This is not a picture or scan of the ballot but an electronic summary of the vote(s) and the ranking(s) from each ballot. Paper ballots or the equivalent can and should be retained for a period of time for legal purposes. The release of CVRs significantly improves the transparency of the RCV process and allows interested parties to evaluate the performance of RCV as a voting system, particularly as the purpose of RCV is to better represent voter preferences among alternatives. Unfortunately, not all constituencies preserve or release CVRs.[8]

The timing of municipal elections may also determine the resources required. For instance, municipal elections for many cities often occur separately from state and federal elections.[9] If the election is conducted separately, then ballots may only have RCV races with a unique set of instructions. However, if traditional single-member district plurality (SMDP) elections are held in some races and RCV contests in others, administrators may need two physical ballots and two mechanisms for counting and reassigning the ballots.[10] That is, ballots are separate, and there are two machines to count the votes, one for plurality ballots and one for RCV ballots. This essentially doubles the costs of technological resources. However, the need to cover the cost of a runoff election is eliminated. The technology exists to count traditional and ranked ballots, but most electoral constituencies do not naturally acquire these devices.

Constituencies vary on how many ranks can be made for each office. In some municipalities, a maximum of three ranks[11] can be made, although in others, such as Portland and Cambridge, a voter can provide as many ranks as there are candidates. The latter can be an important factor for election administration, as a large number of ranks influences both the format and size of the ballot as well as the technology necessary to count ballots.

The larger the number of candidates or rankings, the more space is required on the ballot. San Francisco voters were restricted to rank three candidates when RCV/IRV was initiated in 2004. Beginning in 2020, voters may rank ten candidates. Minneapolis also limited the number of rankings to three; however, this limitation initially depended on the ballot design and on the postelection tabulation process. Election officials in Minneapolis are given flexibility to increase the number of rankings each voter can provide as the technology improves. New York City primary voters may rank five. In St. Paul, the number of candidates voters can rank is six. In Cambridge, Massachusetts, with its STV, voters could rank the full slate in the past but now are limited to rank up to fifteen, including a write-in. As STV elections may involve many seats and more candidates, Election Commission officials note the difficulty of ballot design if the number of alternatives grows too large for the paper, bubble-sheet ballot. The Massachusetts statute governing such elections requires that voters must be able to cast at least fifteen choices for any individual office.[12]

One concern of RCV elections, particularly within a nonpartisan context, is the order of names on the ballot. There is a concern that candidates with names higher on the list will be advantaged in terms of more votes and higher preferences. This claim is not unique to RCV and may hold for elections generally.[13] However, an ordering effect may be amplified for RCV elections, especially for ballots without party identification. For the three-member STV elections in early twentieth-century Boulder, candidate names were listed in alphabetical order. Among seventy-one candidates across nine elections, a substantial majority of those elected to the city council (thirty out of thirty-three) had names beginning with A to H; the remaining elected had names beginning through M.[14] Today, Cambridge rotates names on the ballot, though this adds administrative complexity as the number of candidates increases. As the number of candidates grows, so does the number of uniquely different ballots.[15] Certainly, the alleged effect of candidate order should be a consideration for the construction of RCV ballots.

RCV provides challenges for ballot design because so much more space is needed on the ballot. Both the instructions and the appearance of the ballot must signal to every citizen how to complete a ballot correctly, regardless of prior voting experience or level of education. The constraints on ballot appearance are determined by state law. Local election officials cannot simply design a ballot on their own, although they may have some flexibility. For elections in St. Paul, which uses manual reallocation of ballots to determine a winner, the design is created specifically to provide visual ease for sorting ballots. In Cambridge, space and clarity on ballots are critical for an STV election with many candidates. Where electronic counters (of ballots and of votes) are utilized, ballot design must mesh with the tabulation technology.

Marking the Ballot

In traditional SMDP elections, voters can make inadvertent errors when completing their ballots. As voting becomes more complex, as it does naturally in RCV elections, there are more opportunities for errors in marking ballots. The appearance of the ballot varies by the locality where a citizen casts a ballot and by the technology used to record, verify, and count votes. Within the American federal system, where each state determines the electoral rules, ballots appear differently from one state or constituency to another. These differences in ballot design can be associated with increases in errors in voting. Generally, the number of uncounted ballots, or residual votes, for an elective office may be attributed to ballot design (Knack and Kropf 2003, Kimball and Kropf 2005) or voting technology (Ansolabehere and Stewart 2005, Kimball and Kropf 2008).

Within recent decades, several election outcomes might have been influenced by ballot design. For instance, the 2000 presidential contest between George W. Bush and Al Gore in Florida led to an unusually close election and a subsequent recount of votes, a determination that would decide the winner of the electoral college. Voter completion of punch-card or butterfly ballots was particularly problematic, though ultimately not decisive for the outcome. Officials reexamined individual ballots, making judgments about voter intent from "hanging chads" and other characteristics of punched ballots.[16] Similarly, the outcome of the 2008 US Senate race in Minnesota, between Republican incumbent Norm Coleman and Democratic challenger Al Franken, depended upon voters who had difficulty completing optical scan ballots. The final tally in this particularly close race hinged on the interpretation of voter intent for some poorly marked ballots.[17] Each candidate received less than 42 percent of the total vote, and the election may be a case study in favor of the application of RCV. Of course, RCV elections cannot guarantee elections will not result in close margins.

Ballot errors occur when a vote cannot be counted for a particular elective office or ballot proposition. A few ballots are simply spoiled or invalid and must be discarded. More frequently, a ballot may not count due to an undervote or an overvote. An undervote occurs when no candidate is marked on the ballot by a voter for a particular race. An undervote, intentional or not, is treated as an abstention for that race.[18] An overvote occurs when a voter marks two or more candidates for a race when only one is permissible. The assumption is that the voter meant to express a preference but marked the ballot incorrectly. In the case of an overvote, voter intent cannot be determined as the ballot was completed incorrectly. As noted earlier, existing research suggests that RCV may lower undervotes but increase overvotes. These issues of ballot irregularities are associated with the problem of exhausted ballots discussed earlier.[19]

Sometimes a voter does not register a preference for a particular race. This occurs more often than many people expect because voters are not certain who they prefer, particularly for races down the ballot and with low information (county commissioner or coroner, for instance). So, voters who express preferences for some items on the ballot may abstain from a particular contest, even a prestigious one.[20] In some notably close races, such as the presidential election in Florida in 2000, the US Senate election in Minnesota in 2008, or a scattering of contests in 2020, to cite several memorable instances, a recount may require election workers to reexamine questionably marked ballots to determine voter intent.

Completing an RCV ballot is more complicated than an equivalent plurality election because there are multiple votes for each race.[21] A voter must identify one and only one candidate for each ranking—first, second, and so forth—and should not repeat candidates. There is a greater likelihood of error in the completion of an RCV ballot.[22] A valid ballot may omit preferences from lower rankings. As evident from examples noted earlier, some voters plunk or bullet vote, expressing first preferences in an RCV election and leaving lower rankings blank. A vote that is less than full rank shows some similarity to approval voting. However, this strategy could be a form of tactical voting, or it could be due to a lack of information about or interest in ranking other candidates. Intentional or not, bullet voting does not raise problems for tabulation by election administrators. If the voter does not rank any more votes, then the ranking is considered exhausted. There are no more alternatives given to transfer the ballot. As noted in Chapter 6, this may raise questions about whether RCV/IRV elections are majoritarian, but, like a voter who abstains in a plurality election, such a ballot simply would not count toward the election outcome. Voluntary truncation of voters in

RCV elections is common. This, along with forced truncation by limiting the number of options a voter can mark, influences election outcomes (Kilgour, Grégoire, and Foley 2020).

Repeat rankings for a candidate likewise do not produce tabulation difficulties. The subsequent repeated ranking would only be reached if the candidate was already eliminated, so that repeated ranking would be skipped just as any preference for a previously eliminated or losing candidate. Casting a ballot with repeated ranking is not qualitatively different than plumping or bullet voting.[23]

RCV elections raise questions for administrators as there are multiple rankings to tabulate, rather than a single vote cast. Without a first-round majority winner, each ranking on every ballot may need to be available for transfer. Occasionally, a voter does not complete a ballot as expected for a particular ranking. In RCV elections, a blank or multiple ranking may occur further down the ballot, and that raises issues if ballot transfers are necessary. In other words, for RCV elections, an undervote or an overvote may appear for a particular rank. While a discussion of how to count a poorly marked ballot may at first seem trivial, consideration of these issues is important for the representation of all voters—a primary goal of RCV proponents—and for the determination of winners in RCV elections. The next three tables outline several examples of ballot completion issues raised by our discussions with election administrators.[24] The first example in Table 7.1 shows a fully completed ordering of all (five) preferences that would be counted through any transfer process.[25] This shows how a voter who chooses to rank all five preferences would complete a ballot, O > P > Q > R > S. The second example in Table 7.1 depicts a ballot where the voter plunks for a first choice, just as in a plurality election. Bullet voting for a single candidate, as in a plurality election, is a common activity.[26]

For all or nearly all constituencies, if a voter leaves the first preference blank, the ballot would not be counted in the first round of tabulation to determine whether there is a majority winner in RCV/IRV. In theory, a blank or an overvote in the first round should indicate an undervote—no vote cast for that office or question—that is how it would be treated in a plurality contest. However, many of the election officials we talked to would look for other valid rankings further down the ballot for RCV. In the second and subsequent transfer rounds, a ballot with a blank before a ranked candidate would remain valid.[27] Electoral rules may produce an automatic transfer if, for instance, the first preference is left blank, but a second preference is

Table 7.1 Examples of correctly completed ballots

Example 1: The top three would be counted as Ophelia (first), Patience (second), and Quinn (third)

↓Make one selection per column below↓

	Fill in the bubble for your **first choice** below↓	Fill in the bubble for your **second choice** below↓	Fill in the bubble for your **third choice** below↓	Fill in the bubble for your **fourth choice** below↓	Fill in the bubble for your **fifth choice** below↓
Patience	①	●	③	④	⑤
Quinn	①	②	●	④	⑤
Ophelia	●	②	③	④	⑤
Skeff	①	②	③	④	●
Rosario	①	②	③	●	⑤

Example 2: A ballot that would be counted in the first round for Ophelia only

↓Make one selection per column below↓

	Fill in the bubble for your **first choice** below↓	Fill in the bubble for your **second choice** below↓	Fill in the bubble for your **third choice** below↓	Fill in the bubble for your **fourth choice** below↓	Fill in the bubble for your **fifth choice** below↓
Patience	①	②	③	④	⑤
Quinn	①	②	③	④	⑤
Ophelia	●	②	③	④	⑤
Skeff	①	②	③	④	⑤
Rosario	①	②	③	④	⑤

marked on the ballot, as shown in the third example in Table 7.2.[28] The alternative would be to count this as an undercount (a voided ballot), but more frequent procedures simply transfer the first-round preference to the candidate marked as a second preference. This could be a problem if a voter intended to mark a different candidate (such as for Ophelia in this example), potentially causing that candidate to lose a close race. This problem, however, is no different from a plurality election in which a voter unintentionally abstains. The difference between the two electoral systems is that the voter's ballot remains "live" for transfer to other lower-ranked candidates.

Election rules differ in some of the other cases, including the fourth example outlined in Table 7.2. The voter marks a first-place ranking for Ophelia and then leaves the rest of the ballot blank, except for the fifth-place ranking for Skeff. Determining voter intent can be more difficult here. Did the voter rank Skeff second? Or is Skeff the least acceptable among the five candidates, and the ballot indicates a candidate who is not approved? Some localities, such as St. Paul, apply a cascading method to reallocate votes. If the first candidate is eliminated, then the transfer cascades downward to the next viable candidate. So long as Skeff remains in the pool of eligible candidates, the voter's ballot is transferred to Skeff. Other constituencies utilize a method that assumes voters who divide their choices in this manner do not expect their votes to transfer after a series of blanks. In these constituencies, if a voter leaves one ranking blank, then the vote would cascade down the ballot to the next marked choice. However, two or more consecutive blanks would stop the count for that ballot. Under that determination of voter intent, Ophelia would be the first choice, but no other candidate could receive a vote transfer, not even Skeff.[29]

These rules are applied to determine voter intent from a confusing ballot, from an election official's perspective. With a secret ballot, officials cannot otherwise determine voter intent. St. Paul follows the cascade method, a decision made at the time of the city's adoption of RCV. According to Dave Triplett, Ramsey County election manager, officials ran three simulations of vote counting under three separate rules on a universe of 10,000 strategically generated ballots, and that resulted in three different winners. The cascade method was selected "because we believed it was the most fair, represented the true vote, and gave every ballot the ultimate chance to be counted." Triplett explains the rationale, "we don't know what the voter's trying to do, and if the voter didn't clearly tell us, we're not going to make an assumption." Decisions about electoral systems should be made by the public, and

Table 7.2 Examples of how local rules could determine how ballots are counted

---

Example 3: A ballot with no first choice. Depending on the locality, this could be (1) an invalid ballot (an undervote) or (2) counted as Patience (first), Quinn (second), and Rosario (third)

	↓Make one selection per column below↓				
	Fill in the bubble for your **first choice** below↓	Fill in the bubble for your **second choice** below↓	Fill in the bubble for your **third choice** below↓	Fill in the bubble for your **fourth choice** below↓	Fill in the bubble for your **fifth choice** below↓
Patience	①	●	③	④	⑤
Quinn	①	②	●	④	⑤
Ophelia	①	②	③	④	⑤
Skeff	①	②	③	④	●
Rosario	①	②	③	●	⑤

Example 4: A ballot with skipped rankings. Depending on the locality, this could be counted only as (1) a vote for Ophelia or (2) as Ophelia (first) and Skeff (second).

	↓Make one selection per column below↓				
	Fill in the bubble for your **first choice** below↓	Fill in the bubble for your **second choice** below↓	Fill in the bubble for your **third choice** below↓	Fill in the bubble for your **fourth choice** below↓	Fill in the bubble for your **fifth choice** below↓
Patience	①	②	③	④	⑤
Quinn	①	②	③	④	⑤
Ophelia	●	②	③	④	⑤
Skeff	①	②	③	④	●
Rosario	①	②	③	④	⑤

the city council is the body that should represent public opinion. So far, St. Paul voters seem satisfied with this method. Maine, however, does not use the cascade method; transfers are not made beyond two or more blanks on the ballot. The interpretation here is that a voter separates candidates that are approved at the top of the ballot from others that are disapproved at the bottom, with indifference for the two or more candidates left blank in the middle.

These issues regarding tabulation and voter intent are not merely speculative; they can influence the outcome of an election. In November 2022, a three-way contest for District 4 School Director in the Oakland Unified School District serves as an example. The Alameda County (CA) Registrar of Voters, utilizing software to tally the RCV results, certified Nick Resnick as the election winner. No candidate received a majority of the first-place votes, so the candidate with the fewest first-place ballots, Mike Hutchinson, was dropped. His ballots were redistributed to Resnick and Pecolia Manigo, and Resnick won a majority over Manigo in the second round. Resnick was subsequently sworn in and took his seat on the school board. In December, the California Ranked Choice Voting Coalition, an independent election reform organization that routinely audits RCV election results, identified a tabulation error. As the Registrar of Voters acknowledged, the "RCV tally system was not configured properly" for the election. After resolving the error and reprocessing the results, the County certified Mike Hutchinson as the legitimate RCV winner.[30]

The initial settings for tabulation were not set in compliance with the administrative practice. The software algorithm should have been configured so that blank preferences would have been transferred to the next preference, but it was not. The issue was that 235 ballots left the first preference blank (in a similar manner as Example 3 of Table 7.2), so these ballots were suspended (or unused). When no candidate received a majority in the first round, these 235 votes should have been transferred to the second (or third) preference marked on the ballot. Without those transfers, Hutchinson ranked third among first-place votes. With the transfers, Hutchinson ranked second, and Manigo would be eliminated first. Then, in the head-to-head contest, Hutchinson defeats Resnick and is—or should be—declared the winner. Table 7.3 depicts the original, certified outcome and the corrected tally following the correction. In March 2023, a state judge overturned the certified results so Hutchinson could take the District 4 seat.[31]

Table 7.3 Original tally and recount: Alameda County, California, 2022 General Election for School Director, District 4

Original Tally		Revised Tally	
Round 1		**Round 1**	
Mike Hutchinson	8,112 (30.94%)	Mike Hutchinson	8,112 (30.94%)
Pecolia Manigo	8,153 (31.10%)	Pecolia Manigo	8,153 (31.10%)
Nick Resnick	9,954 (37.96%)	Nick Resnick	9,954 (37.96%)
suspended ballots	235	*suspended ballots*	235
		Round 1 after 235 reassigned	
		Mike Hutchinson	8,227 (31.13%)
		Pecolia Manigo	8,190 (30.99%)
		Nick Resnick	10,015 (37.89%)
Hutchinson eliminated		*Manigo eliminated*	
Round 2		**Round 2**	
Pecolia Manigo	11,753 (48.76%)	Mike Hutchinson	12,421 (50.52%) ✓
Nick Resnick	12,352 (51.24%) ✓	Nick Resnick	12,165 (49.48%)

Source: County of Alameda, California, "Ranked-Choice Voting Tally: November 8, 2022-General Election," n.d., p. 6.

The other examples shown in Table 7.4 demonstrate how ballot marking errors may lead to vote transfers. The voter in the fifth example mistakenly ranks two candidates second. That second-place ranking is an overvote and must be skipped. If Ophelia is eliminated from the candidate pool, the ballot is transferred to candidate Rosario, ranked third on the ballot, and so forth.[32] In the final example, a voter demonstrates enthusiastic support for Ophelia, marking her first through third and fifth. Yet, the ranked ballot counts the same as one for which Ophelia ranks first and Rosario second.

Australia has a long tradition of preferential voting, and higher demands are placed on voters to complete ballots in Australian elections. Ballots for both the House of Representatives and the Senate must be marked with numerals ranking choices. For a House election, a voter must rank *all* candidates in the proper numerical order (1, 2, 3, etc.) or the entire ballot is considered spoiled. For the Senate, a voter must rank candidates in numerical order but does not need to rank all alternatives for a valid ballot. However, a voter must make a choice to mark the ballot among political parties, a vote "above the line," or among candidates who are identified by party, a vote "below the line." Appendix B gives examples of ballot completion for federal elections in Australia.[33]

Table 7.4 Examples of other marked ballots

Example 5: A ballot with an overvote for the second choice. This ballot would be counted as Ophelia (first), Rosario (second), and Skeff (third)

↓Make one selection per column below↓

	Fill in the bubble for your **first choice** below↓	Fill in the bubble for your second choice below↓	Fill in the bubble for your **third choice** below↓	Fill in the bubble for your **fourth choice** below↓	Fill in the bubble for your **fifth choice** below↓
Patience	①	●	③	④	⑤
Quinn	①	●	③	④	⑤
Ophelia	●	②	③	④	⑤
Skeff	①	②	③	●	⑤
Rosario	①	②	●	④	⑤

Example 6: A ballot with the same candidate in several rankings. This ballot would be counted as Ophelia (first) and Patience (second)

↓Make one selection per column below↓

	Fill in the bubble for your **first choice** below↓	Fill in the bubble for your second choice below↓	Fill in the bubble for your **third choice** below↓	Fill in the bubble for your **fourth choice** below↓	Fill in the bubble for your **fifth choice** below↓
Patience	①	②	③	●	⑤
Quinn	①	②	③	④	⑤
Ophelia	●	●	●	④	●
Skeff	①	②	③	④	⑤
Rosario	①	②	③	④	⑤

The requirement for complete and error-free ranking for elections to the Australian House of Representatives can be called "full preferential voting." By contrast, RCV applications in North America might be referred to as "optional preferential voting," allowing as many or as few options as the voter chooses (Bennett and Lundie 2007). No American constituency applies such stringent restrictions as full preferential voting, but these demanding rules on ballot completion largely eliminate the need for election administrators to judge voter intent. It is worth noting that all tabulation in Australia is done manually; there are no mechanical or electronic voting machines or tabulators.[34] It is also worth remembering that American courts historically have ruled that requirements to rank all candidates (rather than one or any preferred number) are compelled speech and a violation of civil liberties.[35]

There are several key points for a voter casting a preferential ballot to remember: First, only one candidate should be marked for each rank. That is, only one first choice, one second choice, and so forth. Failing to rank appropriately may spoil a ballot in some constituencies (such as in Australian elections). However, in most American municipalities, a ballot with an error may apply toward a different, lower-ranked candidate. In any case, your preference ordering for those candidates—and others—will not be recorded correctly. Second, each candidate should be ranked only once. Generally (with the notable exception of Australian elections), this will not eliminate your vote, but only the first ranking will count. If a ballot ranks a candidate first and third, for instance, only the first rank counts, as the candidate would be eliminated before getting to the lower rank. Third, in all American constituencies, a ballot may be cast that identifies only a first choice. That ballot becomes essentially the same as a vote in a plurality election. Similarly, a voter may identify a number of choices fewer than the maximum as long as they are the first few rankings in order. A voter may rank any number of candidates from zero to the maximum allowed. But note that this is different from the procedure used for the Australian House of Representatives.

The need to determine voter intent, or one might say to account for ballot errors, demands a clear process on how to interpret ballots. The Minneapolis Method, the cascading ballot, and so forth are standard operating procedures to count votes in cases of ballot irregularities. Similarly, transparency in the counting process allows representatives from the press, candidates and parties, and concerned citizens to oversee the RCV election process. The release of full information about the election, including vote transfers and CVRs (with undervotes and overvotes), improves the transparency of voting. Election officials must also communicate a relatively complicated process to voters, often those who have little experience with RCV.

Education, Campaigns, and Voters

Because of its comparative difficulty, whether voters understand how an RCV election works and how to complete a ballot correctly has an association with the success of the electoral system. In an election with many candidates, ranking alternatives in accordance with preferences can be daunting. Scholars have expressed concern about voters' ability to complete ballots correctly.[36] While there is little evidence of racial or ethnic inequities in terms of understanding RCV instructions, older voters may have more challenges with comprehension of the procedure (Donovan, Tolbert, and Gracey 2019). Efforts at voter education are associated with a greater understanding of RCV elections. Maloy (2019) concurs that historical and experimental evidence suggests voters may have difficulty completing preferential ballots; however, he concludes optimistically that education, along with further research on the effects of ballot structure, should allow voters to express their preferences effectively.

Poll workers staff the front line of election administration, and education on preferential voting for individuals who may need additional assistance is also an important part of the success of RCV elections. As voters confront difficulties in handling the RCV ballot, polling place officials need to be able to assist. Poll workers, however, typically are restricted from explaining RCV and limited to showing how to complete the ballot. A survey of local election officials in Maine found that they were unenthusiastic about RCV on average. Moreover, support for RCV was divided along party lines (Anthony et al. 2021).[37] On the other hand, a postelection analysis following RCV implementation in Minneapolis found that election supervisors did a good job of educating both voters and election workers (Schultz and Rendahl 2010).

Not only poll workers need training. From 2009 to 2013, the central staff in Minneapolis turned over with a new City Clerk and a new elections supervisor. Education and experience in advance of the next election are key, so codifying procedures and releasing public documents is important. After every election, "we've learned ways to improve the process," says Director of

Elections Grace Wachlarowicz. "We have a philosophy here in Minneapolis of process improvements after every general election, regardless of whether its ranked choice or not, we always do lessons learned: what worked, what didn't. What can we improve on, what did we try that's like no, we're not going to try that again."

Transparency of the transfer process is necessary for support of RCV elections. All the administrators we spoke to described methods of transparency and openness. Candidates and campaign staff (and political parties, as appropriate), members of the press, and even the general public have an opportunity to watch and review the tabulation and transfer process. In Portland, Maine, for instance, the counting and transfer of ballots occur in the City Hall's beautiful State of Maine Room. Observers can monitor the process visibly from a cordoned area alongside the elections staff; this includes the inspection of ballots, scanning, certification, and even the locking and unlocking of materials at night and the next morning. Some localities offer streaming of the proceedings.

Certain technical questions are important to mention. First, dependence on computerized tabulation is an important feature for reporting results in a timely manner. However, at the current time, software and computing equipment for RCV elections are not yet available through all vendors.[38] Moreover, the original ballots and/or the CVRs should be retained in case of a recount or question about the computing technology. The counting procedures themselves have some open questions. Second, ties are always a problem for determining election results. With RCV elections, there are additional problems with ties among candidates to be eliminated. Unless tied candidates are eliminated jointly through batch elimination, choosing one candidate over another may change the order of elimination and the ultimate outcome in close elections.[39] There must be some (random) decision-making rule to eliminate candidates in the case of a tie in the number of votes received. Third, in STV electoral systems, with two or more representatives chosen, the method to calculate vote transfers may also influence the determination of winners. There are many ways to calculate vote transfers for STV elections. Cambridge uses the Cincinnati method for city council and school committee elections; it transfers whole votes only. For its city boards, Minneapolis uses the weighted inclusive Gregory method, which allows transferring fractions of votes. This is a technical, mathematical issue, but it also may impact outcomes for close elections. Most of the administrators we interviewed believed that the general public did not fully understand nor was deeply concerned about the details of the vote transfer process. Nevertheless, the general idea of vote transfers is a component of educational awareness for the public.

Election campaigns can provide voters with educational information, but the empirical support for this is mixed. Candidates sometimes engage in mutual endorsement or coordinate as teams, and this may provide potential voters with information about RCV.[40] Typical campaign communications, however, involve scant information on how to vote using RCV.[41] As observed in the congressional elections in Maine and Alaska, unless candidates try to appeal to extreme or small groups, candidates in a winner-take-all election (RCV/IRV) seem reluctant to encourage supporters to engage in anything but bullet voting or plunking. Effective campaigns are not generally associated with acknowledgment that a candidate is running behind or that winning is unlikely.

RCV/STV elections might have different incentives for campaign education, as multiple winners are selected. Candidates could coordinate voter awareness through a political party or other political slate. Moreover, campaigns may provide education for an individual campaign in the multimember election. Although Oscar winners are chosen by a plurality vote, the five (or so) Oscar nominees are selected through RCV/STV. A nomination can be impactful for the career of a film industry professional. In 2023, a social media movement and grassroots campaign lobbied in favor of a Best Actress nomination for Andrea Riseborough for her role in the critically acclaimed but financially unsuccessful film, *To Leslie*. Supporters estimated that with a sufficient number of first-place rankings by Academy voters, Riseborough could join the likely list of four other actress nominations considered a lock. Members of the movement engaged in an informational strategy to promote their candidate, and they were successful. Election details are not available; the selection process of the Academy of Motion Picture Arts and Sciences is definitely not transparent, but Andrea Riseborough received a Best Actress nomination.[42]

Promoting educational awareness among voters has become a central focus of election administrators. The burden of providing information about RCV falls on election administrators. A wide range of materials can be furnished by these election supervisors. This advertising includes websites and factsheets explaining RCV, voter guides, instructional posters, speeches and interviews with citizens' groups, animated videos, and kiosks in local constituencies. The educational priorities remain a priority, but the sheer amount of effort may decline over time. Where ranked voting is entrenched, most voters learn ballot completion methods. Tanya Ford, executive director of the City of Cambridge Electoral Commission, notes that Cambridge voters have used proportional representation, or STV, for over eighty years. Assistant Director Lesley Waxman observes that "people in Cambridge are pretty used to PR by now," although the need to provide information for young voters and new residents will always continue.

Often, the responsibility for voter education is split between government entities. In some localities, particularly where the county manages the city election, the county and the municipality have mutual responsibilities to promote educational awareness among voters. For example, in Bay Area cities, the primary responsibility for voter education lies with Alameda County, California, but the city clerk offices in Berkeley, Oakland, and San Leandro also make efforts to inform their residents about the voting process. Public interest groups also help with RCV education efforts. These include Democracy Rising and FairVote, national nonprofit organizations that promote RCV.

Our interviews reinforce for us the critical nature of education as part of successful implementation of RCV, especially in the time leading up to the first election to use the system. The experience in Maine is a case in point. As discussed in Chapter 5, the change to RCV was promoted by an organization, Democracy Maine, a joint effort of the Maine League of Women Voters and Maine Citizens for Clean Elections. Anna Kellar, executive director of Democracy Maine, emphasized with us the role of outreach, made easier in part by the League's established reputation for providing a voter's guide. Kellar observed, "There's already a lot of credibility with the voter guide. We were trying to get people to think specifically about ranked choice voting but also trying to make sure that wherever they were getting their basic voting information was including information about ranked choice." The priority was education for everyone, including those who were opposed to or hesitant about RCV.

> For us, it was really important that even people who didn't like ranked choice voting, we were still reaching them, and they still knew how to use it. We were particularly trying to make sure that we were reaching older voters, people in rural areas, people who might not have that much time thinking about it or that had other challenges. We did a bunch of presentations in senior living facilities.

Their efforts expanded to other audiences as well, including school presentations and town clerks.

Part of the goal was to promote RCV as both a normal way to vote and as a means to encourage voter engagement. Kellar explained it was important to emphasize, "This is how we vote in Maine." John Brautigam, senior advisor and counsel for Maine Citizens for Clean Elections, added that they tried to highlight to people that this was a system that gave voters a "meaningful choice." The goal was for voters to react with, "You know what? Now, I remember why I like to vote. I like to participate because I feel like I can have a say. For 20 years, I haven't really cared about having a say." Voter outreach and education are important components for successful implementation of RCV. As noted, our purpose in writing this book is to assist communities and individuals who are considering changes to their election systems. Since RCV is currently gaining in popularity as a potential reform, it is particularly important that specific aspects of the system be fully understood prior to its adoption so that voters can be fully educated about it.

Several of the election administrators that we spoke to mentioned challenges in providing awareness and education for certain blocs of voters, such as nursing home residents, foreign language speakers, and people with disabilities. The process of ranking choices may be more difficult for some members of these groups. Technological challenges also exist in reaching out to these voters, particularly those with accessibility needs.

RCV and Group Representation

One particularly interesting question about RCV is the extent to which it enhances representation for minority groups, particularly racial and ethnic minorities. There is a lack of consensus on this question. As discussed earlier, the 2021 New York City Democratic Party primary resulted in the leading candidates, themselves people of color, disagreeing on this question. One could make an argument that ranking ballots would result in better minority representation simply because voters are freer to prioritize a candidate who they think will best serve their community without concern that the candidate will prove to be a "spoiler" in the outcome of the election. Scott Kendall notes that this argument was persuasive among native peoples in the state of Alaska, although ranking ballots there occurs only after the field of candidates has been narrowed to four. Experimental evidence suggests that although nonpartisan elections generally work against candidates of color, RCV produces no positive or negative effect. This may occur because of the increased cognitive demands and lengthier time to make decisions for RCV compared to other electoral systems (Crowder-Meyer, Gadarian, and Trounstine 2024).

Two separate questions present themselves when thinking about racial/ethnic equity and RCV. The first question concerns the number of candidates that voters can rank. Many places that adopted RCV limit the number of rankings that voters are allowed to make; while this violates the norm of the pure form of RCV, this limitation is generally made for practical reasons of election administration and vote tabulation. But do limits on the number of candidates that can be ranked restrict the impact of communities of color on the outcome of the election? One could argue that allowing a voter to rank more candidates would increase the chances for a minority-preferred candidate to make it into subsequent rounds or even prevail in the election. If true, other leading candidates would then see it in their strategic interest to attempt to capture a place in the top rankings of those voters.

The second question concerns the advantages of RCV over other forms of election. RCV may be better for minority communities when the alternative is an SMDP election in which the outcome would be a plurality winner consisting only of the majority bloc. For example, a Hispanic population consisting of 15 percent of the electorate has the potential for considerable influence in an RCV election over an SMDP election where a homogeneous white plurality dominates with a consistent 45 percent of the vote. But what about RCV over a standard runoff election? Do candidates and voters behave differently in a regular runoff compared to an "instant" runoff?

One former election administrator we spoke to has reflected carefully on these questions. LaTonda Simmons, the assistant city administrator and former city clerk in Oakland, California, sees some ways that RCV has the potential to be a detriment to full levels of inclusion in the electoral process. In 2020, Oakland increased the number of candidates a voter may rank from three to five. But to Simmons, ranking candidates may not fit well with the manner in which African Americans evaluate candidates, and thus increasing the number to be ranked may not be particularly helpful. That is, there may be a limited number of candidates who appeal to voters in this group, and voters may simply only choose to rank one or two. She observes that such an approach does not match the logic of RCV but may make the most sense for many voters. That problem is exacerbated in Oakland, in a mayoral election with a dozen candidates. She notes that even with a full ranking of five candidates, there is a possibility that none of a minority voter's ranked candidates will make it beyond the first round. And simply increasing the number of allowed rankings also increases the "burden" of completing the ballot.

Simmons further suggests the possibility that a simple runoff election might be better for racial minorities. In a runoff, voters have the opportunity for a side-by-side comparison of the two finalists, and those finalists must appeal to a variety of communities. Simmons says of the interaction between voter and candidate in this situation: "If you will represent me, whether I like you or not, and I take this voting process as seriously as it should be taken, I still have the ability to say [to the candidate], 'Then you need to come to me and compel me with your arguments for my representation.'" Putting it humorously, she says that an approach to a candidate in this situation is, "You have got to come court me."

An RCV or an instant runoff procedure does not include this secondary opportunity for candidates to reach out to minority communities. Candidates who aspire to win need as many first and second ranks as possible. This means the likelihood of success involves reaching out to majority communities, or at least to larger groups, large in terms of size and power. In their analysis of the 2013 Minneapolis municipal election, Jacobs and Miller (2014) find that affluent and white voters are overrepresented compared to minority voters in terms of RCV electoral participation. However, other scholars express confidence that RCV elections may increase the representation of women and minorities.[43]

In general, contemporary support for RCV appears stronger from Democrats and the political left than from Republicans and the political right. When Democratic Representative Jamie Raskin sponsored a bill in 2019 to adopt RCV across the United States, the bill had eleven co-sponsors, all Democrats.[44] The bill would have required RCV for primary and general elections for Congress and provided federal funding to states for implementation. Conversely, the Republican National Committee adopted a "Resolution to Officially Oppose Ranked Choice Voting Across the Country" in 2023. The resolution denounced the electoral system's cost, potential for voter confusion, increasing political distrust, and attack on the political party system.[45]

Democratic Party–leaning areas of the country seem more enamored with the system. For example, the Oregon Legislative Assembly placed a measure to conduct all future state and federal elections using RCV on the 2024 ballot. But, voters rejected it. The measure had passed the state House 34–17, with all seventeen nay votes coming from Republicans, and the state Senate 17–8, with seven of the nay votes coming from Republicans. A voter initiative in Colorado to adopt RCV for state and federal elections (combined with an open primary, as in Alaska) followed this general pattern, with the Democratic governor suggesting support for the concept and the Republican Assistant House Minority Leader expressing skepticism. Republican Representative Lauren Boebert declared on social media that the initiative was an attempt to "rig our electoral system" and promised to oppose it "with everything I have." In April 2024, Democratic Governor Andy Beshear of Kentucky vetoed an election law bill that included a provision to ban RCV, but the legislature, with its Republican supermajority, overrode the veto a week later. Eleven Republican-leaning states (AL, FL, ID, KY, LA, MO, MS, MT, OK, SD, TN) banned the use of RCV, and others are considering it.[46] In most of the states prohibiting RCV, Republicans control the executive office as well as the upper and lower chambers of the state legislature. The right-leaning Heritage Foundation published a report describing RCV as "Rigging the System" and warning that it "destroys your clear and knowing choices as a political consumer," and the conservative website *The Federalist* referred to RCV as "the monster under the bed of American elections."[47]

But it would be a mistake to suggest partisan consensus across the United States about RCV. In an opinion piece in *The Hill*, Saul Anuzis, a former chairman of the Michigan Republican Party, and Stan Lockhart, a former chairman of the Utah Republican Party, put forward many of the usual arguments in favor of RCV and suggested that it would have been potentially useful in the 2024 GOP presidential primary contests with its large number of candidates. Arguing primarily for its use in primaries, they observed that Republicans used it in Virginia in 2021 to nominate their successful gubernatorial candidate Glenn Youngkin, and that its use in that state's congressional nomination primaries resulted in candidates deemed more appealing to the voters.[48] The State of Idaho currently bans RCV, but former Governor Butch Otter is among several Republicans seeking to repeal the ban. And despite being heavily Republican states, Alaska and Utah (for cities) adopted the system in recent years. Support for RCV on the political left is not universal either. In 2021, the Washington, DC, Democratic Party voted to oppose the use of RCV. The District did adopt the system along with an open primary, and the Democratic Party subsequently sued to stop the implementation.[49] In 2016, Democratic California Governor Jerry Brown vetoed a statewide extension of RCV. More recently, Democratic Governor Gavin Newsom vetoed legislation that would have permitted the adoption of RCV in that state's local elections, citing "voter confusion" and insufficient evidence of its effectiveness. It is noteworthy that Newsom was elected as mayor of San Francisco under RCV in 2007.[50]

As a general rule, incumbents are unlikely to propose or support changes to an electoral environment that brought them to office. They have little incentive to alter the electoral system, promote increased voter turnout, or enhance competition favoring challengers, particularly if this produces a greater chance of future electoral defeat. The political lines in Canada are drawn in a similar fashion as in the US Conservatives tend to oppose RCV and some other electoral reforms, while the Liberals and the NDP lend more support. When Liberals were out of power, third in the number of seats in the House of Commons, election reform—RCV or another system—became a priority issue. Party leader Justin Trudeau campaigned for electoral system change, promising the end of plurality federal elections. However, after Trudeau and the Liberals won the election and again became entrenched as the governing party, the desire for reform waned. Milner (2017) provides a fascinating account of this electoral reform odyssey. Once it became clear that the Liberal Party could control the government for the foreseeable future, RCV and other election reforms slid back down the public agenda to a subject of debate for academics and policy wonks (Scarpaleggia 2016).

We reject the notion that RCV, or any other electoral system, is explicitly partisan in orientation. It is true that many of the municipalities that adopted preferential elections since the turn of the century have tended to be more liberal or progressive in orientation, and some may perceive this as evidence that the system is designed to elect representatives from certain groups. However, it may be simply that these communities are more willing to accept alternative structures of government that upset the status quo. For instance, younger generations may exhibit greater dissatisfaction with politics and be more willing to accept reforms like RCV (McCarthy and Santucci 2021). Support for the system may be dependent on the political dynamic in a particular area or perceived short-term political advantage; however, such dynamics are likely to change over time, and thus partisanship is an unreliable basis for adopting or rejecting RCV.

The evidence that voters perceive campaigns in RCV municipal elections as more satisfying or civil is not strong.[51] Donovan, Tolbert, and Gracey (2016), analyzing survey responses, investigate the perception of voters under RCV and plurality elections. They discover that voters in RCV cities perceive less negativity in campaigns and less rancor between candidates. However, Kropf (2021) compares RCV and plurality elections with a text analysis of campaign communications and finds mixed results. Newspaper content is somewhat more positive in RCV elections, but social media (Twitter) is more negative. Juelich and Coll (2021) conclude that RCV municipal elections do not lead to overall gains with increased voter turnout, perceptions of positive campaigns, or feelings of campaign civility, although young voters are more likely to be mobilized and to turn out. The notion that RCV elections result in greater mobilization efforts aligns with other research on alternative electoral systems, particularly cumulative voting (Bowler, Donovan, and Brockington 2003). Experimental evidence suggests that citizens are no more likely to express confidence in RCV than in plurality or majoritarian elections (Nielson 2017). They do not feel results are fairer, nor do they prefer voting in an RCV election.

Voter dissatisfaction may occur in nonpolitical contexts as well. As an example, some in the music branch of AMPAS express frustration with the RCV nomination process for an Oscar. They feel that the nominees are not always reflective of members' best work, participation rates are too low, information demands to assess nominees fairly are huge, and the administrative process is not transparent.[52]

For municipalities that adopted RCV, there has seldom been a majority expression of dissatisfaction with the electoral system. Yet many communities also have an undercurrent of opposition. Many locations, in the early twentieth century and again in the early twenty-first century in communities like Aspen, adopted and repealed RCV, returning to plurality elections. A 2024 initiative petition in Alaska was circulated to eliminate the open primary and top four general election. In Vermont, Burlington voters, however, adopted and then rejected RCV, only to reintroduce and expand it for all elected city officials in 2024. Only Cambridge has maintained its STV electoral system over the long term. Only time will tell whether the trend toward the adoption of ranked choice in North American elections will continue into the future.

As noted throughout this book, the ability of RCV to meet reformers' goals may simply depend on the local political environment within the area adopting the voting method. One election method cannot address concerns in all communities. In fact, external pressures on communities to adopt this method may be counterproductive. Don Frantz, Mayor Pro Tem of Cary, put it this way, "I think each municipality needs to do what's best or what works for them. I do think anytime you have outside organizations, national movements, and things coming in and telling us what to do, that can often rub... the wrong way." Like the old aphorism "all politics is local," the conditions within the community, state, or nation determine the appropriate electoral system for its citizens.

8
Evaluating RCV

> Political science is, perhaps of all studies, the most difficult, from the boundless variety of its phenomena. The apparent simplicity of much that is upon the surface leads us to think that we comprehend it; and the depth of complexity of what is beneath and behind, which eludes our sight, seem to mock our attempts to penetrate its secrets.
>
> Thomas Hare, *The Election of Representatives, Parliamentary and Municipal*[1]

A goal of this book is to help citizens understand ranked choice voting (RCV) and to evaluate whether RCV is a good option in their communities. So far, we have done this by providing descriptions, explanations, and examples of how RCV has been and could be used. We hope that our discussion of advantages and disadvantages proves useful. As Oxford philosopher Michael Dummett (1997, vii) wrote, "to make a sensible choice of an electoral system, quite a lot of thought is needed. It is thought of which almost all those who have a vote are capable, one they have grasped the issues involved; the issues are virtually never put to them by politicians or journalist." In that spirit, this book outlines the theoretical and empirical concerns related to preferential voting systems.

For some contexts, RCV may be a good method for deciding among policy options within an informed electorate. Any collective decision made by a large group might successfully utilize RCV. These decisions could fall within a broad range: the selection of board members for an association or society, smaller group decisions such as the International Olympic Committee's selection of a future Olympic venue, multiple-option referred questions on ballot propositions, or information-gathering from the public on policy priorities. For example, in recent years, many school boards across the country sought information about parents' preferences regarding how to handle the coronavirus pandemic. Some of those inquiries involved multiple choices, such as should classes be shifted entirely online, should classes

Ranked Choice Voting. James W. Endersby and Michael J. Towle, Oxford University Press.
© Oxford University Press (2025). DOI: 10.1093/9780197798959.003.0009

remain in person, should in person and online classes be alternated in some predetermined fashion, or should classes be delayed? To our knowledge, most of these requests sought a single outcome, a plurality winner. A reasonable request for such preferences might be more informative if the citizens, here parents, could provide a full ordering of preferences. The information produced might have been more satisfying with more effective consultation. Likewise, public questions on where to locate the new city hall or a new school, and so forth, might well be more satisfactory with more complete public input.[2]

Although it is easier to compare RCV elections with plurality elections from a traditional single-member district, this may not be the most appropriate comparison. The more apt comparison might be to standard runoff elections, in which the top two alternatives are paired if neither receives a majority vote.[3] This is the notion that caught on in twentieth- and twenty-first-century North America, that in a case with no first-ballot majority winner, a runoff would be held instantly, without the demands of a subsequent election.[4]

The typical rationale is to produce majority winners without the cost of a later runoff. In addition, the electorate selecting the winner would be the same, and there would be no additional campaign between the top two. But if we value another opportunity to reconsider the top two candidates, that is, we want another campaign limited to the top two alternatives, then a traditional runoff is the better method. These are choices for citizens to weigh, and there is no definitive answer.

To return to an example mentioned briefly earlier, the case of the 2020 Senate runoff in Georgia may be illustrative. For those who remember the election, it may also bring all partisan biases to the forefront. This is because the control of the US Senate hung in the balance based on the outcome of the 2020 Georgia runoff election. Republicans needed one more victory to control the US Senate, and Democrats needed to win both seats to control the Senate for the first two years of the Biden Administration. In the end, the Democrats were successful in winning both seats in this traditional Republican state. The campaigns, general and runoff, were divisive, and they involved substantial out-of-state money and campaign support. See Table 8.1, which summarizes the outcomes of these senate elections in Georgia.

In the general election, Republican incumbent David Perdue received 49.73 percent of the vote, and the trailing Democrat Jon Ossoff gathered 47.95 percent. The only other candidate was Libertarian candidate Shane

Table 8.1 2020 Georgia runoffs for US Senate

	Nov. 2020 General		Jan. 2021 Runoff	
Candidate	Votes	Percent	Votes	Percent
General (6-year term)				
David A. Perdue (I, R)	2,462,617	49.7%	2,214,979	49.4%
Jon Ossoff (D)	2,374,519	47.9%	2,269,923	50.6%
Shane Hazel (L)	115,039	2.3%		
Total	4,952,175	100.0%	4,484,902	100.0%
Ballots Cast	5,025,683		4,492,050	
Special (2-year)				
Rafael Warnock (D)	1,617,035	32.9%	2,289,113	51.0%
Kelly Loeffler (I, R)	1,273,214	25.9%	2,195,841	49.0%
Doug Collins (R)	980,454	20.0%		
Deborah Jackson	324,118	6.6%		
16 Others	719,540	14.6%		
Total	4,914,361	100.0%	4,484,954	100.0%
Ballots Cast	5,025,683		4,492,050	

Hazel. We cannot know the second preferences of the Georgia voters in the general election as the election did not involve RCV. However, the second preference votes would need to have been in favor of Ossoff by nearly 8 to 1. Given the evidence from other races examined in earlier chapters, it seems unfathomable that Ossoff could have gathered eight second-choice ballots for everyone for Perdue. In short, Perdue almost certainly would have won an RCV election, and the Republicans would have maintained control of the US Senate.

For the other 2020 Georgia Senate seat, the outcome is much less clear. The ultimate victor Democrat Raphael Warnock led the field of twenty candidates with 32.9 percent. Appointed incumbent Republican Kelly Loeffler followed with 25.9 percent, and Republican Doug Collins trailed with 20.0 percent. It is more difficult to know how the second preferences would break in this hypothetical RCV election, but, following decades of political science research, we know that Republicans tend to vote for Republicans and Democrats for Democrats. The outcome of the special election, still likely to be very close, would depend on who and how many voters would list a second choice and how many votes would be dropped as exhausted or nontransferable. The influence of RCV (or single transferable vote [STV]) on election results is likely to be different in partisan and nonpartisan contexts.[5]

What explains the ultimate victories by Ossoff and Warnock? Although the campaign and the additional attention received may have influenced the outcome, it was the difference in the electorate that probably mattered most. A half million fewer Georgians participated in the runoff election than in the general election. If there is a rationale for implementing RCV, this disparity in participation between general and runoff elections seems key. But opponents may also legitimately claim that a second campaign is preferred to an instant runoff, which places significant cognitive demands on voters. Choosing a single best choice is difficult for many,[6] ranking three candidates in order may be daunting for many more. Determining an ordered preference among twenty alternatives seems extremely difficult for any voter to accomplish in a meaningful way.

As an aside, the evidence questions whether RCV elections would really lead to more candidates and greater diversity of opinion. Considering this example, would the GA special election have been more reflective of public attitudes with even more than twenty candidates? If voter participation improves following a greater breadth of choices, one assumption behind proponents of ranked choice, why is the number of voters casting a November ballot in the special election with twenty candidates lower than the general election with only three.

For most applications of RCV, it is not clear that the full transfer process is necessary. For instance, it may be that transfers should only be made between the top two candidates if the leading candidate does not attain a majority. A provision could include transfers among the top three candidates if no candidate receives at least 40 percent of the vote. These benchmarks are admittedly arbitrary, but they catch the flavor of the search for a consensus winner.

Cautions and Questions for Reformers

The pressure for electoral reform will continue to increase in the near future. The general public holds dissatisfaction and distrust of political institutions and political elites. One common measure of trust in government hit a postwar low in 2016 and 2020.[7] Preferential voting mechanisms offer the promise of systematic change. Advocacy organizations such as FairVote,

New America, and Common Cause are pushing for RCV or related electoral reform measures. There is a trend for state legislative bills and ballot questions proposing the adoption of some form of RCV or related methods. A number of academic sponsors have offered their support for RCV as well. The American Academy of Arts & Sciences calls for RCV for presidential, congressional, and state elections, along with allowing states to hold multimember (STV) elections.[8] New variations of the traditional RCV will continue to be improvised, such as Alaska's top four runoff and a similar, recently proposed single-vote primary with a final-five instant runoff election.[9] However, with such limited and recent experience with RCV in actual elections, caution with acceptance of the more grandiose claims of reformers may be wise.[10] Although the opportunity for improvements to elections exists, the evidence in favor of many of the purported claims of RCV is imperfect. Indeed, cross-national studies indicate that the public is no longer satisfied with ranking alternatives and that casting preferential votes has a small but negative effect on satisfaction with democracy.[11]

The remainder of this final chapter addresses two points. First, based on the experiences of communities that have used RCV, we present cautions for communities preparing to adopt an RCV system. Second, we pose several questions to consider before adopting an RCV system.[12] These cautions and questions are founded in political science scholarship on electoral systems, on observations regarding the historical experience of preferential voting in North America, and from election administrators, public officials, and political activists whose work keeps them involved with RCV elections. Communities giving serious consideration to RCV, or another electoral system, should ask the following questions.

What is the problem we are trying to solve? As with any change in policy, perhaps the best place to start is to think about what the problem is that you are trying to solve. For example, is there a sizeable group that is unable to be recognized because of the election system you are using? Are there people in your community who do not bother to vote because they have no chance of having a meaningful impact on the election? Does your area have three or more main political parties, such that no party can ever claim to govern with a majority? Or perhaps there may be three different ethnic groups, with each group feeling uncertain about its saliency in the community? Do you live in an area that is not particularly partisan or ideological, but the elected officials always seem to come from the extremes of their parties? Does your area have divisive issues that separate people? These are the types of questions that reformers should think about before proposing any change.

It is important to keep in mind that the election system you use will not only determine who is elected, but also can affect who the candidates are, how they campaign, and the types of issues that they address. In short, changes to the election system can shake things up in a community. Each of us may think these changes are good or bad, but others may disagree. The impact of electoral changes may depend on where you live and who is being affected.

How does the government structure relate to the electoral system? If your community is considering RCV for one office—for example, the mayor—it is important to consider the entire context of the elected government, not just that one office. If you live in a community that has a large group that feels underrepresented by the government, attempts to address this problem might best be focused on the overall structure of the government. While it is possible for a small minority in an election using RCV to become a part of a coalition that gives a mayoral candidate a majority, this outcome is not guaranteed; it might make more sense to look to other parts of the government for diversity in representation. How is the city council elected? Is the method of election to all elected offices conducive to creating a diverse outcome? If not, your community may want to consider such things as the number of people elected to the council or the methods used to elect that council. Representation for ethnic minorities can often be better addressed by enlarging the size of the representative body or adjusting the districts from which representatives are elected, especially if the minority group is dominant in certain geographic areas.

It is also important to consider whether every elected office would be elected using RCV, or just one. At first glance, in a community with a separately elected mayor and city council, it would probably make sense to elect all of those positions using RCV. But there can be a risk here for some; for example, an underrepresented group might find it easier in some districts to achieve a plurality rather than a majority. It is possible that the RCV requirement for a majority in every district might reduce the representation of some voices, such as a group that can only elect one of its own from a district using a plurality method. Our point is simply that communities should not look at the election of one individual in isolation from the context of the entire government.

What is the partisan or factional situation where you live? For communities that have two major political parties and barely any other political divisions, RCV might not be particularly helpful. This is particularly true if there is one party that clearly dominates. For example, in a city where mayoral elections typically have a 60 percent level of support for one political party, little is to be gained by RCV since it is unlikely that there would be a second round. Admittedly, even this is uncertain. For example, it is possible that the use of RCV might expose a rift in the dominant party since candidates might be willing to create a division in order to bring themselves into a runoff. Shaking things up can be good, but it can also lead to unproductive political chaos and infighting. On the other hand, if one party (or both) is divided into factions, RCV has the potential to break down party polarization to reach more of a consensus outcome.

What are the sizes of the divisions to be represented? Of course, a community with a 60/40 split where the 60 percent wins every election does leave a sizeable portion of the community without a voice. STV or another election system encouraging minority representation (on councils or legislative bodies, not for solitary political offices such as mayor or governor), such as cumulative voting, might give the 40 percent a louder voice. Of course, political reality suggests that an area with one-party domination is unlikely to willingly make changes to weaken its own influence. The situation is different if your community has three competing political factions, with none having a majority. Such scenarios can lead to resentment when the governing group does not have majority support. Communities with this type of longstanding split would have the most to gain from RCV. For example, a city with a 40 percent–30 percent–30 percent split might benefit from the outreach that each group would attempt to make to others in order to achieve—*and sustain*—a majority.

Is politics the most effective way to deal with divisions in your community? Not all divisions within a community can be remedied by politics alone. For example, if you live in an area that has problems among racial, ethnic, or socioeconomic groups, it would be a mistake to assume that any election system would be a sufficient way to address these differences. While politics can address community divisions, it can also exacerbate them. If bridge-building and cultural understanding are the objectives, other approaches should come first.

To the extent that politics might help, it makes a big difference whether there is one isolated minority group that constitutes a relatively small fraction of the community or several different groups. For example, a community that is 15 percent African American in an otherwise white community faces different challenges than a community that is 30 percent African

American, 30 percent Hispanic, and 40 percent white. In the former situation, it is possible that the need to get to 50 percent might result in more outreach, but it is not guaranteed; in fact, the 15 percent could just as easily be scapegoated as a way to create a political majority. But the latter situation is more likely to result in cooperation since none of these groups can get a majority without the assistance of others. It is tempting when thinking about elections to assume that a different voting system will address a community's divisions. But politics might not address the underlying problem.

Will voters understand—and welcome—the changes being proposed? Change is frequently unwelcome, especially in politics. Even with the best of intentions, many will be suspicious of the motives of those who are advocating for change. And since changes to election methods often translate into changes in who gets elected, would-be reformers will be accused of partisan motivations.

Our interviews reinforce for us the critical nature of education as part of the successful implementation of RCV, especially in the time leading up to the first election to use the system. Municipalities that successfully implemented the system carefully planned their education efforts. For example, advocates in Maine and Alaska spoke with us about the importance of outreach, especially to people who might oppose the system or find it challenging; part of their strategy was to promote the idea that RCV gives voters better options in voting. But whatever approach is used, getting basic information to the voters is an essential prerequisite for an election they trust.

The act of voting in a preferential system is not complicated. Voters simply have to rank-order their preferences. However, the cognitive demands of creating a full or lengthy preference ordering are large. It may be relatively simple for a small group of friends to decide amicably which of three restaurants where they would like to have lunch. However, the demands are radically more difficult if each friend is required to rank personal preferences across ten, twenty, or fifty restaurants. Anecdotal evidence suggests that insisting on RCV as a method of choosing a restaurant leads to fewer friends and eating alone. For many voters, there is a learning curve to RCV. Moreover, it would be a mistake to underestimate the degree to which some individuals may be put off by an unfamiliar way of voting. Clearly, any change must be accompanied by a substantial public information campaign.

Explaining how to vote is the easy part. In the intermediate and long term, voters in a ranked-choice system must be able to see what actually happens to their vote. The typical voter spends little effort thinking about voting systems, and this is especially true where the counting stops as soon as all of the ballots have been tallied. RCV adds a second layer of complexity, and it would be a mistake to assume that voters will immediately understand what is happening. The legitimacy of the election outcome is dependent on voters believing that the system is rational and fair.[13]

We underline the importance of this for any area considering the use of STV. Our experience suggests individuals need a few opportunities to examine the system before they understand it. A casual voter is unlikely to comprehend the system with a cursory public relations campaign. STV is not truly proportional unless a large number of representatives are selected. STV may produce more diverse representation, but an assumption is that voters focus on their own self- and group-interest. Moreover, the process of vote transfers is typically less transparent.

It is worth noting that the cities in the United States that are most associated with RCV systems are also among the most educated. According to an analysis by the Brookings Institution of the top 100 most populated urban areas, the Washington, DC, metropolitan area, which includes Takoma Park, MD, had the highest percentage of the population with college degrees. The San Francisco Bay area ranked 4th, Boston/Cambridge ranked 6th, and Minneapolis/St. Paul ranked 10th.[14] These are the areas where municipal RCV elections have been adopted and become entrenched. Education may be an important factor in the relatively uncontroversial use of this system in these areas.

This gives another reason for caution. Any effort to improve representation must be cognizant of the fact that citizens with less education may be more intimidated by voting and feel most uncomfortable with the added complexity of RCV. It would be elitist to simply dismiss voters who have trouble grasping what happens with ranking preferences. Presumably, the entire reason to reform an election system is to make sure that voters do not feel dismissed in the election process.

Rules matter—pay close attention to the procedures used. In our discussions with election administrators across the United States, we were impressed by their skill and dedication to fair and open democratic governance. These election administrators, of course, are constrained by the rules established by city, county, and state public officials. For us, it is clear that these officials do their best in their service to the public. However, the rules themselves are a hodgepodge of policies, each designed to fit the politics of a specific locale.

Pertinent issues—such as the number of preferences a voter can rank, ballot design, technology (or lack of it) to count and transfer ballots, and how to handle cast ballot deviations such as overvotes, undervotes, and skipped rankings—lead to little consistency across jurisdictions. To be fair, American elections, even for plurality contests, resemble a crazy quilt of election standards and practices.[15] Variation and experimentation can be healthy for democracy. However, in the RCV arena, these differences in the voters' experiences may have substantial consequences. More objective research on these standards and practices would be a fruitful endeavor.

Consider other voting systems too. Lobbying for RCV may push out other viable alternatives such as approval or cumulative voting. The conversation about electoral systems could be broader than the discussion of RCV as a lone substitute for plurality elections. As noted in the discussion of municipal elections, most RCV communities do not truly use RCV. Instead, in some locations, a limited RCV is used; the number of possible rankings (such as three) may be restricted to less than the number of alternatives.[16] Moreover, STV or multiwinner ranked vote (MRV), that is, a multimember RCV election, may elect too few alternatives to be proportional. Proportionality depends on the election of multiple officials at-large, not in districts with a small number of representatives.

We question the utility of the MRV used in some constituencies. MRV, a particular version of multimember instant runoff voting (IRV), is not particularly different from block voting for at-large constituencies. MRV tends to reflect preferences among the majority only, not those of minority groups. In a community with a homogeneous majority coalition, MRV produces outcomes no different than block voting. The majority elects both their higher preferences, and a minority, even a large one, will be unable to attain representation. Ranking preferences in this situation is a sham. Of course, not all majorities are monolithic, but the aim of instituting RCV is usually to enhance representation, not buttress malapportionment.

Multimember districts with STV or other methods such as cumulative voting or approval voting are worthy of more consideration. Much of the current agenda on electoral systems focuses on RCV/IRV, but RCV/STV or other systems may better achieve some goals such as proportional representation. These systems work better for at-large, or at least more highly aggregated, representation. The trade-off is that election administration and demands on voter knowledge and awareness are substantially higher. If at-large representation is desirable, and this may be the case in smaller communities and towns, a better option—in terms of administration and information costs—may be to create individual at-large seats elected separately (whether RCV or not).

Assessment and Future of RCV

Education—for election administrators, candidates, and voters—seems key to success for RCV elections. Even for more complicated electoral systems, such as STV elections for city council and school board in Cambridge, casting ballots may become the norm over time. Yet the need for education on ballot completion (for voters and poll workers) and transfers and counting (for election administrators) would need to be ongoing for new voters. A strength of plurality voting (with or without runoffs) is that it is easy to understand, to vote, and to tabulate. Concern is justified for RCV in rural areas and in resource-poor urban areas, constituencies often underserved by staff and expertise. Certainly, instant runoff elections are not instant compared to simple plurality, though they lead to official results much faster than standard runoff elections. As American elections progress into the mid-twenty-first century, a lengthier time to obtain final election results may become standard, certainly, if the 2016 and 2020 federal elections indicate the future. RCV elections may be part of that delay. In any case, we should be more concerned about the accuracy of elections rather than how quickly they are calculated.[17]

Is all the education and change from RCV worth it? Acceptance of RCV/alternative vote (AV) has become the norm in Australia. But Douglas Rae (1971), in his analysis of various national electoral systems, provocatively concluded that Australia's AV "behaves in all its particulars as if it were a single member district plurality formula."[18] While Australians might disagree with that assessment, the evidence here largely supports this view that IRV/AV produces results similar to SMDP.

RCV initially appears to benefit smaller parties or factions and independent candidates, while plurality elections are more difficult for them. Third-party candidates—or the factional, nonpartisan equivalent—may open the conversation and raise issues of environmental policy, indigenous rights, religious perspectives, or whatever is important to people that receive less attention from the current political agenda. Broadening voices will not take away from legitimate, contemporary discourse. In addition, minor candidates may no longer take on the role of spoiler.

There are many open questions regarding RCV elections in North America. Will RCV be more likely to produce outcomes characterized more by moderation or by extremism? So far, there appear to be more anecdotes than evidence. Neither moderation nor extremism is evident in the experience of municipal elections. Will RCV provide more satisfaction with democracy? Certainly, some RCV elections involve mutual candidate endorsement, and voter experience with elections may be improved if candidates are not arguing about who is a legitimate candidate and who is a spoiler. Will turnout increase with more experience with RCV elections? Perhaps, but at this time, confidence in the positive effect on voter turnout requires a political leap of faith.

In the end, whether a constituency should stay with plurality elections or move toward preferential elections may be a question of political philosophy. Is the priority of securing majorities truly consistent with the protection of minority rights? Yet, RCV may offer an opportunity for fundamental reform to break the polarization, antagonism, and deadlock that seem to confront contemporary American politics (Diamond 2019). One characteristic of the American federal system too often undervalued is the ability of states and constituencies to experiment with political reforms in order to test whether they achieve their goals and objectives.

Throughout this book, we have resisted the urge to either advocate for or oppose preferential voting. To repeat our earlier caution, there is no perfect voting system. The decision between plurality or ranked choice elections, for instance, simply involves a balancing of pros and cons. One electoral system is not decidedly better than another. RCV has both potentially significant benefits as well as some major drawbacks. In the spirit of Thomas Hare, an early scholar of preferential voting, who is quoted at the beginning of this chapter, our task is to shed light on many of the issues to consider when evaluating the potential of RCV.

Appendices

Appendix A

Table A.1 Preferential voting systems

Ranked Choice Voting (RCV) System (Abbreviation)	# Elected	Runoff If No Majority	# Rankings Maximum	# Rankings Required
Instant Runoff /Alternative Vote (**IRV, AV**)	1	Sequential elimination from bottom	Varies	None
US Cities	1	"	3 to all candidates	None
Australian House	1	"	# Candidates	# Candidates
Contingent Vote (**CV**)	1	2	All	None
Supplementary Vote (**SV**)	1	2	3	
Multiwinner Ranked Vote (**MRV**)	Multiple	Sequential elimination from bottom	Varies	None
US Cities	2–3	"	Varies	None
Australian Senate	6	"	6	6
Single Transferable Vote (**STV**)	Multiple	Sequential elimination from excess votes at top and votes from bottom		
Ireland	3–5	"	# Candidates	None
Cambridge	9 Council 6 School Committee	"	# Candidates	None
Minneapolis	2–3	"	# Candidates	None

APPENDICES 171

Appendix B

Figure B.1 Ballots for the Australian House of Representatives.
Reproduced from Australian Electoral Commission (2021) at https://aec.gov.au/Voting/How_to_vote/practice/practice-house-of-reps.htm. For a formal ballot paper, a voter must number all candidates in sequence.

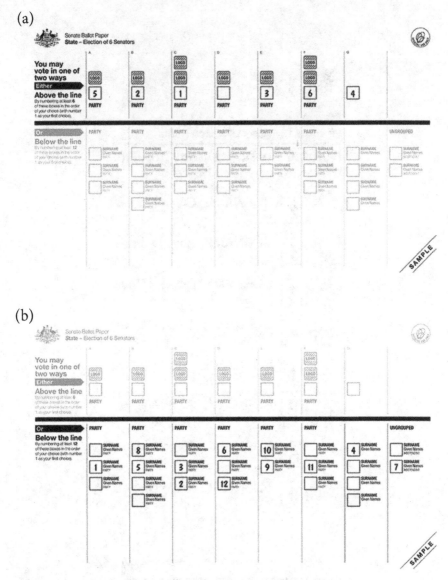

Figure B.2 Ballot for the Australian Senate.

Reproduced from Australian Election Commission (2021) at https://aec.gov.au/Voting/How_to_vote/Voting_Senate.htm. To cast a formal ballot paper, a voter must either (a) mark at least six parties in order above the line or (b) at least twelve candidates below the line (but not both).

Interviews

In the process of researching the material for this book, we discussed ranked choice voting (RCV) and related issues with the following individuals (and others unidentified). We were struck by the knowledge and devotion of the election administrators who implement rank choice voting and by the concern of the advocates (for and against) RCV. We appreciate the information provided by those whose names are listed below. Any errors in our discussion are ours alone.

Names in alphabetical order by last name but listed FN LN and followed by title.

John Brautigam, Senior Advisor and Counsel, Maine Citizens for Clean Elections
Melissa Caiazzo, Election Administrator, City of Portland, Maine
Julie Flynn, Deputy Secretary of State, State of Maine
Tanya L. Ford, Executive Director, City of Cambridge Election Commission, Massachusetts
Don Frantz, Mayor Pro Tem, Cary Town Council, North Carolina
Katherine Jones, City Clerk, City of Portland, Maine
Anna Kellar, Executive Director, Democracy Maine (League of Women Voters Maine and Maine Citizens for Clean Elections)
Scott Kendall, Counsel, Alaskans for Better Elections
LaTonda Simmons, Assistant City Administrator, City of Oakland, California
Aki Soga, Engagement Editor, former Editorial Page Editor, *Burlington Free Press*
David Triplett, Elections Manager, Ramsey County, Minnesota
Jim True, City Attorney, City of Aspen, Colorado
Grace Wachlarowicz, Assistant City Clerk, City of Minneapolis, Minnesota
Lesley Waxman, Assistant Director, City of Cambridge Election Commission, Massachusetts

Notes

Introduction

1. We temporarily ignore the problem of ties with an even number of votes. Social scientists typically assume a large decision-making group combined with an approved method of randomly selecting a winner in the case of a tie.
2. Another analogy for RCV we find compelling is decision-making on the U.S. Supreme Court. Justices vote to decide on the outcome of a case and prepare a majority opinion. Those opposed may write a dissenting opinion. However, in cases where a majority is divided, one or more of the Justices may prepare a concurring opinion. A concurrence expresses general agreement with the decision of the majority but expresses a preference for a third alternative, which is described in the concurring opinion.
3. Maine's electoral law applies to all federal elections. It also applies to state primary elections. For the 2018 election to the US senate, independent incumbent Angus King also won the election in the first round of counting with approximately 54 percent of the vote.

Chapter 1

1. For example, legislators may vote to pass a bill or not, for an amendment to a bill or not, for a substitute to the bill or not. There is usually a specific order to consider these options, but there are two alternatives for each vote except in rare circumstances.
2. A mathematical proof that majority rule meets commonly accepted conditions of fairness (anonymity, neutrality, and positive responsiveness) is provided by Kenneth May (1952). For extensions, see May (1953), Fey (2004), and Surekha and Bhaskara Rao (2010). Nearly all legislative votes are pairwise. Bill passage with amendments involves a series of pairwise votes, with a number of amendments considered sequentially in a predetermined manner. For cases of a tie, some (predetermined) random decision process, such as a coin toss or drawing from a deck of cards, must determine the outcome. For the unlikely case of a tie with an even number of voters, the winner receives 50 percent, not quite a majority, but a majority did not vote against the arbitrarily selected winner either. Note that the commonplace term "50% plus one" to identify a majority is accurate only for elections with an even number of voters. For an odd number of voters, "50% plus one" overstates the definition of a majority.
3. We might consider the frequency of plurality elections to be even higher, as some of these elections, particularly for the US House of Representatives, included only one or two candidates listed on the ballot. State election law may limit the number of nominees to two or make it difficult for minor party or independent candidates to reach the ballot.
4. The minority elections listed from 2018 exclude the 2nd Congressional District in Maine but include the election for the 9th Congressional District in North Carolina, which was voided due to evidence of ballot tampering and election fraud. Some states require runoff elections between the top two candidates (even if from the same political party). This underestimates the frequency of elections with a minority vote, as there are only two candidates in the general election.
5. The literature on voting rights is vast; for one excellent account of voting rights throughout American history, see Keyssar (2000). With regard to Constitutional Amendments, we might add the 17th, requiring the popular election of US senators, the 23rd granting voting rights in the District of Columbia; the 24th, eliminating the poll tax; and the 22nd, limiting presidential terms to two.
6. The US senate is an unusual case. Each state elects two senators, though for staggered six-year terms. Each senate election selects a single plurality winner, although both senators represent the same statewide constituency. Similarly, some cities have multiple at-large seats, but votes are cast separately for each at-large seat on the city council. State judicial officials are selected

by voters through a wide array of mechanisms. In all these instances, one political representative is selected independently by voters, even if the incumbents overlap in their geographical representation. Although congressional elections are the prototypical SMDP elections, Dow (2017) describes substantial variation in congressional elections across American political development.
7. On runoff elections in the US, see Bullock and Johnson (1992). Louisiana law specifies that ballots and election brochures for the runoff must be distributed "not less than 20 nor more than twenty-five days after the completion of the counting of the votes in the initial election." LA Rev Stat § 42:1360.
8. Luke's faction might like Coombs' rule, which is similar to RCV but works through voters' preferences in the opposite order. For Coombs (1964), the candidate with the most last-place votes is dropped first. In the example, Kate is dropped first with 8,000 third-place rankings. That leaves a runoff between Luke and Jane, and as noted earlier Luke wins in the pairwise contest. See also Chamberlin, Cohen, and Coombs (1984) and Grofman and Feld (2004) for more on Coombs' Rule.
9. For most political offices, districts are created on the basis of geography, that is, residence. But we can imagine other nongeographical divisions, such as representation based on occupation (for union elections), employment level (tenure-track or adjunct in higher education), ethnic group, or age cohort. A 'district' for electoral purposes is typically geographical, but it need not be so. We might distinguish the concept of districting—dividing the population into groups—from mandates on representation. For instance, political parties in some states elect a man and a woman separately as ward leaders, but the full party electorate votes on each party official. The Maine legislature reserves three seats for representatives from Native American tribes. The Seanad or Senate of Ireland has six seats elected by graduates of two Irish universities and 43 elected to represent vocational interests (of 60 total).
10. The literature on redistricting is vast.
11. Most, though not all, at-large multimember councils in the US hold staggered elections, so that half run every two years or a third every three years. With a strong, coalesced faction, it matters little: the majority has the potential of winning all the seats.
12. Or even multiple nontransferable voting. Voters could cast ballots for candidates from different parties, but empirical evidence suggests they seldom do.
13. There are 2,000 total votes cast, with 1,000 voters casting two votes each. Peter receives 600 of 2,000 votes or 30 percent, Patrick 600 of 2,000 votes, 30 percent, and so on.
14. There is historical evidence for this as well. For instance, several states were not able to redistrict for Congress after the 1930 Census and reapportionment. The 1932 congressional elections in four states were held at-large. Democrats won all seats in Congress in Kentucky (9 members), Missouri (12), and Virginia (9). Republicans held several seats in those states before the election (2 of 7 districts in KY, 4 of 12 in MO, and 1 of 9 in VA). Only Minnesota went from solidly Republican, with 9 of 10 districts in 1930, to a majority Farmer-Labor Party on the at-large ballot (5 Farmer-Labor, 3 Republicans, and 1 Democrat). Following partisan redistricting, Republicans captured a majority of congressional districts in Minnesota and one each in Kentucky and Missouri in the 1934 elections. Since 1967, law requires that all states with more than one representative in the US House must use single-member districts through 2 US §2c. However, Congress failed to repeal Section 2a(c), which mandates at-large elections in certain circumstances when states fail to redistrict after the decennial census.
15. By a minority population, we mean any group, from an ethnic minority – such as African Americans – to a political minority – such as a group in town who oppose the construction of a new road – that comprises less than 50 percent of the overall political constituency. We generally think of the minority as sizeable and concentrated; one person is technically a minority in any polity of three or more individuals, but we would not expect legislative representation for each individual.
16. This division is an ideal setting. In the real world, Democrats tend to live near Democrats, and Republicans near Republicans. Likewise, racial, ethnic, income, and education groups also tend to congregate together residentially.
17. Other electoral systems, such as the block vote, allow a voter to cast multiple votes in an at-large election, but they are less common. Other electoral systems are discussed further in the next chapter.

18. Thomas Hare will be discussed later. For the contribution of Henry Raymond Droop, see Droop (1881). However, there are many other calculations of quotas, particularly for political elections.
19. For instance, a recent controversy over film nominees involves their requirement for theatrical distribution in Los Angeles, New York, or other major American cities. Public distribution in theaters has traditionally distinguished the Oscars from other awards for television and video film releases. Some Academy members questioned the validity of nominees such as those from the 2019 award-winning film Roma, which was produced primarily for a digital audience and received no broad release in theaters. However, the growth of streaming services, particularly during the coronavirus pandemic, strengthened the eligibility of digital releases. Questions of voter eligibility may also influence results. For instance, bending the rules at the time, Barbra Streisand was fast-tracked for active Academy membership and subsequently nominated for her first film role in Funny Girl. The final result was a tie between Streisand and Hollywood legend Katharine Hepburn for The Lion in Winter. Assuming Streisand voted for herself, her eligibility and her vote made her an Oscar winner and deprived Hepburn of winning outright.
20. This was five and is now up to ten ranked films. It seems unlikely that many Academy voters complete the full profile, but maybe they do.
21. See "Academy Awards of Merit" from the AMPAS Board of Governors (2020). As we shall see, there are many variations of RCV. The particular method used by the Academy is the reweighted range voting system.
22. The 2020 Georgia general and special elections became the most expensive senate elections in history, as the runoffs attracted hundreds of millions of additional dollars in campaign spending. Much of the campaign contributions originated from out-of-state. Nearly five million voters cast ballots for each race in the November elections, but despite all this additional spending, 500,000 fewer voters participated in the runoff elections.
23. Most of the academic literature refers to this behavior of misrepresenting true preferences as strategic voting, although it may also be termed sophisticated voting or, for mass elections, tactical voting (Fisher 2004). On strategic voting, see Cox (1997). The observation that SMDP elections lead to two-party systems is known as Duverger's Law (see Duverger 1954, Riker 1982b, and Grofman, Blais, and Bowler 2009, but see Colomer 2005).
24. Even under plurality voting, candidates may have an incentive to be ambiguous about their positions on many issues (Page 1976; Alesina and Cukierman 1990). Heightening the need to broaden the base rather than attracting core supporters might encourage even greater ambiguity.

Chapter 2

1. A similar point of view is that essentially half of all votes are wasted in a majority election. Only the votes needed to pass the majority threshold are effective; even the nearly 10 percent of extra votes for the winning candidate are wasted. This leads to the paradox of voting, the conundrum noted by Anthony Downs (1957). If rational citizens are concerned only about whether their votes are effective or wasted, then no one will vote. Yet if rational citizens believe that no one else will vote, then everyone will vote. Neither is what we observe in mass elections. An effective vote is sometimes referred to as a used vote (Cohan, McKinlay, and Mughan 1975).
2. Of course, the districts could be gerrymandered or drawn differently to artificially represent some Democrats, but the focus here is on the electoral system, not on other political factors such as apportionment, redistricting, and campaign finance.
3. RCV/IRV includes only transfers of the second type, votes from eliminated candidates. There is no need to transfer surplus votes from a winning candidate as there is no other alternative to elect. What we discuss as multiwinner ranked vote, MRV, is different from both of these and will be discussed later.
4. We can imagine a utilitarian election in which each voter assigns votes or points to each alternative, but this seems extremely difficult to implement. Riker gives a utilitarian example (from Dyer and Miles 1976) of a decision at the Jet Propulsion Laboratory at Cal Tech to determine which of many possible trajectories should be taken by the Voyager space probe in 1977. Because of the value of one path versus another, informed scientists could assign cardinal utility to each possibility. An analogous example of utilitarian political decision-making can be found in Seattle municipal elections. Although it does not affect the election outcome directly, Seattle residents receive four vouchers worth $25 each, which they can contribute to one to four candidates. A candidate may, in turn, use accumulated vouchers to cover the costs of a campaign.

5. Theoretically, that is, because determining the "best" means making comparisons with all the other alternatives. A buyer in the economic market makes a similar decision about which product or service has the best value.
6. For four candidates, the Borda count from first to last place would be 4, 3, 2, 1. However, one could also assign points of 3, 2, 1, 0, consistently subtracting 1 across all scores, or make any linear transformation of the original counts. The relative total scores for the candidates would be the same. The Borda count is similar to methods used to award a sweepstakes trophy to a team or school across a series of events. For Borda, results for all events are assigned points, but most sweepstakes awards assign points only for the top three contenders of each event.
7. Duncan Black (1958) provides an excellent treatment of the development of social choice methods. Another scholar Black identifies is Charles Dodgson, better known to many as Lewis Carroll, the writer of Alice in Wonderland and other works. Contributions of both Condorcet and Borda were eclipsed by the earlier writings of the Majorcan/Spanish scholar Ramon Llull in the thirteenth century. For an anthology of classic works on social decision-making, see McLean and Urken (1995).
8. We take this notion from Jim Endersby (2009: 1498) who dichotomizes botanists as "a 'lumper,' one who defines species broadly, submerging many minor varieties under a single name, [or] a splitter who does the opposite, naming the varieties as subspecies or even full species."
9. Like so many discussions of electoral systems, the categorization for both of these large democracies is due to generalization. Some states use elections other than SMDP for seats in the US House of Representatives (runoff and RCV), and US senators are chosen separately but with dual membership from each state. In India, voters select the larger, lower chamber, the Lok Sabha, through SMDP elections, but members of the upper chamber, the Rajya Sabha, are selected through state legislatures using STV. Most scholars generalize a polity's electoral system in terms of its most frequently used method of selection for the lower chamber of parliament.
10. A notable exception is Thomas Gilpen (1844), who advocated strongly for list PR in city elections of the mid-nineteenth-century Philadelphia, Pennsylvania.
11. See Bogdanor (1984), Grofman and Bowler (1997), Amy (2000), Farrell and McAllister (2000), and Reilly and Maley (2000).
12. Article I, Section 4, of the US Constitution gives Congress the power to "alter" state methods of electing congress, but US regulations are fairly limited.
13. Within the United Kingdom, several systems are used. The 90 members of the Northern Ireland Assembly are elected to five-year terms through STV. The Scottish Parliament has 129 members selected through a mixed electoral system. A voter casts a ballot in their constituency and a separate ballot for the region. Similarly, the 69 members of the Welsh Parliament are elected through MMP. Elections for the 650 members of the UK Parliament are conducted in constituencies using FPTP/SMDP. Local councillors are elected through FPTP in England and Wales, but through STV in Scotland and Northern Ireland. The United States, in particular, is often characterized as SMDP, but local and regional elections involve a maze of voting systems, including ranked choice and others.
14. See Reilly 2002 and Fraenkel and Grofman 2014. After independence from Australia in 1968, Nauru imported Australia's alternative vote method of elections but changed to Dowdall's method in 1971. The alternative vote, RCV-IRV, was used in special elections to fill vacancies until repealed in 2017.
15. For more on Nanson's method, see Nanson (1882, 1990), Niou (1987), McLean and Urken (1995), and McLean (1996).
16. There are 160 Teachtaí Dála, or members of the Dáil, elected from 39 multimember constituencies.
17. Marsh (2000, 2007) and Farrell and Katz (2014). Of course, this brings into question what we actually mean by the term proportional. Proportional representation of what? Voter preferences, we might assume by the whole method of ranking candidates, are more complex than a choice for one political party only. List proportional elections are only representative of revealed first preferences, not of preferences generally. Moreover, many governments elected through PR are coalitional in nature. Perhaps voters influence the structure of those coalitions, but only if they behave strategically (thus, not a first preference). We could similar debate what we effectively mean by representation (Chamberlin and Courant 1983).
18. See Hircsy de Mino and Lane (2000). An incumbent representative who switched to a third party was reelected in 2017, the first minor party candidate elected in over 50 years.

19. See Taagepera (1996), Grofman, Mikkel, and Taagepera (1999), and Coakley and Fraenkel (2007) on national RCV systems generally.
20. If eight candidates are listed, but only seven consecutive rankings from 1 to 7 are marked, the ballot would still be counted as a formal ballot. The candidate with the blank box would be considered the last choice.
21. Much later, we will return to the complication of election administration. It is worth noting that the Australians use paper ballots, not computerized voting, and separate ballots for elections to each national chamber.
22. Quotes at pages 156, 153, and 153. It is worth noting that, like Jeremy Bentham, J.S. Mill believed in utilitarianism, although ordinal preferences are not a utilitarian method of decision-making.
23. Jenifer Hart (1992) provides an excellent discussion of the forces for RCV/AV and PR in Great Britain from the nineteenth-century through World War II.
24. See Bogdanor (1984), Homeshaw (2001). Andrae served as Speaker, then Finance Minister. He was re-elected to the Danish parliament in 1856 and was selected as prime minister in the new government. See also Andrae (1926).
25. RTE. "Constitutional Convention to be established." February 22, 2012.
26. Bohan, Christine. "At last: Constitutional Convention to hold first meeting in December." The Journal.IE. November 5, 2012.
27. O'Connell, Hugh. "Do you want to change the way we elect TDs?" The Journal.IE. May 2, 2013.
28. "Constitutional Convention votes in favour of current voting system." The Irish Times. June 9, 2013.
29. Even pure proportional representation would simply produce a legislature with three minority parties. A coalition government could be formed, but this is an elite-driven solution, whereas flipping coins or drawing a high card yields a random solution. Neither tie-breaking procedure comes from the voters themselves, violating a decision-making condition generally called citizens' sovereignty.
30. In this example, the Condorcet loser is Cauliflower. But this presumes that voters give preferences in a sincere, not a strategic, manner. Here, A > B > C.
31. Eggers and Nowacki (2024) show that plurality elections are typically more susceptible to strategic behavior, though RCV may encourage more strategic voting under certain circumstances.
32. Of course, friend 5 would need to estimate the ranked preferences of his friends accurately to deliberately eliminate Broccoli this way. But in this example, friend 2 could apply the same strategy to select asparagus. What this suggests is that individuals with better information overall tend to be able to manipulate the outcome more easily.
33. Of course, it becomes quite difficult to use theoretical models to determine the frequency of nonmonotonic outcomes when the number of candidates is increased beyond three because the number of potential vote combinations grows considerably. Ornstein and Norman (2014, 9) conclude their article with the statement that, "The general case with more than three candidates is a promising topic for future research."
34. The 2009 Burlington election is also unusual because RCV was used only for mayoral elections. Seven City Councilors were elected concurrently from individual wards. No candidate received a majority in Ward 7, so a standard runoff election was held between the two candidates receiving the most votes. Typically, one advantage of adopting RCV is to eliminate the need for traditional runoff elections.
35. Although Graham-Squire and Zayatz (2020) reach different substantive conclusions, they also find the 2009 Burlington election to be a case of nonmonotonicity.
36. See Fishburn and Brams (1983), Felsenthal (2012), Gierzynski (2011, 165–166).

Chapter 3

1. Nearly all candidates for national elections, the subject of the previous chapter, are partisan. The original development of ranked methods does not require that candidates be labeled with political party or faction affiliation. Though the discussion of PR generally assumes party or a similar representation, this is not required for STV or other electoral systems.
2. Article XX, Section 6. Klemme (1964) suggests that the home rule option was not considered particularly important at the time of adoption.

3. The Grand Junction plan included the commission government (imported from Galveston, Texas), the initiative and referendum, local control and simplification of taxation, and regulation of public service corporations with the goal of destroying political machines. The electoral component was only a part of this broader plan; "The preferential ballot for cities is a plan to restore majority elections and true representative government" (Bucklin 1911, 90).
4. Kneier 1947, 439–445, Barber 1995, Barber 2000, 50–51, 167. New Jersey accounted for over half of the cities adopting Bucklin voting.
5. The 1915 Duluth election involved choosing a municipal judge. The Court ruled the municipal judge to be a state officer who could not be elected using preferential voting. Although the Court deemed preferential voting to violate Minnesota state voting rights, it refused to void municipal preferential elections definitively, much to the consternation of local public officials who were not sure how to conduct elections. See Brown v. Smallwood, 130 Minn. 492 (1915).
6. This addresses the key question of voting rights for the Bucklin method as well. By accumulating second preferences when no candidate receives a majority of first-place votes, some voters count twice as much as others. As noted by a legal commentator (Editors, 1915, HLR: 214), "The fundamental principle to be generally applied is that there must be no discrimination between the various electors; the voting strength of one must be exactly equal to the voting strength of another." Traditional RCV methods do not violate this standard, as voters' preferences are equally weighted.
7. This is particularly true in cities with partisan elections. Independents were more likely to rank a second choice than party supporters, who plunked or voted only for their top choice.
8. Each Bank's Board is comprised of nine directors, and six are elected through Bucklin voting. See 12 USC 304, clauses 17 and 19.
9. Formal political theorists note that Bucklin voting violates a separate set of fairness conditions compared to RCV (Tideman 2006).
10. For example, the New Jersey Supreme Court upheld Bucklin voting for a five-person commission in New Brunswick in a decision that mischaracterized vote transfers as traditional ranked choice voting. See Orpen v. Watson, 87 N.J.L. 69 (1915), 88 N.J.L. 379 (1915).
11. Article II, Section 16, State ex rel. v. Portland 65 Or. 273, 133 Pac. 62 (1913). A new charter ratified by Portland voters narrowly approved a five-member commission government with four-year terms. In addition to the mayor, only two at-large commissioners were elected in each election. The use of ranked ballots depended on the number of candidates running.
12. Santucci (2022) provides a detailed analysis of adoption and repeal in some of these cities. Frazier (2020) offers an excellent discussion on the experience in Lowell, Massachusetts.
13. Quotes in Hallett and Hoag (1940: 107) from Taft's City Management: The Cincinnati Experiment (1933).
14. Hallett and Hoag (1940: 105–121), Robert J. Kolesar in Barber (1995: 160–208), Barber (2000: 101–107).
15. Maxey (1922), Moley (1923), 652, Hallett and Hoag (1940), 123.
16. On the value of a citywide perspective, see Miller and Tucker (1998), 15–16, Barber (2000), 52.
17. The more general lesson from the Cleveland experience may be that rewriting the rules of government and elections, aka political reform, simply substitutes one set of elites for another (Trounstine 2008). Often, these conflicts centered on class politics (Bridges 1997, Bridges and Kronick 1999).
18. Cities in which voters rejected a referendum for STV/PR before and during the 1920s include St. Louis, MO (1916), Flint, MI (1919), Minneapolis, MN (1926), West Allis, WI (1926), and several cities in Ohio—Coshocton, Canton, Toledo, and Zanesville (Harris 1930).
19. Connecticut, Michigan, and Ohio
20. The editors of the Harvard Law Review (1941: 114) note that Michigan, California, and Rhode Island rejected it, and New York, Ohio, and Massachusetts allowed it. The debate over whether RCV may satisfy state constitutional provisions continues, see Pildes and Parsons 2021 for an extensive discussion.
21. Wattles ex rel. Johnson v. Upjohn, 211 Mich 514 (1920), McBain (1922: 281–282). Because seven council members were elected at-large, but only one vote was cast, the Michigan court wrote in its opinion: "To the average elector the destiny of his vote is a mystery, however easy it may be for him to follow instructions in marking his ballot."

22. Barber (2000), 113–114. Evaluating effects on voter turnout is also imprecise due to women's suffrage. In Ashtabula, for example, turnout appears to decline, but part of this may be due to the fact that women newly granted franchise rights participated in lower numbers (Moley and Bloomfield 1926).
23. For example, see Burnham (1965, 1981).
24. In Ashtabula, the number of candidates dropped from 21-29 under plurality to 12-17 under STV. Tenure in office seemed unaffected by STV, though the quality of candidates, judged by a five-person panel selected for "fair-mindedness and good judgment" and civic knowledge, rated elected councilmen as marginally better (Moley and Bloomfield 1926). For partisan, local elections, Moley (1923: 665) observes that: "Parties under the Hare system will nominate the same sort of candidates as they always have—the best 'vote-getters.' In several instances in Cleveland men who were elected were not rated even by the leaders of their own parties as of sufficient ability to make desirable councilmen. They were elected because of wide acquaintance or long service, or, in one case, because of wide advertising."
25. In Boulder, invalid ballots ranged from 6 percent to 11 percent (Sowers 1934), and in Ashtabula from 3 percent to 13.5 percent (Moley and Bloomfield 1926).
26. Moley (1923: 657) notes that fifteen of 25 candidates in Cleveland did not reach the quota and that 26 percent of ballots could not be applied toward any candidate.
27. Moley (1923: 663–665).
28. Brooks (1923: 445). At least ten other towns used a "preferential ballot," but existing descriptions remain vague as to whether this is STV, Bucklin, or Nanson methods (Weaver 1971).
29. Hoag and Hallett (1926), McLean (1996).
30. Some commentators describe Marquette's municipal elections as Condorcet voting, though this is not strictly correct.
31. Jansen (1998).
32. Block voting, described earlier, permits each voter to cast multiple separable and nontransferable votes equal to the number of at-large winners elected.
33. Massachusetts General Laws, Chapter 54a. This chapter does not refer to the method as the single transferable vote, although this term describes the procedure. The chapter also includes parameters for ballot design, method of tabulation, and so forth, that are largely at the discretion of other contemporary cities with RCV.
34. There are different operational definitions of how to calculate a quota. The City of Cambridge uses the Droop quota (Droop Quota = [(Number of Voters)/(Number of Seats + 1)] + 1). This quota is generally considered better than other methods, including the quota proposed by Thomas Hare. See Gallagher (1992) for a useful discussion of quotas, calculations, and proportionality.
35. Adding that extra vote guarantees that no more candidates can be elected than there should be. For instance, if 20,000 voters cast ballots to elect nine candidates, then the quota must be 2,001 (or more accurately, more than 2,000); otherwise, ten candidates would be elected to nine seats. This threshold is the Droop quota (or Hagenbach–Bischoff quota if the extra vote is unnecessary).
36. The process of rounding off surplus transfers to a given number of digits may vary outcomes and produce different winners; see Endersby and Towle (2010). Some talented scholars have claimed that a satisfactory program to transfer surplus votes will always elect the same alternatives; see Meek (1994), Hill, Wichmann, and Woodall (1987), and Tideman and Richardson (2000). But we maintain a healthy skepticism regarding these claims and rounding of transfers and results.
37. Massachusetts General Laws, Chapter 54a, Section 16(b). Of course, there was neither computing technology nor accepted transfer algorithms in 1938.
38. Whether Cambridge always used the Cincinnati Method is an open historical question. Robert Winters, political observer, editor of the Cambridge Civic Journal, and self-appointed archivist of municipal elections, believes Cambridge adopted the Cincinnati method in 1973. See rwinters.com. The Massachusetts Supreme Court upheld the constitutionality of the electoral system in Moore v. Election Commissioners of Cambridge, 35 N.E. (2d) 222 Mass. (1941).
39. This skip number is the nearest whole number to the ratio of (total votes for winner)/(surplus votes).
40. A viable alternative is one which neither has already won nor lost. Ballots cannot be transferred to candidates who have already won a seat on the multimember body. Likewise, ballots cannot

be transferred to a candidate who has been dropped. The STV election includes both of these—winning and losing alternatives—while tabulation for single-member RCV/IRV elections ends when the lone winning alternative is identified.
41. In Cambridge, vacancies before the next election are filled by the next-ranking candidate.
42. Hoag (1914: 9). He believed that Nanson's method, though not necessarily the version as implemented in the Michigan U.P., was the superior option for single-winner elections and would surpass Bucklin and RCV in practice. Hoag referred to AV/IRV as the Ware method, named after noted architect William Robert Ware, who developed the preferential ballot and contributed an appendix to Hare's fourth edition. Hoag attributes further improvements in ballot design and vote tabulation to Daniel S. Remsen (1896) of New York.
43. George H. Hallett, Jr., leader of the Citizens Union and, alongside Hoag, the Proportional Representation Society, was instrumental in establishment of the New York school board and other STV elections.
44. Within this wave of STV reform, a few communities adopted ranked choice for single-member elections. RCV was used in locations such as Ann Arbor, Michigan, for a single election in 1975 (Eldersveld 1995), but this did not spread to other communities.
45. www.fairvote.org. Interestingly, the earlier proportional representation advocate, George Hallett, is Richie's great uncle.
46. Hill continues to advocate for RCV among other government reforms (e.g. Hill 2002). Data analysts associated with New America advocate for a wide range of political and electoral reforms, including RCV. See, for example, Drutman (2020) and Drutman and Strano (2021). But also see a less fervent view of RCV in Lee Drutman, "How I Updated My Views on Ranked Choice Voting," September 18, 1923, leedrutman.substack.com.
47. Philip Rojc, "Who's Behind a Long Shot Effort to Fundamentally Reform Voting," January 31, 2018, www.insidephilanthropy.com.
48. Richie and Hill (1999), Richie, Hill, and Kleppner (2000). The term for the alternative vote in the US has shifted from IRV to RCV as well.
49. Sanders had previously been active in another party, Liberty Union, and ran unsuccessfully for a range of offices. His decision to leave and run as an independent was more successful (Endersby and Thomason 1994).
50. That many Republican voters ranked the Progressive second provides evidence for the monotonicity problem discussed earlier.
51. The 2010 repeal passed with 52 percent (3,972-3,662). Over half of the yes votes (2,209) came from two of the city's seven wards; the others rejected the RCV repeal.
52. The bill, H.744, became law without the signature of Governor Phil Scott; the Burlington Council suspended the rules to approve the ordinance for city council races on June 5, 2022.
53. We are unaware of any election scholar who supports this type of election that we label MRV. Generally, scholars are skeptical of block voting generally as the method simply solidifies support for a majority faction.
54. With such a low quota, three candidates could reasonably be elected to fill two seats (theoretically, four!). Presumably, under the rules for block voting, the two candidates with the largest pluralities would be elected.
55. See Matt Shipman, "New Data Support Use of Instant Runoff Voting," North Carolina State University, December 3, 2009, https://news.ncsu.edu/2009/12/wmscobbhirv09/.
56. Aspen officials examined the Minneapolis election system for parks and taxation boards, but they opted to go in a slightly different direction.
57. See the election certificate of November 3, 2009. The city council then placed a charter amendment to return to plurality/runoffs, and the proposition was approved by voters.
58. November 2, 2010, Referendum 2B. The higher turnout was due to the amendment's location on the general election ballot.
59. NM HB 98. The bill standardized the date for local elections and required all-mail elections for others.
60. Moreover, 71 percent of voters ranked all seven candidates in Payson, and 59 percent ranked all five candidates in Vineyard. See "Ranked Choice in Utah Cities" from Utah RCV. A separate survey in 2021 found that 86 percent of voters in RCV communities were satisfied with their voting experience; however, voters in non-RCV municipalities were 89 percent satisfied with their voting experience (Y2 Analytics, "Utah Ranked Choice Voting Municipal Election Survey: Voter Experience in the 2021 Utah RCV Pilot Program").

61. The first ballot leader, Brennan, was elected after the 15th round with 55.8 percent of remaining valid ballots. However, the transferred vote total was only 45.9 percent of the total valid votes from the first round.
62. See, for example, Phil Hirschkorn, "Ranked-choice plays significant Role in Portland Charter Commission," WMTW news, June 19, 2021. The charter commission has twelve members, three chosen by the city council. People First Portland, a group supported by the Democratic Socialists of America, endorsed six of the nine elected members.
63. Mayra Flores de Marcotte, "Sunnyvale Council Changes the Way it Chooses the Mayor," Mercury News, May 20, 2010. Through 2007, the most senior member became mayor. The IRV method allowed members to rank first and second preferences only. Two potential problems discussed were a 3-2-2 vote among three candidates and abstentions, particularly in the case of a tie. In 2010, a mayor was elected between two candidates with four votes for one and three abstentions. As noted earlier, effective RCV methods in small groups demand full participation and full preference orderings.
64. Cityofpalmdesert.org/our-city/represent-pd/.
65. Harris quotes Cleveland Mayor Newton D. Baker: "The councilmen are elected by a so-called proportional representation ballot. Just what proportion and what the proportion is, I have never been able to discover." Harris preferred the term "choice voting," a term not commonly used until much later.
66. McBain (1922, 284–285).
67. For example, the court in Pennsylvania upheld limited voting, but those in New Jersey and Rhode Island judged it unconstitutional (HLR 1941: 114–115).
68. Some applications of cumulative voting for three votes and two candidates would give 1½ votes to each candidate.
69. State courts often considered cumulative voting as a variation of limited voting since the number of candidates receiving a vote, from some voters at least, was less than the number elected. Michigan and Ohio judged cumulative voting unconstitutional, but Illinois and North Dakota sustained it (HLR 1941: 115).
70. Guinier (1994) champions cumulative voting as a means to represent voters within racial and ethnic groups. See Graber (1996) for an alternative view on representation.
71. See, for instance, Weaver (1984), Engstrom, Taebel, and Cole (1989), Cole, Taebel, and Engstrom (1990), Engstrom and Barrilleaux (1991), and Engstrom, Still, and Kirksey (2017).
72. Bucklin voting shares some similarities with voter preferences. In the Grand Junction method, voters ranked acceptable candidates and lined through unacceptable candidates (Bucklin 1911: 90). Later implementations dropped the second component as unnecessary.
73. Brams and Fishburn (2005). Brams (1979) and Kiewiet (1979) suggest a possible application of approval voting for presidential elections.
74. Local organizations include Reform Fargo and Reform St. Louis. These offshoots have significant support from the Center for Election Science. The Center also supports star voting.
75. A total of 18,805 ballots were cast with 42,855 total votes. The two winners received 10,393 (55.3 percent) and 9,893 (52.6 percent) votes. A trailing third candidate received 9,196 (48.9 percent) of approval votes, the remaining candidates each received approval rates of less than 21 percent. As for block voting, election administrators must report the total number of ballots cast within the constituency as well as the number of votes. Allowance for write-in candidates complicates the ballot as well; Fargo voters could cast ballots for up to nine alternatives in 2020.
76. Turnout was 44,571 in March and 58,707 in April. In Ward 4, for instance, only two candidates competed in the nonpartisan primary. In March, Tammika Hubbard led with 62.3 percent over James Page with 40.8 percent approval. In April, however, Page won with 52.4 percent over Hubbard with 47.2 percent. (Keep in mind that percentages in approval elections do not sum to 100 percent. Instead, voters can check "approve" for any number of candidates from zero to all.)
77. For elections in the United States with a long ballot of many different elections, roll-off is common. Voters may skip contests they are unfamiliar with or find alienating and mark others where they have a preference. However, even on a short ballot (with only one or a few contests), voters may cast a blank ballot (Galatas 2008).
78. Not ranking a candidate could be a measure of disapproval, as in approval voting. But in a ranked system, by assumption, it is better to rank the lesser of (two or more) evils higher to reduce the likelihood of a worse outcome.

79. Voters could list up to three rankings. Races for mayor and three councillor races went beyond the first ballot.
80. Supporting Ontario's Recovery and Municipal Elections Act, 2020. Voters in Kingston, ON, had endorsed an RCV proposal, but no election was conducted before repeal.
81. Maya Wiley, "I lost the NYC mayoral race, but women and minorities win with ranked-choice voting." Washington Post, July 11, 2021.
82. Brian M. Rosenthal and Michael Rothfeld, "Inside Decades of Nepotism and Bungling at the N.Y.C. Elections Board," New York Times, October 26, 2020 (November 2, 2020).
83. The Board of Elections did not respond to an offer of help from members of the Ranked Choice Voting Resource Center. See Courtney Gross, "Ballot Blunders: NYC Board of Elections Dismisses Help with Ranked-choice Count," Spectrum News, October 4, 2021.

Chapter 4

1. Smith v. Allwright, 321 U.S. 649. The Minnesota Supreme Court discusses the distinction between primaries and elections as an explanation for the diverging state opinions regarding preferential voting in Brown v. Smallwood (1915).
2. Weeks (1937).
3. Williams (1923: 113).
4. Merriam and Overacker (1928: 52, 84). The quote emphasizes the empirical conclusion reached later—that many RCV winners do not, in fact, receive majorities.
5. Georgia also had a non-RCV primary with county elections and delegates making nomination decisions at a state convention.
6. This is Nanson's method, discussed in the previous chapter and used in the city of Marquette in the upper peninsula of Michigan.
7. Dove v. Oglesby (1926), 244 Pacific 798, per Article III, Section 5 of the Oklahoma Constitution. See Barth (1925), Cushman (1926: 588), and Merriam and Overacker (1928: 84–85). The system was ruled unconstitutional before implemented.
8. Williams (1923), Kettleborough (1921).
9. Weeks (1937: 65) attributes this failure to rank second preferences in part to poor efforts at voter education by party leaders and to "ignorance of the voter; his desire not to have his vote counted for any but his first choice; or his refusal to accept what was thought to be a complicated system, which, it was felt, could be easily corrupted or readily subject to mistakes in the count, or which seemed to provide for an unfair method of evaluating choices."
10. Merriam and Overacker (1928: 85).
11. Lee Davidson, "Poll: Utah GOP Primary Voters Are Wary of 'Ranked-choice Voting," Salt Lake Tribune, June 15, 2020.
12. Whether there were absolute majorities is unclear, because votes were weighted depending on the number of delegates representing voting units throughout the state. Electors did not have to complete their ballots fully.
13. Michigan courts, which had judged STV/PR in municipal elections unconstitutional, also declared void a law for cumulative voting for state legislative districts, Maynard v. Board of Commissioners, 84 Mich. 228 (1890). Two legislators were elected from a single district in Grand Rapids under cumulative voting. The court ruled that the inequalities of weighted votes are "frauds upon the rights of the majority of the electors." Although the case did not involve RCV, the decision also opined that the Hare system "is too intricate and tedious ever to be adopted for popular elections by the people" (at 243, 233).
14. For studies on the Illinois experience with cumulative voting, see Blair (1958), Sawyer and MacRae (1962), Kuklinski (1973), Wiggins and Petty (1979).
15. An early, vocal proponent of cumulative voting was Pennsylvania Congressman Charles Buckalew. In 1867, Buckalew introduced a bill in Congress to elect members through what he referred to as the "free vote" that would allow representation of minorities, particularly African Americans in the South, reduce corruption, and provide some level of proportional representation (Barber 2000: 21–22, Dow 2017: 142). Buckalew was successful in getting Pennsylvania and several other states to adopt cumulative voting for stockholders in corporate elections.
16. Retention elections typically occur as part of the Missouri Plan, in which the Governor makes an initial judicial appointment (typically from a list provided by an independent panel). Following the judge's first term, a ballot question asks voters whether the judge should be retained in office. Since voters can only vote Yes or No, there is no need for an instant runoff.

17. Judicial elections may improve perceptions of legitimacy. See, for instance, Bonneau and Hall (2009) and Gibson (2012).
18. North Carolina judicial elections were partisan prior to the passage of the 2002 Judicial Campaign Reform Act, which enacted many election reforms beyond nonpartisan elections. After the 2008 Court of Appeals election with eight candidates and a winner with only 22 percent of votes, North Carolina opted for a limited version of RCV for vacancies that occurred after the primary election but 60 days before the election (N. C. General Statute §163-329). The state's pilot project leading to the 2009 election in Cary, NC, occurred around this time. The state returned to partisan elections in 2012.
19. McCullough was first elected to the Court of Appeals in 2000 but lost his 2008 reelection bid, 42.6 percent –57.4 percent.
20. Thigpen was appointed to another vacancy on the Court of Appeals in 2012, but he also lost the 2012 election narrowly to Chris Dillon, 47.3 percent –53.7 percent.
21. Although party preference was not identified on the ballot, it appears that there were many Democratic/liberal candidates on the ballot and fewer Republican/conservative candidates. A combination of coordination problems (with partisans) and limitation to three candidates may have produced a bias for McCullough's win.
22. The 2009 Military and Overseas Voter Empowerment Act (MOVE) amended and broadened UOCAVA to improve access to the polls for citizens out of the country.
23. On the impact of regionalism in Canadian politics, see Schwartz (1974) and Young and Archer (2002). See Dyck (1986) on provincial party and election systems. The SMDP electoral system may exaggerate regional divisions in Canada (Cairns 1968).
24. Qualter 1970, 130–131.
25. Qualter 1970, 131–133.
26. If no party has a majority of seats in the House of Commons, Canada tends to create a minority government from the party with more seats than any other. European parliaments with multiple parties tend to create a coalition government among multiple parties to ensure majority status. Canada's minority governments, for instance, followed the 2006 and 2009 elections when the Conservatives under PM Stephen Harper and 2019 and 2021 when Liberal PM Justin Trudeau formed minority governments.
27. The lengthiest nomination was the 1924 Democratic Convention which lasted 103 ballots.
28. The Progressive Conservative Party used a weighted voting, ranked method in 1998. The movement toward OMOV also occurred in the United Kingdom. The first OMOV leadership election in Canada was held by the Parti Québécois within the province of Quebec in 1985. The Bloc Québécois, the federal cousin of the PQ used OMOV in 1997. It was adopted by Progressive Conservative provincial parties first in Manitoba and then in Alberta. The federal party application of OMOV includes RCV. Technically, in the federal party context, OMOV is a misnomer, as weighted votes vary across electoral constituencies.
29. This is unlike party membership in the United States; a voter can register and/or cast a ballot in a party primary simply by claiming to be a party identifier.
30. Bernier bolted from the Conservative Party and led the People's Party in the 2019 general election. Although People's Party candidates competed nationwide, none were elected to the House of Commons, not even Bernier himself.
31. Although the weighted system intends to represent party voters geographically, this party leadership election does signal the peril of combining RCV with other electoral methods. Lewis received 71 percent of the second place transferable ballots from supporters of the fourth place candidate (Derek Sloan). On the second round, Lewis led both remaining candidates, and she would have made it to the final against O'Toole except for the weighting by riding.

Chapter 5

1. LD 1714. Other bills were proposed in later sessions as well.
2. Although there is a national League of Women Voters, policy positions are typically made at the state level.
3. Democracy Maine would later attract a third collaborator, Maine Students Vote.
4. The others include cofounder Cara McCormick, political activist and owner of Smart Campaigns, and campaign manager Kyle Bailey.
5. A popular referendum could produce speedy results. Traditional lobbying might lead to the same result, but it would take time and consume resources over a long period. See Santucci

(2018) for a discussion of partisan and other coalitions important for passage of an RCV ballot proposition.
6. 2017 ME 100, Art. IV, pt. 1, sect 3 & 5, and pt. 2, sect. 4. The Court's nonbinding decision declared "determining the winner of an election through plurality voting is inconsistent with determining the winner through a ranked-choice voting process."
7. LD 1646, P.L. 2017, chapter 316. The legislature met in a special session, and the act became law without the Governor's signature.
8. Art. 4, Pt. 3, Sect. 17.
9. The vote was 149,900 to 128,291. People's vetoes are not uncommon in Maine; this proposition was the 31st to appear on a Maine statewide ballot since 1909.
10. 21-A M.R.S. sect. 723.
11. Maine Senate v. Secretary of State et al. 2018 ME 52, at 21. When the Maine Supreme Judicial Court hears an appellate case, it is said to be Sitting as the Law Court.
12. Poliquin requested the recount on November 26, and it began on December 6.
13. Brett Baber et al. v. Matthew Dunlap et al. (2018), 376 F. Supp. 3d 125.
14. 2019 LD 1083.
15. There was significant legal activity after the bill's passage, but the actions were more informative about Maine electoral law than about RCV. The Maine Republican Party mounted an attempt for a people's veto to override the presidential primary law. The Committee on Ranked Choice sought to disallow the petition, but the Court rejected that claim (Payne v. Dunlap, Docket No. AUGSC-CV-20-50, 2020). However, the Republican initiative did not consist of enough valid signatures, so the Secretary of State rejected it. The Republicans filed a lawsuit to challenge that administrative decision, but the Court and, when remanded, the Secretary of State confirmed that the initiative petition did not include enough signatures to be valid (Jones v. Dunlap, Docket No. AP 20-0016 (Me. Super.), 2020). No people's veto question regarding RCV for presidential elections appeared on the ballot.
16. Hagopian v. Dunlap, 480 F.Supp.3d 288 (2020). The federal case involves voting for the US senate election rather than the presidential election.
17. The vote was 174,032 to 170,251.
18. Kendall also worked for Murkowski in her write-in campaign in 2010. This scenario of a political moderate losing to a more extreme candidate in a closed primary, but who was the overall preferred option (the Condorcet winner) among all voters, seems key to the plan he developed.
19. Shea Siegert, one of the first to join, enlisted as campaign manager.
20. Other organizations, including the League of Women Voters of Alaska, endorsed the proposal.
21. Typically, state elections administration falls within the purview of the Secretary of State; however, in Alaska, the office is supervised by the Lieutenant Governor.
22. Alaska Constitution, Art. II, Sect. 13; Alaska Statutes Sec. 15.45.040. The single-subject rule is a common standard for American legislatures.
23. Meyer v. Alaskans for Better Elections, 465 P.3d 477 (2020), S-17629. See also Young v Alaska (2022).
24. Edgmon was an independent selected as Speaker through a bipartisan coalition. Republican Louise Stutes also endorsed the initiative; she would be elected the next Speaker under a split partisan legislature.
25. In November, Myers beat two independent candidates (one who withdrew unofficially), receiving 57 percent of the vote. The general election had five times as many voters as the Republican primary.
26. Article XI, Sect. 6. This same constitutional section also requires the Lieutenant Governor to certify election returns.
27. The plaintiffs include members of the Libertarian, Republican, and Alaska Independence Parties. In Superior Court, this was Kohlhaas v. Alaska (2020).
28. Kohlhaas v. Alaska (2022). The Court upheld the decision but did not immediately release a full written opinion.
29. Palin received 29.8 percent of special primary votes, Begich received 19.3 percent, Gross 12.5 percent, and Pelota 7.4 percent. Begich's grandfather was the incumbent Representative in 1972 who defeated challenger Don Young. However, Begich disappeared and was presumed dead following a plane crash en route to a campaign event. Young won the US House seat in special election that followed in 1973.
30. Alaska law permits the fifth-place candidate (Tara Sweeney) to substitute, but Gross' withdrawal occurred too late for this.

31. Twenty-one percent of the ballots from Begich supporters could not be transferred to either candidate. A slim majority ranked Palin second, but almost 29 percent marked the Democrat second.
32. Peltola's final count was 91,266, about 48.4 percent of the 188,582 total ballots cast. In addition, another 3,707 ballots were blank or voided.
33. Republican Buzz Kelley suspended his campaign and urged his supporters to vote for Tshibaka, although he did not remove his name from the general election ballot (Lisa Phu, "Fourth-place Finisher Buzz Kelley Suspends Campaign for U.S. Senate, Backs Tshibaka," Alaska Beacon, September 12, 2022). Less than half of ballots ranking Kelley first (37 percent) were transferred to Tshibaka. The number of ballots for the fourth-place candidate, however, was too small to change the outcome, as two-thirds of the Democrat's supporters' ballots were transferred to Murkowski. It is noteworthy that turnout among registered voters in the general election (44.4 percent) was much larger than in the primary and special election for Representative (32.2 percent) held concurrently on August 16. Whether Peltola is the more moderate candidate is less clear, but arguably so.
34. The success of implementation in both states has lead groups such as FairVote and Article IV, a funding organization also backing systems like the Alaska model, and their financiers to strengthen their support for lobbying and ballot propositions for other states.
35. S.B. 2162 was approved by the legislature and signed into law by the governor on June 17, 2022. The law also applies to special elections for county council seats.
36. Question 3 passed in 2022 with a margin of 53 percent –47 percent. In 2024, Nevada voters opposed the question, 53-47 percent. For information on the amendment process, see Article 19, Section 2, of the Nevada Constitution.
37. Presidential election reform has been a priority of RCV proponents throughout this century (Richie, Hill, and Kleppner 2000, Tolbert and Gracey 2018).
38. Of course, this simple description omits a number of factors influencing whether a candidate remains in or stays out of the race. These include campaign finance contributions, media attention, endorsements, organization, momentum, perceptions of viability, and so forth.
39. The Democrats also have assigned delegates or superdelegates, though since 2020 they do not have a meaningful vote in the first round of balloting.
40. Another challenge occurs when there is a large number of candidates seeking the nomination (often when there is no incumbent running), and support is spread thinly among them. For example, according to the 2020 Democratic rules, if no candidate meets the 15 percent requirement, a new threshold is set at 10 percent below the proportion received by the top candidate, and the delegates are divided among those who receive more than that. In such a scenario, delegates would be awarded to candidates who have low levels of support. Using RCV instead, while keeping the 15 percent threshold, might allow the party to ensure that delegates are awarded to candidates who have relatively more appeal, even if only as a second or third choice for many primary voters.
41. If no candidate receives an absolute majority in the Electoral College, then a runoff is held. The three presidential candidates with the highest number of electoral votes go to the House of Representatives for final election, with each state getting one vote. The top two vice presidential candidates go to the senate.
42. It could be argued that James Madison supported both the district plan for selecting electors as well as something like RCV for decision-making within the Electoral College (Dewey 1962, Foley 2020 pp.182–183 n.15 and 213 n. 22).
43. Voters in most states actually cast a ballot for a slate of electors from the political party of that candidate, not for the candidate directly. In the past, the names of those electors would appear on the ballot.
44. Foley (2020) notes that the Electoral College is majoritarian by its very nature, and generally, he supports some sort of runoff for presidential elections.
45. Arizona, Colorado, Florida, Maine (statewide only), Michigan, Minnesota, Nevada, New Hampshire, New Mexico, North Carolina, Pennsylvania, Utah, Virginia, and Wisconsin. In addition, there was no majority winner in the 2nd District in Nebraska.
46. Arizona, Georgia, North Carolina, and Wisconsin. In 2024, there were only two: MI, WI.

Chapter 6

1. Excluded are Pierce County, Washington (Tacoma), which implemented RCV in 2008–2009, and Benton County, Oregon (Corvallis), which held its first RCV election in 2020. Also excluded are state and federal elections. These cases are not municipalities, and election results may be influenced by other factors.

2. Although many reformist competitors champion approval voting, we do not consider that system here, as it is not directly comparable to RCV methods. Cities with cumulative voting and other electoral systems are also omitted as not directly comparable.
3. At least one community did not implement RCV because of technological and educational complexities that could not be resolved in the short-term for its first implementation.
4. So why exclude these towns? Basalt, a small mountain community in Colorado, adopted RCV in 2002. However, there was never a need to devise and implement RCV procedures fully, until 2020, when three candidates ran for mayor. Thus, the data set includes Basalt elections only for 2020.
5. For partisan elections, this is often a rationale for RCV in open primaries, such as the Alaska model, as well as other two-round systems such as the top-two elections in California and Washington state, the jungle primary in Louisiana, and runoff elections generally. The argument that RCV should elicit more candidates of greater ideological variety (a rationale for adoption in Maine) and that RCV will produce more moderate winners (a rationale for adoption in Alaska) seems somewhat inconsistent. However, both expectations assume more candidates may compete.
6. At present, there is no known theoretical prediction of an equilibrium number of candidates for RCV. The conjectures of Duverger (1954) and others discussed earlier predict two parties or major candidates for SMDP elections, and the presumed number of competitive candidates for preferential elections should be higher than two.
7. STV council elections are limited to Cambridge, Massachusetts, and Eastpointe, Michigan.
8. STV elections are held in Cambridge and, depending on the number of open seats, in Minneapolis. RCV/IRV elections are held in Oakland, Portland, ME (although only one election occurs in this time span), and sometimes Minneapolis.
9. Candidate numbers include those whose names appear on the ballot and exclude write-in candidates. City electoral rules vary in terms of whether write-ins need to be approved and how write-in votes are handled. This cleaner measure only counts official candidates.
10. More candidates tend to enter a race for open seats than for those with an incumbent seeking reelection. Excluding three outliers with more than nineteen candidates running for a single seat, the average number of candidates for mayor falls to 4.6 (n = 40) and for council to 3.3 (n = 241).
11. A majority of the races for nonmayoral executives often have candidates that are unopposed (21/36), though these may still be prestigious positions. For instance, Kamala Harris ran unopposed for District Attorney in San Francisco in 2007. She later was elected to the US senate and as vice president. The number of candidates is also influenced by population size. Two-thirds of municipal elections in the small Maryland community of Takoma Park, for instance, are unopposed (34/51).
12. Breaking down the number of mayoral and council candidates by city does not reveal an obvious pattern of increasing competition. Except for occasional spikes of competition for individual high-salience elections without an incumbent, the variation in candidate competition by city across time appears relatively small.
13. Since special elections are included in the RCV dataset, they are also included, if they occurred, in the pre-RCV election calculations. Special elections tend to draw more candidates on the ballot since there is no incumbent. Generally, the number of general election cycles is three, although the number varies based on data availability, the frequency of mayoral or council races, and other contextual factors.
14. Municipal primary returns for Minneapolis in these early years are unavailable.
15. The four cities are also selected because they have larger populations. Obtaining numbers of registered or eligible voters over time for small communities can be a demanding and troublesome task.
16. We set aside the issue of voter roll-off, the tendency of some voters to omit marking the ballot for down-ballot races such as these city races. Our discussion would involve an additional layer of complexity but little useful information. The political science literature on why a voter might skip one office after making the effort to otherwise complete a ballot is scant. A voter's level of information about the office or question appears to be a major explanatory factor. There is roll-off even among RCV voters; for instance, some vote for mayor but skip casting a vote for city council.
17. Of course, it is possible that new voters are brought in, and old voters are dissuaded from participation, and these offset so that net turnout remains similar. In that case, the electorate may be qualitatively different. For instance, younger voters may be more likely to participate and seniors less likely, thus changing the composition of the electorate. Regarding institutional

factors, it appears that these explain much of the variation in voter turnout. Concurrent elections (especially in presidential years) lead to greater rates of participation. The appearance of a mayoral race on the ballot likewise draws more voters, which accounts for much of the fluctuation. Competition also increases turnout (consistent with the findings on the number of candidates for an office), although it is difficult to isolate the magnitude of this effect with multiple races on a long ballot. Statistically, the adoption of RCV has no significant effect on voter turnout. For a discussion of a variety of factors influencing voter turnout in national elections, see Endersby and Krieckhaus (2008).

18. From our point of view, a wasted ballot is the one left uncast. A related argument is that RCV elections may encourage higher turnout, both in terms of new voters going to the polls and, perhaps, from voters skipping an office or leaving a contest unmarked when submitting a ballot (voter roll-off). This important argument is not fully considered here. The claims of a "wasted vote," however, are based on ballots cast by voters.

19. The notion of increased satisfaction with the electoral process presumably can be linked to the transfer process. Ranking the top three preferences among a list of candidates when a fourth is elected does not seem more satisfying than seeing the first preference lose in a plurality election. However, voter perceptions of satisfaction and civility may be distinct from election outcomes, as the data analyzed here suggests.

20. Neely and Cook (2008) and Burnett and Kogan (2015) also note that a voided ballot or a missing candidate preference may also occur, as well as an overvote. We return to the topic of over- and under-votes in the subsequent discussion of election administration. For now, the focus is on nontransferred ballots, those that no longer contribute to the overall (final) vote tally.

21. If a voter marks preferences for all candidates except for the least preferred candidate, the sixth place of six candidates in the example in the text, then the voter's ranking is full. This is because no rational voter would ever choose the least preferred candidate when paired with any other. Note this is different from leaving a blank space earlier in the order of preferences—marking 1st, 2nd, 4th, 5th, and 6th, for example. As will be discussed later, this ordering produces an administrative issue about the interpretation of voter intention.

22. In 2010, Malia Cohen was elected to represent the Tenth District of the San Francisco Board of Supervisors on the 20th round of vote transfers. Minneapolis Mayor Betsy Hodges was elected after 33 rounds of vote transfers in 2013. The tabulation process in Minneapolis took two days to complete.

23. In other words, if voters can mark only the top three rankings, ballots become exhausted in rounds four or five.

24. If a candidate wins a majority in the first round, there are no subsequent rounds of vote transfer in RCV/IRV elections. This average of 3.3 percent significantly underestimates transfers for RCV/IRV in particular.

25. These are RCV voters who plunk or cast a ballot for one and only one candidate. This proportion is higher for IRV elections (2.7 percent) than for STV (0.3 percent).

26. It also seems peculiar to write-in any option after the first few rankings. What would be the logic of including a write-in candidate down ballot, such as in fourth place, for instance, after ranking other candidates officially on the ballot? This seems to imply that a voter has no confidence that any of her preferences among announced candidates will remain after several transfers and counts, but a write-in candidate could come from behind with transferred votes. But write-in options would surely be eliminated quickly in all but the most unusual elections. We can imagine a case of a write-in candidate winning after starting in early rounds as a leading contender. But the notion of a write-in rising through multiple counts strikes us as political science fiction.

27. McCune and McCune (2022) observe similar findings when comparing RCV to SMDP elections, as well as to Borda, Condorcet, and Bucklin voting methods.

28. As these state primaries allowed two rankings and restricted the subsequent round to a top two runoff, this is really an example of the Limited Vote (LV).

29. Alex Acquisto, "Poliquin's legal team takes a new jab at ranked-choice voting," Bangor Daily News, December 5, 2018.

30. A secondary runoff typically has fewer voters casting ballots, but abstention then is a choice. Since a law may limit the number of preferences allowed, the electoral rule may logically limit voters from giving preferences between a given two candidates in a hypothetical (instant)

runoff. It also seems a burden to expect a voter to have an identifiable choice among any two candidates who might make the final round, particularly as the purpose of RCV is to discourage strategic behavior on the part of the voter.
31. In the Telluride mayoral election of 2015, a tie occurred between the top two candidates, so we coded only one as the leader. For RCV, there is a possibility of a tie in the final tabulation, but ties may occur among potential candidates for elimination. Encountering a tie at either point requires a method of random selection to determine which alternative is eliminated. Except for Telluride (not involving a candidate elimination), no ties are found in the set of municipal elections analyzed here.
32. The comparison is more directly a comparison with another election system, the single nontransferable vote (SNTV), which was used in Japan until 1993. SNTV might be considered a plurality system for multimember elections. A comparison cannot be made to multimember at-large elections since one voter has multiple votes to cast, not just one.
33. Since the quota is fixed, the early and intermediate rounds lead to elections that are 100 percent of the quota. However, the final round frequently selects the candidate(s) with the most votes without attaining the quota.
34. First-round victors under STV are loosely associated with the number of representatives chosen. Many of these winners come from elections of only two or three, not nine (Cambridge City Council).
35. For instance, after the first RCV election in Minneapolis, Schultz and Rendahl (2010) found that voters overall were satisfied with the new electoral system, although they also disliked the delay in learning the outcome of the election. However, there was little evidence that many of the claims for the reform—higher turnout, an increased number of candidates, more third-party support, or even reduced election cost—were achieved.
36. STV elections with multiple officials selected simultaneously fare somewhat better at fulfilling this last point, but this is achieved with additional information costs. However, Quinlan and Schwarz (2022) find that lower preference rankings influence outcomes only about 10 percent of the time in STV elections in European countries.

Chapter 7

1. Another likely possibility is that many voters simply do not understand how preferential voting works, perhaps in theory but certainly in application. Providing more information on RCV is our intention for this book.
2. Municipalities are often responsible for their elections. Some localities, like St. Paul, MN, contract with the county to manage the election under the constraints set by the city.
3. Dave Triplett of Ramsey County notes that, when RCV in St. Paul was first established, "we set it up to be a recount. We thought the recount laws really applied well to this type of activity. One of our goals was transparency. We wanted to be fast, transparent, and accurate. So, we treated it like a recount."
4. The legal interpretation is that a Microsoft Excel spreadsheet is not voting machine software, as it merely serves the function of a calculator.
5. RCV political junkies who experienced both hand counting and computerization often express nostalgia for manual tabulation. For example, the hand count "was a big production," says Executive Director of the Cambridge Election Commission, Tanya Ford. Lesley Waxman, Assistant Director, adds that there is "an element of drama to the hand count where people would get excited to see who was reaching quota or who was getting the transfers when somebody was defeated ... computerizing took that drama away." Both add that "we don't want to go back to the hand count," and neither do the candidates who seek quick determination of the winners.
6. See, for instance, Maya King and Zach Montellaro, "New York's 'head-swirling' mistake puts harsh spotlight on ranked-choice voting," Politico, July 6, 2021.
7. Over 16,000 electronic ballots from Bangor and Hampden were reported incorrectly. This 2022 election included the second congressional district contest between incumbent Jared Golden and former incumbent Bruce Poliquin, a rematch of the 2018 contest discussed earlier. Second-place ballots of voters for third-party candidate Tiffany Bond again re-elected Golden, who received less than a majority of first-place votes. Unlike New York, Maine requires that transfers are calculated only after all ballots are collected, a process with which we strongly

agree. See Phil Hirschkorn, "Delay in ranked-choice voting deciding Maine 2nd Congressional District race" and Jack Molmud, "Ballot error delays outcome for CD-2 race," News Center Maine, November 15, 2022.

8. The secrecy of the ballot is maintained since we do not know which voter cast a ballot. Some cities release the full cast vote record for all races, while others release CVR for each contest individually. McCune and McCune (2022: 9–10) identify localities and reasons for which CVRs are unavailable. A complicating factor is that American elections are typically supervised by counties, but RCV currently occurs within cities.

9. One common assumption is that off-cycle local election voters are more engaged and informed than average. Overall voter turnout tends to be lower for off-cycle local elections.

10. Alternatively, RCV and plurality races could be on opposite sides of the ballot.

11. The limitation to three rankings echoes the Bucklin method from a century earlier, as well as supplementary voting in London and elsewhere. Limiting the number of rankings to two corresponds to the contingent vote.

12. Massachusetts General Laws, Chapter 54a, Section 16(a).

13. See Bain and Hecock (1957) and Miller and Krosnick (1998). Darcy and McAllister (1990) provide other explanations for this behavior. For Australian ranked choice elections, see Mackerras (1970) and Orr (2002).

14. Sowers (1934: 29). Most of the candidates had names from A to H, forty out of seventy-one, but the election rate remains higher (over 82 percent). Three were elected I to M among ten candidates (30 percent). For the twenty-one candidates from N to Z, Sowers notes, "No candidate has ever been elected whose name began with a letter in the last half of the alphabet … ". An editorial note to Sowers notes that Cincinnati and Hamilton did rotate names on ballots.

15. Moreover, the relative order of candidates has minimal effect with rotation. A solution to eliminate the effect of order would be to randomize candidate names. With only twelve candidates, that would require 12! or 479,001,600 ballots, a number that exceeds the population of the United States by about 100 million. Cambridge routinely has more than 20 STV candidates running for the city council.

16. The closeness of the race was particularly evident in Palm Beach County, which used punch-card ballot technology. There were more candidates than would fit on a single page, and some voters punched candidates listed on the first and second pages, thus voiding their vote for the presidency. See Brady et al. (2001) and Wand et al. (2001).

17. The optical scan ballot—like a "bubble sheet" answer on a classroom exam—had various marks that were judged by electronic tabulators as invalid ballots. The initial count found Coleman winning by 215 out of about 2.9 million votes cast; the final count resulted in Franken's victory by 225 votes. The legal issue also involved whether some rejected absentee ballots should be included. Both the Bush-Gore contest and the Franken-Coleman election led to judicial decisions confirming the election winners. A three-judge state District Court panel awarded Franken a 312-vote victory margin.

18. Typically, election administrations treat these as if no ballot is cast at all. An exception from the past was ballot referendums which required an absolute majority of all voters to pass, what was sometimes called the "silent vote." For those ballot questions, nonvotes or abstentions were counted as voting no on the proposition. In North America, the requirement of an absolute majority in mass elections no longer appears to exist. Such requirements may occur, however, for voting in the Electoral College and on some questions in legislatures. For example, in the US senate, cloture, the rule to end a filibuster, requires three-fifths (60) of all sworn senators (100).

19. See Neely and Cook (2008), Endersby and Towle (2014), and Burnett and Kogan (2015). Cormack (2023) finds that New York City 2021 Democratic primary voters were more likely to cast overvotes. Moreover, overvotes are more likely to occur in marginalized communities, in areas with lower levels of education and income, and on absentee (rather than in-person) ballots.

20. For example, Knack and Kropf (2003) and Stewart et al. (2020) show that 1–2 percent of American voters may skip casting a ballot for the top of the ticket in presidential elections, often intentionally due to dissatisfaction, indifference, or alienation. Galatas (2008) looks at blank and null ballots in the Canadian province of Ontario and finds that certain factors, such as party competition and demographic characteristics, may be associated with blank or spoiled ballots.

21. Portland City Clerk Katherine Jones noted that approximately 2,600 votes in the mayoral race involved ballots with incomplete ovals. An election judge had to determine voter intent in each instance.
22. Maloy and Ward (2021) find there is a greater likelihood of mismarked ballots for ranked choices, and the frequency of error increases with the number of candidates. However, they do not observe an increase in voided ballots.
23. The Maine Republican Party recommended filling in all ovals on an optical scan ballot for a single candidate to make a ballot 'complete' (see "Secretary of State Matthew Dunlap's statement regarding ranked-choice voting ballot-marking guidance," October 21, 2021). Such a ballot would be a valid vote, but repeating the same candidate has no effect on the outcome past the first choice.
24. We largely omit the discussion of technology although this pertains to how to deal with ballot completion errors. A manual count of paper ballots may present one set of challenges that differ from software that makes electronic tabulations. The software's algorithm resolves many of these issues in advance without reconsideration by election officials, but, as noted above, in some constituencies, election workers may not be fluent in their understanding of the software engineering.
25. Some constituencies limit voters to a fewer number of rankings, such as two or three. We opt for five in order to show undervote/overvote issues for tabulation. For elections where voters may rank all candidates on the ballot, they technically have no need to rank their lowest or last preference.
26. Kurlowski (2019) examines cast vote records for the 2018 gubernatorial election in Maine and observes that plumping, a single shot vote, is the most frequent ballot cast, followed by a blank ballot, an undervote.
27. For statewide elections in Maine, if both the first and second choices are blank, the ballot is considered an undervote—exhausted—even if there is a third or subsequent choice marked. Two consecutive blanks void the remainder of the ranked preferences.
28. For example, in the 2018 race for City Council District 1 in Berkeley, "[t]he RCV report for round 1 combines the accumulated totals of first-choice rankings as well as the second- or third-choice selections transferred to the first-choice ranking selections when the first-choice rankings were skipped." Overall, 3,411 voters ranked Rashi Kesarwani first, but 89 voters marked no candidate first and Kesarwani second. These 89 ballots were transferred to her.
29. We found the variety of interpretations surprising and unpredictable. For instance, for state elections in Maine, two skips would exhaust the ballot, however, in Portland—Maine's most populous city—a ballot with a first- and last-place marking would be transferred to the lowest ranked candidate if the voter's first choice is removed.
30. Following calls for a recount from the NAACP, and other organizations, Alameda County conducted a recount for all RCV races and updated the results. The final victors only changed for School Director District 4, although the transfer numbers changed for other races. This example also reinforces the need for transparency by elections administrators.
31. The actual circumstances are even more unusual. Mike Hutchinson already served as the district 5 director, but, due to modified boundary map, his residence was now in district 4. So, for a time, Hutchinson and Nick Resnick simultaneously served on the school board. Resnick expressed the belief that he was legitimately elected (after all, he was certified as the winner), but he eventually resigned his position under pressure, prior to the court ruling. Hutchinson is Black; Resnick was, or would have been, the first transgender person elected to the Oakland USD. (See Brian Krans, Darwin BondGraham, Jacob Simas, and Tasneem Raja, "Timeline: How the Alameda County Registrar of Voters Ran—and Fumbled—the November Election," Oaklandside, January 6, 2023; Ashley McBride, "Judge Declares Mike Hutchinson Winner of OUSD School Board Race," Oaklandside, March 7, 2023.)
32. The possibility of an overvote presumably is greater for a bubble sheet or optical scan ballot. Computerization may eliminate this possibility of an overvote at the cost of frustration on the part of some voters.
33. For House of Representatives elections, the last place ranking need not be marked, as long as all others are. For senate elections, at least six parties must be ordered if voting above the line, and twelve must be marked in order if voting below the line. See Australia Election Commission (2019), "How to make your vote count." See Appendix Figure B.2 for an Australian House of Representatives ballot and Appendix Figure B.2 for an Australian Senate ballot.

34. Australia also has compulsory or mandatory voting. For an excellent discussion of Australian elections, see Farrell and McAllister (2006).
35. See, for instance, Dove v. Oglesby (1926) and Hagopian v. Dunlap (2020).
36. See Neely and Cook (2008), Burnett and Kogan (2015), Neely and McDaniel (2015), and McDaniel (2016). The disparities may lead to lower turnout among racial and ethnic groups or ballot completion errors.
37. In Maine, members of the Democratic Party by and large favor RCV, and the Republican Party supporters oppose RCV. This carries over to the perceptions of RCV in terms of local election supervisors. Support for RCV tends to break along party lines. If a town is primarily Democratic, then the clerk is typically favorable toward RCV. However, regardless of partisan preferences, all election officers agree to follow whatever the law requires.
38. Vendors of tabulation software for RCV elections work diligently for clean and fair results, although we are unaware of any external standards or checks imposed for RCV election software development generally. Moreover, the examples here and for New York City provide some evidence of the demands for technical skills and knowledge that may be difficult for some constituencies to develop and maintain.
39. Changing the order of elimination may benefit different surviving candidates in the transfer process, leading to the selection of a different winner. There may be other implications, such as encouraging candidates to run again in a subsequent election. Moreover, the City of Cambridge fills vacancies with eliminated candidates, so it may influence who would fill a seat following death or resignation of an incumbent.
40. As noted earlier, Kathryn A. Garcia and Andrew Yang campaigned together in the 2021 New York City primary. Other examples include co-endorsements of Mark Eves and Betsy Sweet in the 2018 gubernatorial primary in Maine and an alliance between Treva Reed and Loren Taylor in the 2022 Oakland mayoral contest.
41. In the NYC 2021 elections, Cormack (2023) finds few mentions of RCV in campaign emails. Eric Adams, the ultimate victor, mentioned RCV most often, in 15 percent of these communications; prominent RCV advocate Andrew Yang addressed RCV in only 6 percent.
42. She did not win. The Oscar went to Michelle Yeoh. A campaign for an Oscar nomination violates the Academy's rules. A subsequent investigation decided there was insufficient evidence to rescind the nomination. The movement was criticized for reducing the likelihood that a Black actress could make the nominee list. See Glenn Whipp, "How Andrea Riseborough Pulled Off that Shocking Oscar Nomination," Los Angeles Times, January 24, 2023, and Kyle Buchanan, "The Oscars' Andrea Riseborough Controversy, Thoroughly Explained," New York Times, February 8, 2023.
43. John, Smith, and Zack (2018) find mixed results for the representation of women and ethnic minorities, and their findings seem largely due to a decline in representation for SMDP elections over time rather than a significant increase in representation from RCV/AV elections. Donovan, Tolbert, and Gracey (2019) report no evidence of racial or ethnic bias in understanding instructions of RCV, although women and Asians had lower levels of understanding. Benjamin and Burden (2021) express confidence that a related reform with a five-candidate instant runoff election, similar to Alaska's top four runoff, will enhance minority representation. Many of these assumptions regarding improved representation, however, assume a notable increase in the number of candidates competing in RCV elections as well as less contentious political campaigns. Comparative national evidence on the representative of ethnic minorities is mixed. For instance, although scholars disagree, ethnic representation was not successful with Fiji's experience with RCV/AV (Grofman and Fraenkel 2006a, 2006b, Horowitz 2006, Lal and Larmour 2012, Reilly 2012, and see Horowitz 1991 regarding RCV for South Africa and Reilly 1997 for Papua New Guinea).
44. This was H.R. 4464, the Ranked Choice Voting Act. See Office of Jamie Raskin press release, "Rep. Raskin, House Democrats Introduce Ranked Choice Voting Bill." September 25, 2019. FairVote was identified as a partner organization for the bill. A more recent version of the bill (S 3313, Voter Choice Act) has five Democratic sponsors, along with one independent, Senator Angus King of Maine.
45. Republican National Committee, "Resolution to Officially Oppose Ranked Choice Voting Across the Country," February 6, 2023.

46. See, for instance, Adam Edelman, "Oregon becomes the latest state to put ranked choice voting on the ballot," NBC News, June 27, 2023; Sandra Fish, "2024 ballot measure would make Colorado's primaries open, enact ranked-choice voting for general elections," Colorado Sun, November 20, 2023; Natalie Venegas, "Lauren Boebert Rages against Plan that Could Keep Republicans Off Ballots," Newsweek, November 20, 2023; Mercedes Yanora, "The Daily Brew," Ballotpedia.org, April 18, 2024; and Michael Wines, "Some on the Right Flirt With a Voting Method the Left Loves," New York Times, February 8, 2024.
47. Hans A. von Spakovsky and J. Christian Adams, "Ranked Choice Voting Is a Bad Choice." Heritage Foundation. Issue Brief, No. 4996, August 23, 2019, and Shawn Fleetwood, "Ranked-Choice Voting Is the Monster Under the Bed of American Elections," The Federalist. October 31, 2023.
48. Saul Anuzis and Stan Lockhart, "Why ranked-choice voting is a win for Republicans," The Hill, June 2, 2023.
49. Martin Austermuhle, "D.C. Democratic Party Sues to Keep Ranked Choice Voting and Open Primaries Off the Ballot," The DCist, August 7, 2023. DC Voters approved RCV in 2024.
50. Brown vetoed SB 1288 on September 29, 2016, For Newsom's veto of SB 212, see Veto Message, October 13, 2019. Newsom was elected mayor on the first ballot from a field comprising eleven other candidates.
51. Without pointing to any individual races, RCV campaigns from Bay Area mayoral elections to federal and state elections in Maine strike us as just as full of negativity and vitriol as are similar plurality elections.
52. Jon Burlingame, "How Oscar's Music Branch is Plagued by Voting Issues," Variety, February 21, 2024.

Chapter 8

1. Hare (1865: 74).
2. Our focus as political scientists is on social and political questions, however, a wide variety of organizational and business questions might lead to more satisfying outcomes for the stakeholders if some form of ranked choice decision-making was used. On the schools in the pandemic question, for example, the most important piece of information is often not which alternative "wins"—the obvious result when only plurality methods are used, but it is how the public actually perceives and assesses the options in a summary form.
3. A runoff is not a "top two" election such as in California, Nebraska, or Washington state, as the runoff between the top two candidates occurs regardless of whether either receives a majority in the primary election. There is no traditional runoff if a candidate receives a majority of votes.
4. The observation that comparing three alternative electoral systems may produce a voting cycle is not lost on us. RCV>Runoff>Plurality>RCV> ... or the like.
5. Party matters for voters in partisan contests. However, in nonpartisan preferential elections, voters rely on other cues and heuristics to evaluate candidates (Alvarez, Hall, and Levin 2018).
6. A sizable number of voters in the US do not vote for candidates listed lower down on the ballot, a phenomenon known as roll-off, even after they have received a ballot. Presumably, voters know less about more localized races. With less information on those elections, citizens are less likely to cast a vote in those contests.
7. The American National Election Studies (2022) has posed a series of questions on political trust to respondents for election surveys since 1952. The percentage who respond that the federal government can be trusted "just about always" or "most of the time" fell from 76 percent, about three out of four respondents, in 1964 to 22 percent, less than one out of four, in 2020. The average trust in government score declined from a high of 61 in 1966 to 17 in 2016 and 2020. Similarly, an index for political efficacy, questions about whether the government cares about citizens' opinions, slipped from a high of 74 in 1960 to a record low of 28 in 2020.
8. The introduction of RCV is listed second on the Academy's list of 31 recommendations for reform. See Commission on the Practice of Democratic Citizenship (2020: 24–26).
9. Gehl and Porter (2020), Reilly, Lublin, and Leven (2021). This option is advancing in Nevada.
10. See, for instance, Daniel DiSalvo, "The Promise and Peril of Ranked-Choice Voting," City Journal, Manhattan Institute for Policy Research, April 24, 2021.

11. For experimental studies in four countries, see Blais et al. (2021). For lower satisfaction in Belgium for voters who make candidate preferences within party lists, see Bol et al. (2018).
12. For a similar discussion, see Amy (2000). He lists "seven common mistakes" regarding excitement for trendy electoral system changes.
13. For instance, many members of the public expressed doubts about the legitimacy of the electoral process in the 2016 and, particularly, the 2020 presidential elections, even though election administrators presented outcomes in an open and transparent process, subject to review. RCV tabulation is more difficult to present in an open forum.
14. Sabrina Tavernisemay, "A Gap in College Graduates Leaves Some Cities Behind," New York Times, May 30, 2012. See also the accompanying graphic "Cities with the Most College-Educated Residents"; the data are from 2010.
15. For instance, see Kropf (2016) and Stewart (2020).
16. This is due to the way a ballot must be constructed in advance of the election—providing rankings for an unknown number of candidates may be difficult.
17. A necessary delay for accuracy is worthwhile generally, as well as for RCV elections. This is particularly true for the new electoral world with absentee and provisional ballots, overseas voting, and vote-by-mail, in addition to ranked choice elections. See Michael J. Towle, "Accurate Election Results Are Worth Waiting For," Baltimore Sun, March 29, 2019.
18. Rae (1971: 108). See also Jansen (2004). Note that this seems at odds with the theoretical expectations from Duverger's law about party systems resulting from electoral systems.

References

Abramson, Paul R., John H. Aldrich, Phil Paolino, and David W. Rohde. 1995. "Third-Party and Independent Candidates in American Politics: Wallace, Anderson, and Perot." *Political Science Quarterly* 110(3): 349–367.

Alesina, Alberto, and Alex Cukierman. 1990. "The Politics of Ambiguity." *Quarterly Journal of Economics* 105(4): 829–850.

Alvarez, R. Michael, Thad Hall, and Ines Levin. 2018. "Low-Information Voting: Evidence from Instant-Runoff Elections." *American Politics Research*, 46: 1012–1038.

Andrae, Poul. 1926. *Andrae and His Invention: The Proportional Representation Method*, trans. Vaughn Meisling. Philadelphia: Meisling.

American National Election Studies. 2022. ANES Time Series Cumulative Data File [dataset and documentation]. September 16, 2022, version. www.electionstudies.org

Ansolabehere, Steven, and Charles Stewart III. 2005. "Residual Votes Attributable to Technology." *Journal of Politics* 67: 365–389.

Amy, Douglas. 1993. *Real Choices, New Voices: The Case for PR Elections in the United States*. New York: Columbia University Press.

Amy, Douglas. 2000. *Behind the Ballot Box: A Citizen's Guide to Voting Systems*. Westport, CT: Praeger.

Anthony, Joseph, Amy Fried, Robert Glover, and David C. Kimball. 2021. "Ranked Choice Voting in Maine from the Perspective of Local Election Officials." *Election Law Journal* 20(3): 254–271.

Arrow, Kenneth. 1963. *Social Choice and Individual Values*, 2nd ed. New York: Wiley.

Bain, Henry M., Jr., and Donald S. Hecock. 1957. *Ballot Position and Voter's Choice: The Arrangement of Names on the Ballot and Its Effect on the Voter*. Detroit: Wayne State University Press. 1957.

Barber, Kathleen. 1995. *Proportional Representation and Election Reform in Ohio*. Columbus: Ohio State University Press.

Barber, Kathleen. 2000. *A Right to Representation*. Columbus, OH: Ohio State University Press.

Barth, Harry. 1925. "Oklahoma Adopts Preferential Voting in the Primary." *National Municipal Review* 14(7): 410–413.

Benjamin, Andrea, and Barry C. Burden. 2021. *Consequences of Final-Five Voting for Communities of Color*. Cambridge, MA: Institute for Political Innovation.

Bennett, Scott, and Rob Lundie. 2007. "Australian Electoral Systems." Canberra: Department of Parliamentary Services, Parliament of Australia.

Black, Duncan. 1958. *Theory of Committees and Elections*. Cambridge, UK: University Press.

Blair, George S. 1958. "Cumulative Voting: Patterns of Party Allegiance and Rational Choice in Illinois State Legislative Contests." *American Political Science Review* 52(1): 123–130.

Blais, Andre, Carolina Plescia, John Hogstrom, and Gabrielle Peloquin-Skulski. 2021. "Do (Many) Voters Like Ranking?" *Party Politics* 27(6): 1223–1228.

Board of Governors, Academy of Motion Picture Arts and Sciences. 2020. "93rd Academy Awards of Merit: Amended Version."

Bogdanor, Vernon. 1984. *What is Proportional Representation? A Guide to the Issues.* Oxford, UK: Martin Robertson.

Bol, Damien, Andre Blais, Xavier Gillard, Lidia Nunez Lopez, and Jean-Benoit Pilet. 2018. "Voting and Satisfaction with Democracy in Flexible-list PR." *Electoral Studies* 56: 23–34.

Bonneau, Chris W., and Melinda Gann Hall. 2009. *In Defense of Judicial Elections.* New York: Routledge.

Bowler, Shaun, Todd Donovan, and David Brockington. 2003. *Electoral Reform and Minority Representation: Local Experiments with Alternative Elections.* Columbus: Ohio State University Press.

Boynton, William E. 1917. "Proportional Representation in Ashtabula." *National Municipal Review* 6(1): 87–90.

Brady, Henry E., et al. 2001. "'Law and Data': The Butterfly Ballot Episode." *PS: Political Science and Politics* 34(1): 59–69.

Brams, Steven J. 1979. *The Presidential Election Game*, 2nd ed. New Haven: Yale University Press.

Brams, Steven J., and Peter C. Fishburn. 1978. "Approval Voting." *American Political Science Review* 72: 831–847.

Brams, Steven J., and Peter C. Fishburn. 2005. "Going from Theory to Practice: The Mixed Success of Approval Voting." *Social Choice and Welfare* 25: 457–474.

Brams, Steven J., and Peter C. Fishburn. 2007. *Approval Voting*, 2nd ed. Springer.

Bridges, Amy. 1997. *Morning Glories: Municipal Reform in the Southwest.* Princeton, NJ: Princeton University Press.

Bridges, Amy, and Richard Kronick. 1999. "Writing the Rules to Win the Game: The Middle-Class Regimes of Municipal Reformers." *Urban Affairs Review* 34: 691–706.

Brooks, Robert C. 1923. *Political Parties and Electoral Problems.* New York: Harper.

Bucklin, James W. 1911. "The Grand Junction Plan of City Government and Its Results." *Annals of the American Academy of Political and Social Science* 38: 87–102.

Bullock III, Charles S., and Loch K. Johnson. 1992. *Runoff Elections in the United States.* Chapel Hill: University of North Carolina Press.

Burnett, Craig M., and Vladimir Kogan. 2015. "Ballot (and Voter) "Exhaustion" under Instant Runoff Voting: An Examination of Four Ranked-choice Elections." *Electoral Studies* 37: 41–49.

Burnham, Walter Dean. 1965. "The Changing Shape of the American Political Universe." *American Political Science Review* 59: 7–28.

Burnham, Walter Dean. 1981. "The System of 189: An Analysis." In Paul Kleppner, ed., *The Evolution of American Electoral Systems*, pp. 147–202. Westport, CT: Greenwood.

Cairns, Alan. 1968. "The Electoral System and the Party System in Canada, 1921, 1965." *Canadian Journal of Political Science* 1(1): 55–80.

Chamberlin, John R., Jerry L. Cohen, and Clyde H. Coombs. 1984. "Social Choice Observed: Five Presidential Elections of the American Psychological Association." *Journal of Politics* 46, 479–502.

Chamberlin, John R., and Paul N. Courant. 1983. "Representative Deliberations and Representative Decisions: Proportional Representation and the Borda Rule." *American Political Science Review* 77(3): 718–733.

Coakley, John, and Jon Fraenkel. 2017. "The Ethnic Implications of Preferential Voting." *Government and Opposition* 52(4): 671–697.

Coghlan, Denis. 1999. "A Hidden Landmine at the Heart of the FF Plans for PR." *Irish Times*, August 7.

Cohan, A. S., R.D. McKinlay, and Anthony Mughan. 1975. "The Used Vote and Electoral Outcomes: The Irish General Election of 1973." *British Journal of Political Science* 5(3): 363–383.

Cole, Richard L., Delbert A. Taebel, and Richard L. Engstrom. 1990. "Cumulative Voting in a Municipal Election: A Note of Voter Reactions and Electoral Consequences." *Western Political Quarterly* 43(1): 191–199.

Colomer, Josep M. 2005. "It's Parties that Choose Electoral Systems (or, Duverger's Laws Upside Down)." *Political Studies* 53: 1–21.

Commission on the Practice of Democratic Citizenship. 2020. *Our Common Purpose: Reinventing American Democracy for the 21st Century*. Cambridge, MA: American Academy of Arts & Sciences.

Condorcet, Marquis de. 1785. *Essai sur l'Application de l'Analyse a la Probabilité des Décisions Rendues à la Pluralité des Voix*. Paris.

Coombs, Clyde H., 1964. *A Theory of Data*. New York: John Wiley.

Cormack, Lindsey. 2023 "More Choices, More Problems? Ranked Choice Voting Errors in New York City." *American Politics Research* 52(3): 306–319.

Cox, Gary W. 1997. *Making Votes Count: Strategic Coordination in the World's Electoral Systems*. New York: Cambridge University Press.

Crowder-Meyer, Melody, Shana Kushner Gadarian, and Jessica Trounstine. 2024. "Ranking Candidates in Local Elections: Neither Panacea nor Catastrophe for Candidates of Color." *Journal of Experimental Political Science* 11: 117–134.

Cushman, Robert E. 1926. "Public Law in the State Courts in 1925-1926." *American Political Science Review* 20(3): 583–603.

Darcy, Robert, and Ian McAllister. 1990. "Ballot Position Effects." *Electoral Studies* 9: 5–17.

Dewey, Donald O. 1962. "Madison's Views on Electoral Reform." *Western Political Quarterly* 15(1): 140–145.

Diamond, Larry. 2019. "The Long Game of Democratic Reform." *American Interest*.

Donohoe, Miriam. 2000. "Backbenchers opposed to Electoral Reform Plans." *Irish Times*, January 5.

Donovan, Todd, Caroline Tolbert, and Kellen Gracey. 2016. "Campaign Civility under Preferential and Plurality Voting." *Electoral Studies* 42: 157–163.

Donovan, Todd, Caroline Tolbert, and Kellen Gracey. 2019. "Self-Reported Understanding of Ranked-Choice Voting." *Social Science Quarterly* 100(5): 1768–1766.

Doron, Gideon. 1979a. "The Hare Voting System is Inconsistent." *Political Studies* 27(June): 283–286.

Doron, Gideon. 1979b. "Is the Hare Voting Scheme Representative?" *Journal of Politics*, 41(3): 918–922.

Doron, Gideon, and Richard Kronick. 1977. "Single Transferable Vote: An Example of a Perverse Social Choice Function." *American Journal of Political Science* 21(2): 303–311.

Dow, Jay K. 2017. *Electing the House: The Adoption and Performance of the U.S. Single-member District Electoral System*. Lawrence: University of Kansas Press.

Downs, Anthony. 1957. *An Economic Theory of Democracy*. New York: Harper & Row.

Droop, H.R. 1881. "On methods of electing representatives." *Journal of the Statistical Society of London* 44(2): 141–196.

Drutman, Lee. 2020. *Breaking the Two-Party Doom Loop: The Case for Multiparty Democracy in America*. New York: Oxford University Press.

Drutman, Lee, and Maresa Strano. 2021. "What We Know About Ranked-Choice Voting." Report, New America.

Dummett, Michael. 1984. *Voting Procedures*. New York: Clarendon, Oxford University Press.

Dummett, Michael. 1997. *Principles of Electoral Reform*. New York: Oxford University Press.

Duverger, Maurice. 1954. *Political Parties: Their Organization and Activity in the Modern State*. Barbara North and Robert North, tr. New York: Wiley.

Dyck, Rand. 1986. *Provincial Politics in Canada*. Scarborough, ON: Prentice-Hall.

Dyer, James S., and Ralph E. Miles, Jr. 1976. "An Actual Application of Collective Choice Theory to the Selection of Trajectories for the Mariner Jupiter/Saturn 1977 Project." *Operations Research* 24: 220–244.

Editors. 1915. "Are Preferential Voting Statutes Unconstitutional?" *Harvard Law Review* 29: 213–215.

Editors. 1941. "Constitutionality of Unorthodox Election Methods?" *Harvard Law Review* 55: 114–120.

Eggers, Andrew C., and Tobias Nowacki. 2024. "Susceptibility to Strategic Voting: A Comparison of Plurality and Instant-Runoff Elections." *Journal of Politics* 86(2): 521–534.

Eldersveld, Samuel J. 1995. *Party Conflict and Community Development: Postwar Politics in Ann Arbor*. Ann Arbor: University of Michigan Press.

Endersby, James W. 2022. "The Timing of Missouri Municipal Elections: Advantages and Disadvantages of Merging Municipal and Federal Elections." Institute for Public Policy, Report #01-2022, University of Missouri.

Endersby, James W., and W. David Thomason. 1994. "Spotlight on Vermont: Third Party Success in the 1990 Congressional Election." *Social Science Journal* 31(3): 251–262.

Endersby, James W., and Michael J. Towle. 2010. "Counting on the STV." Paper presented at the meetings of Midwest Political Science Association, Chicago, IL.

Endersby, James W., and Michael J. Towle. 2014. "Making Wasted Votes Count: Turnout, Transfers, and Preferential Voting in Practice." *Electoral Studies* 33: 144–152.

Endersby, James W., and Jonathan T. Krieckhaus. 2008. "Turnout around the Globe: The Influence of Electoral Institutions on National Voter Participation, 1972-2000." *Electoral Studies* 27(4): 601–610.

Endersby, Jim. 2009. "Lumpers and Splitters: Darwin, Hooker, and the Search for Order." *Science* 326(11): 1496–1499.

Engstrom, Richard L., and Charles J. Barrilleaux. 1991. "Native Americans and Cumulative Voting: The Sisseton-Wahpeton Sioux." *Social Science Quarterly* 72(2), 388–393.

Engstrom, Richard L., Edward Still, and Jason E. Kirksey. 2017. In Georgia A. Persons, ed., *Race and Representation*. Routledge.

Engstrom, Richard L., Delbert A. Taebel, and Richard L. Cole. 1989. "Cumulative Voting as a Remedy for Minority Vote Dilution: The Case of Alamogordo, New Mexico." *Journal of Law and Politics* 5(3): 469–498.

Farrell, David M. 2001. *Electoral Systems: A Comparative Introduction*. Basingstoke: Palgrave.

Farrell, David M., and Richard S. Katz. 2014. "Assessing the Proportionality of the Single Transferable Vote." *Representation* 50(1): 13–26.

Farrell, David M., and Ian McAllister. 2000. "Through a Glass Darkly: Understanding the World of the STV." In Shaun Bowler and Bernard Grofman, eds., *Elections in Australia, Ireland, and Malta under the Single Transferable Vote: Reflections on an Embedded Institution*, pp. 17–36. Ann Arbor: University of Michigan Press.

Farrell, David M., and Ian McAllister. 2006. *The Australian Electoral System: Origins, Variations, and Consequences*. Sydney: UNSW Press.

Felsenthal, Dan S. 2012. "Review of Paradoxes Afflicting Procedures for Electing a Single Candidate." In Dan S. Felsenthal and Moshe Machover, eds., *Electoral Systems: Paradoxes, Assumptions, and Procedures*, pp. 19–91. Berlin: Springer.

Fey, Mark. 2004. "May's Theorem with an Infinite Population." *Social Choice and Welfare* 23: 275–293.

Fishburn, Peter C., and Steven Brams. 1983. "Paradoxes of Preferential Voting." *Mathematics Magazine* 56(4): 207–214.

Fisher, Stephen D. 2004. "Definition and Measurement of Tactical Voting: The Role of Rational Choice." *British Journal of Political Science* 34(1): 152–166.

FitzGerald, Garret. 2000. "People Entitled to have Voting System Choice Put Before Them." *Irish Times*, February 26.

Foley, Edward B. 2020. *Presidential Elections and Majority Rule*. New York: Oxford University Press.

Fraenkel, Jon, and Bernard Grofman. 2006a. "Does the Alternative Vote Foster Moderation in Ethnically Divided Societies? The Case of Fiji." *Comparative Political Studies* 39(5): 623–651.

Fraenkel, Jon, and Bernard Grofman. 2006b. "The Failure of the Alternative Vote as a Tool for Ethnic Moderation in Fiji: A Rejoinder to Horowitz." *Comparative Political Studies* 39(5): 623–651.

Fraenkel, Jon, and Bernard Grofman. 2014. "The Borda Count and Its Real-world Alternatives: Comparative Scoring Rules in Nauru and Slovenia." *Australian Journal of Political Science* 49(2): 186–206.

Frazier, Erica. 2020. "The Single Transferable Vote Then and Now: Lowell, Massachusetts." Paper presented at the Southern Political Science Association.

Galatas, Steven E. 2008. "'None of the Above?' Casting Blank Ballots in Ontario." *Politics and Policy* 36(3): 448–473.

Gallagher, Michael. 1992. "Comparing Proportional Representation Electoral Systems: Quotas Thresholds, Paradoxes and Majorities." *British Journal of Political Science*, 22(4, October): 469–496.

Gallagher, Michael. 1996. "The Constitution." In John Coakley and Michael Gallagher, eds., *Politics in the Republic of Ireland*, 2nd ed., pp. 49–66. Limerick: PSAI Press.

Gallagher, Tom. 2000. "The San Francisco Voter Revolt of 1999." *Social Policy* 31: 24–34.

Garland, Jess, and Chris Terry. 2017. *The 2017 General Election: Volatile Voting, Random Results*. London: Electoral Reform Society.

Gehl, Katherine M., and Michael E. Porter. 2020. *The Politics Industry: How Political Innovation Can Break Partisan Gridlock and Save Our Democracy*. Cambridge, MA: Harvard Business Review Press.

Gilpen, Thomas. 1884. *On the Representation of Minorities of Electors to Act with the Majority in Electoral Assemblies*. Philadelphia: Clark.

Grigg, Kenneth. 1981. "The Value of the Voter." *Australian Quarterly* 53: 40–45.

Gibbard, Allan. 1973. "Manipulation of Voting Schemes: A General Result." *Econometrica* 41: 587–601.

Gibson, James L. 2012. *Electing Judges: The Surprising Effects of Campaigning on Judicial Legitimacy*. Chicago, IL: University of Chicago Press.

Gierzynski, Anthony. 2011. *Saving American Elections*. Amherst, NY: Cambria Press.

Gilpin, Thomas. 1844. *On the Representation of Minorities of Electors to Act with the Majority, in Elected Assemblies*. Philadelphia, PA: J. C. Clark, printer.

Graber, Mark A. 1996. "Conflicting Representations: Lani Guinier and James Madison on Electoral Systems." *Constitutional Commentary* 13: 291–307.

Graham-Squire, Adam, and Nick Zayatz. 2020. "Lack of Monotonicity Anomalies in Empirical Data of Instant-runoff Elections." *Representation* 57(4): 565–573.

Grigg, Kenneth. 1981. "The Value of the Voter." *Australian Quarterly* 53(1): 40–45.

Grofman, Bernard, and Shaun Bowler. 1997. "STV in the Family of Electoral Systems." *Representation* 34(1 Winter): 43–47.

Grofman, Bernard, and Scott L. Feld. 2004. "If You Like the Alternative Vote (a.k.a. the Instant Runoff), Then You Ought to Know about the Coombs Rule." *Electoral Studies* 23: 641–659.

Grofman, Bernard, Evald Mikkel, and Rein Taagepera. 1999. "Electoral Systems Change in Estonia, 1989–1993." *Journal of Baltic Studies* 30(3): 227–249.

Grofman, Bernard, André Blais, and Shaun Bowler, eds. 2009. *Duverger's Law of Plurality Voting*. New York: Springer.
Gronke, Paul, Eva Galenas Rosenbaum, and Peter A. Miller. 2007. "Early Voting and Turnout." *PS: Political Science and Politics* 40(4): 639–645.
Gronke, Paul, and Peter Miller. 2012. "Voting by Mail and Turnout in Oregon." *American Politics Research* 40(6): 976–997.
Guinier, Lani. 1994. *The Tyranny of the Majority: Fundamental Fairness in Representative Democracy*. New York: Free Press.
Hajnal, Zoltan L., and Paul G. Lewis. 2003. "Voter Turnout in Local Elections," *Urban Affairs Review* 38(5): 645–668.
Hallett, Jr., George Hervey, with Clarence Gilbert Hoag. 1940. *Proportional Representation: The Key to Democracy*. New York: National Municipal League.
Hare, Thomas. [1861] 1865. *The Election of Representatives, Parliamentary and Municipal: A Treatise*, 3rd ed. London: Longman, Green.
Harris, Joseph P. 1930. "The Practical Workings of Proportional Representation in the United States and Canada." *National Municipal Review* 19(5 Supp): 2–50.
Hart, Jenifer. 1992. *Proportional Representation: Critics of the British Electoral System, 1820-1945*. Oxford: Clarendon Press.
Hatton, Augustus R. 1916. "The Ashtabula Plan: The Latest Step in Municipal Organization." *National Municipal Review* 5(1): 56–65.
Herron, Erik S., Robert J. Pekkanen, and Matthew S. Shugart. 2018. *Oxford Handbook of Electoral Systems*. New York: Oxford University Press.
Hill, I.D., Wichmann, B.A., and D.R. Woodall. 1987. "Algorithm 123: Single Transferable Vote by Meek's Method." *Computer Journal* 30(3): 277–281.
Hill, Steven. 2002. *Fixing Elections: The Failure of America's Winner Take All Politics*." New York: Routledge.
Hill, Steven and Rob Richie. 2004. "Despoiling the Election." *The Nation* 279(July 12): 28–78.
Hirczy de Mino, Wolfgang, and John C. Lane. 2000. "Malta: STV in a Two-Party System." In Shaun Bowler and Bernard Grofman, *Elections in Australia, Ireland, and Malta under the Single Transferable Vote*, pp. 205–247. Ann Arbor: University of Michigan Press.
Hoag, Clarence Gilbert, and George Hervey Hallett, Jr. 1926. *Proportional Representation*. New York: Macmillan.
Hoag, C.G. 1914. "Effective Voting." U.S. Senate, Document No. 250, 63rd Congress, 2nd Session.
Homeshaw, Judith. 2001. "Inventing Hare-Clark: The Model Arithmetocracy." In Marian Sawer, ed., *Elections: Full, Free and Fair*, pp. 96–114. Sydney: Federation Press.
Horowitz, Donald L. 1991. *A Democratic South Africa? Constitutional Engineering in a Divided Society*. Berkeley: University of California Press.
Horowitz, Donald L. 2006. "Strategy Takes a Holiday: Fraenkel and Grofman on the Alternative Vote." *Comparative Political Studies* 39(5): 652–662.

Jacobs, Lawrence R., and Joanne M. Miller. 2014. "Ranked Choice Voting: By the Data, Still Flawed." *Minneapolis Star-Tribune*, February 12.

Jacobs, Lawrence R., and Joanne M. Miller. 2014. "Ranked Choice Voting and the 2013 Minneapolis Elections." Unpublished manuscript.

James, Edmund J. 1896. "An Early Essay on Proportional Representation." *Annals of the American Academy of Political and Social Science* 7: 61–80.

James, Herman G. 1916. "Proportional Representation: A Fundamental or a Fad?" *National Municipal Review* 5: 273–277.

Jansen, Harold John. 1998. *The Single Transferable Vote in Alberta and Manitoba.* Dissertation, University of Alberta.

Jansen, Harold. 2004. "The Political Consequences of the Alternative Vote: Lessons from Western Canada." *Canadian Journal of Political Science* 37(3): 647–669.

John, Sarah, Haley Smith, and Elizabeth Zack. 2018. "The Alternative Vote: Do Changes in Single-member Voting Systems Affect Descriptive Representation of Women and Minorities?" *Electoral Studies* 54: 90–102.

Johnston, J. Paul, and Miriam Koene. 2000. "Learning Histories Lessons Anew: The Use of STV in Canadian Municipal Elections." In Shaun Bowler and Bernard Grofman, *Elections in Australia, Ireland, and Malta under the Single Transferable Vote*, pp. 205–247. Ann Arbor: University of Michigan Press.

Juelich, Courtney, and Joseph Coll. 2021. "Ranked Choice Voting and Youth Voter Turnout: The Roles of Campaign Civility and Candidate Contact." *Politics and Governance* 9(2): 319–331.

Kettleborough, Charles. 1921. "The Direct Primary in Indiana." *National Municipal Review* 10(3): 166–170.

Keyssar, Alexander. 2000. *The Right to Vote: The Contested History of Democracy in the United States.* New York: Basic Books.

Kiewiet, D. Roderick. 1979. "Approval Voting: The Case of the 1968 Election." *Polity* 12(1): 170–181.

Kilgour, D. Marc, Jean-Charles Grégoire, and Angèle M. Foley. 2020. "The Prevalence and Consequences of Ballot Truncation in Ranked-choice Elections." *Public Choice* 184(1-2): 197–218.

Kimball, David C., and Joseph Anthony. 2016. "Voter Participation with Ranked Choice Voting in the United States." Paper presented at the annual meeting of the American Political Science Association, Philadelphia, PA.

Kimball, David C., and Joseph Anthony. 2017. "Ranked Choice Voting: A Different Way of Casting and Counting Votes." In Todd Donovan, ed., *Changing How America Votes.* Lanham, MD: Rowman & Littlefield, pp. 100–112.

Kimball, David C., and Martha Kropf. 2005. "Ballot Design and Unrecorded Votes on Paper-Based Ballots." *Public Opinion Quarterly* 69(4): 508–529.

Kimball, David C., and Martha Kropf. 2008. "Voting Technology, Ballot Measures, and Residual Votes." *American Politics Research* 36(4): 479–509.

Klemme, Howard C. 1964. "The Powers of Home Rule Cities in Colorado." *University of Colorado Law Review* 36: 321–363.

Knack, Stephen, and Martha Kropf. 2003. "Roll-Off at the Top of the Ballot." *Politics & Policy* 31(4): 575–594.

Knack, Stephen, and Martha Kropf. 2003. "Voided Ballots in the 1996 Presidential Election." *Journal of Politics* 65: 881–897.

Kneier, Charles M. 1947. *City Government in the United States*, rev. ed. New York: Harper.

Kropf, Martha E. 2016. *Institutions and the Right to Vote in America*. New York: Palgrave Macmillan.

Kropf, Martha. 2021. "Using Campaign Communications to Analyze Civility in Ranked Choice Voting Elections." *Politics and Governance* 9(2): 280–292.

Kuklinski, James. 1973. "Cumulative and Plurality Voting: An Analysis of Illinois' Unique Electoral System." *Western Political Quarterly* 26(4): 726–746.

Kurlowski, Drew. 2019. "Adventures in Ranked Choice Voting: Examining Maine's 2018 Gubernatorial Primary." Paper presented at the Election Sciences, Reform, & Administration Conference, Philadelphia (July 11).

Lakeman, Enid. 1970. *How Democracies Vote: A Study of Majority and Proportional Electoral Systems*, 3rd ed. London: Faber and Faber.

Lal, Brij V., and Peter Larmour, eds. 2012. *Electoral Systems in Divided Societies: The Fiji Constitution Review*. Canberra: ANU E Press.

Laatu, Juho, and Warren D. Smith. 2009. "The Rank-order Votes in the 2009 Burlington Mayoral Election." Unpublished manuscript.

Lijphart, Arend. 1990. "The Political Consequences of Electoral Laws, 1945-85." *American Political Science Review*, 84(2, June): 48–496.

Lijphart, Arend. 1999. *Patterns of Democracy: Government Forms and Performance in Thirty-Six Countries*.

Mackerras, Malcolm. 1970. "Preference Voting and the 'Donkey Vote.'" *Politics* 5: 69–76.

Maloy, J.S. 2019. *Smarter Ballots: Electoral Realism and Reform*. Palgrave MacMillan.

Maloy, J.S., and Matthew Ward. 2021. "The Impact of Input Rules and Ballot Options on Voting Error." *Politics and Governance* 9(2): 306–318.

Marsh, Michael. 2000. "Candidate Centered but Party Wrapped: Campaigning in Ireland under STV." In Shaun Bowler and Bernard Grofman, eds., *Elections in Australia, Ireland, and Malta under the Single Transferable Vote: Reflections on an Embedded Institution*, pp. 114–130. Ann Arbor: University of Michigan Press.

Marsh, Michael. 2007. "Candidates or Parties? Objects of Electoral Choice in Ireland." *Party Politics* 13(4): 500–527.

Martinez, Michael. 2010. "Why is American Turnout So Low, and Why Should We Care?" in Jan E. Leighley, ed., *The Oxford Handbook of American Elections*, pp. 107–124. New York: Oxford University Press.

Maxey, Chester Collins. 1922. "The Cleveland Election and the New Charter." *American Political Science Review* 16(1): 83–86.

May, Kenneth O. 1952. "A Set of Independent Necessary and Sufficient Conditions for Simple Majority Decision." *Econometrica* 20: 580–684.

May, Kenneth O. 1953. "A Note on the Complete Independence of the Conditions for Simple Majority Decision." *Econometrica* 21: 172–173.

McBain, Howard Lee. 1922. "Proportional Representation in American Cities," *Political Science Quarterly* 37: 281–298.

McCarthy, Devin, and Jack Santucci. 2021. "Ranked-Choice Voting as a Generational Issue in Modern American Politics." *Politics & Policy* 49(1): 33–60.

McCune, David, and Lori McCune. 2022. "Does the Choice of Preferential Voting Method Matter? An Empirical Study Using Ranked Choice Elections in the United States." *Representation*.

McDaniel, Jason A. 2016. "Writing the Rules to Rank the Candidates." *Journal of Urban Affairs* 38(3): 387–408.

McDonald, Michael P., and Samuel L. Popkin. 2001. "The Myth of the Vanishing Voter." *American Political Science Review* 95(4): 963–974.

McLean, Iain. 1996. "E.J. Nanson, Social Choice and Electoral Reform." *Australian Journal of Political Science* 31(3): 369–385.

McLean, Ian, and Arnold B. Urken. 1995. *Classics of Social Choice*. Ann Arbor: University of Michigan Press.

Meek, Brian L. 1994. "A New Approach to the Single Transferable Vote." *Voting Matters* 1: 1–11. [Translation of "Une Nouvelle Approche du Scrutin Transférable". *Mathématiques et Sciences Humaines* 25(1969): 13-23 and 29(1970): 33-39.]

Mercer, Marsha. 2016. "Are 'Instant Runoffs' a Better Way to Vote?" Stateline, Pew Charitable Trusts, September 2, 2016.

Merriam, Charles E., and Louise Overacker. 1928. *Primary Elections*. Chicago: University of Chicago Press.

Mill, John Stuart. [1862] 1958. *Consideration on Representative Government*. Indianapolis: Bobbs-Merrill.

Miller, Joanne, and Jon Krosnick. 1998. "The Impact of Candidate Name Order on Election Outcomes." *Public Opinion Quarterly* 62(3): 291–330.

Miller, Nicholas R. 2017. "Closeness Matters: Monotonicity Failure in IRV Elections with Three Candidates." *Public Choice* 173: 91–108.

Miller, Zane L., and Bruce Tucker. 1998. *Changing Plans for America's Inner Cities*. Columbus: Ohio State University Press.

Milner, Henry. 2017. "Electoral System Reform, the Canadian Experience." *Election Law Journal* 16(3): 349–356.

Moley, Raymond. 1918. "Representation in Dayton and Ashtabula." *National Municipal Review* 7: 27–38.

Moley, Raymond. 1923. "Proportional Representation in Cleveland," *Political Science Quarterly* 38: 652–669.

Moley, Raymond, and Charles A. Bloomfield. 1926. "Ashtabula's Ten Years' Trial of P.R." *National Municipal Review* 15: 651–660.

Moser, Robert G., and Ethan Scheiner. 2012. *Election Systems and Political Context: How the Effects of Rules Vary Across New and Established Democracies*. New York: Cambridge University Press.

Nanson, E.J. 1882. "Methods of Election." *Transactions and Proceedings of the Royal Society of Victoria* 19: 197–240.

Nanson, E. J. 1900. "The Real Value of a Vote and How to Get it at the Coming Federal Elections."

Neely, Francis, and Corey Cook. 2008. "Whose Votes Count? Undervotes, Overvotes and Ranking in San Francisco's Instant-Runoff Elections." *American Politics Research* 36: 530–554.

Neely, Francis, and Jason McDaniel. 2015. "Overvoting and the Equality of Voice Under Instant-runoff Voting in San Francisco." *California Journal of Politics & Policy* 7(4): 1027.

Nielson, Lindsay. 2017. "Ranked Choice Voting and Attitudes toward Democracy in the United States: Results from a Survey Experiment." *Politics and Policy* 4: 535–570.

Niou, Emerson M.J. 1987. "A Note on Nanson's Rule." *Public Choice* 54(2): 191–193.

Ntounias, Theodoros. 2023. "Voter Information Search and Ranked Choice Voting." *Election Law Journal* 22(4): 337–362.

Norris, Pippa. 2004. *Electoral Engineering: Voting Rules and Political Behavior*. Cambridge: Cambridge University Press.

Ornstein, Joseph T., and Robert Z. Norman. 2014. "Frequency of Monotonicity Failure under Instant Runoff Voting. Estimates Based on a Spatial Model of Elections." *Public Choice* 161: 1–9.

Orr, Graeme. 2002. "Ballot Order: Donkey Voting in Australia." *Election Law Journal* 1(4): 573–578.

Overacker, Louise. 1930. "Direct Primary Legislation in 1928-29." *American Political Science Review* 24(2): 370–380.

Page, Benjamin I. 1976. "The Theory of Political Ambiguity." *American Political Science Review* 70(3): 742–752.

Passarelli, Gianluca. 2020. *Preferential Voting Systems: Influence on Intra-Party Competition and Voting Behavior*. Palgrave MacMillan.

Pildes, Richard H., and G. Michael Parsons. 2021. "The Legality of Ranked Choice Voting." *California Law Review* 109: 1773–1845.

Pilon, Dennis. 1996. "The Drive for Proportional Representation in British Columbia, 1917-23." MA thesis (History), Simon Fraser University.

Plassmann, Florenz, and T. Nicolaus Tideman. 2014. "How Frequently Do Different Voting Rules Encounter Paradoxes in Three-candidate Elections?" *Social Choice and Welfare* 42: 31–75.

Potthoff, Richard F. 2023. "Is Hare (aka IRV and RCV) Better But Not Best?" *Election Law Journal* 22(1): 1–26.

Potthoff, Richard F., and Michael C. Munger. 2021. "Condorcet Loser in 2016: Apparently Trump; Condorcet Winner: Not Clinton?" *American Politics Research* 49(6): 618–636.

Qualter, Terrence H. 1970. *The Election Process in Canada*. Toronto, ON: McGraw-Hill.

Quinlan, Stephen, and Hannah Schwarz. 2022. "The Transfers Game: A Comparative Analysis of the Mechanical Effect of Lower Preference Votes in STV Systems." *International Political Science Review* 43(1):118–135.

Rae, Douglas W. 1967. *The Political Consequence of Electoral Laws*. New Haven, CT: Yale University Press.

Rae, Douglas W. 1971 The Political Consequence of Electoral Laws, rev. ed. New Haven, CT: Yale University Press.

Reilly, Ben. 1997. "The Alternative Vote and Ethnic Accommodation: New Evidence from Papua New Guinea." *Electoral Studies* 16(1): 1–11.

Reilly, Benjamin. 2002. "Social Choice in the South Seas: Electoral Innovation and the Borda Count in the Pacific Island Countries." *International Political Science Review* 23: 355–372.

Reilly, Ben. 2012. "Constitutional Engineering and the Alternative Vote in Fiji: An Assessment." In Lal, Brij V. and Peter Larmour, eds., *Electoral Systems in Divided Societies: the Fiji Constitution Review*, pp. 73–96. Canberra: ANU E Press.

Reilly, Benjamin, David Lublin, and Rachel Leven. 2021. *Final-Five Voting: Comparative Evidence on a Novel Election System*. Cambridge, MA: Institute for Political Innovation.

Reilly, Ben, and Michael Maley. 2000. "The Single Transferable Vote and the Alternate Vote Compared." In Shaun Bowler and Bernard Grofman, eds., *Elections in Australia, Ireland, and Malta under the Single Transferable Vote: Reflections on an Embedded Institution*, pp. 37–58. Ann Arbor: University of Michigan Press.

Remsen, Daniel S. 1896. "The Fusion of Political Parties." *Annals of the American Academic of Political and Social Science* 8: 32–49.

Reynolds, Andrew, Ben Reilly, and Ellis. 2005. *Electoral System Design*. Stockholm: International Institute for Democracy and Electoral Assistance.

Richie, Robert, and Steven Hill, eds. 1999. *Reflecting All of Us: The Case for Proportional Representation*. Boston: Beacon Press. [Also published as Whose Vote Counts?]

Richie, Rob, Steven Hill, and Caleb Kleppner. 2000. "Reclaiming Democracy in the 21st Century: Instant Runoffs, Proportional Representation, and Cumulative Voting." *Social Policy* 31: 35–42.

Riker, William H. 1982a. *Liberalism against Populism*. Prospect Heights, IL: Waveland Press.

Riker, William H. 1982. "The Two-party System and Duverger's Law: An Essay on the History of Political Science." *American Political Science Review* 76(4): 753–766.

Scarpaleggia, Francis, et al. 2016. "Strengthening Democracy in Canada: Principles, Process and Public Engagement for Electoral Reform." Ottawa, ON: House of Commons, Report of the Special Committee on Electoral Reform.

Slaughter, Anne-Marie, Francis Fukuyama, and Larry Diamond. 2019. "Ranked Choice Voting." *Politico Magazine*.

Santucci, Jack. 2017. "Party Splits, not Progressives: The Origins of Proportional Representation in American Local Government." *American Politics Research* 45: 494–526.

Santucci, Jack. 2018. "Maine Ranked-choice Voting as a Case of Electoral-system Change." *Representation* 54(3): 297–311.

Santucci, Jack. 2022. *More Parties or No Parties: The Politics of Electoral Reform in America*. New York: Oxford University Press.

Satterthwaite, Mark. 1975. "Strategy Proofness and Arrow's Conditions." *Journal of Economic Theory* 10: 187–217.

Sawyer, Jack, and Duncan MacRae, Jr. 1962. "Game Theory and Cumulative Voting in Illinois, 1902-1954." *American Political Science Review* 56(4): 936-946.

Schultz, David, and Kristi Rendahl. 2010. "Evaluation Ranked Choice Voting in the 2009 Minneapolis Elections: A report for the Minneapolis Elections Department," v. 2.

Schwartz, Mildred A. 1974. *Politics and Territory: The Sociology of Regional Persistence in Canada.* Montreal: McGill-Queen's University Press.

Shugart, Matthew Soberg, and Martin P. Wattenberg, eds. 2001. *Mixed Member Electoral Systems: The Best of Both Worlds?* New York: Oxford University Press.

Sinnott, Richard. 1996. "The Electoral System," in John Coakley and Michael Gallagher, eds., *Politics in the Republic of Ireland*, 2nd edition, pp. 67–85. Limerick: PSAI Press).

Slaughter, Anne-Marie, Francis Fukuyama and Larry Diamond. 2019. "How to Fix Polarization: Ranked Choice Voting." Politico Magazine.

Sowers, Don C. 1936. "Sixteen Years of P.R. in Boulder." *National Municipal Review* 23(1): 27–30.

Spence, Catherine Helen. 1861. *A Plea for Pure Democracy: Mr. Hare's Reform Bill Applied to South Australia.* Adelaide.

Stewart, Charles III. 2020. "The Elections Performance Index," in Mitchell Brown, Bridgett A. King, and Kathleen Hale, eds., *The Future of Election Administration,* pp. 119–153. Palgrave MacMillan.

Stewart, Charles III, R. Michael Alvarez, Stephen S. Pettigrew, and Cameron Wimpy. 2020. "Abstention, Protest, and Residual Votes in the 2016 Election." *Social Science Quarterly* 101(2): 925-939.

Still, Edward. 1992. "Cumulative Voting and Limited Voting in Alabama." In In Wilma Rule and Joseph F. Zimmerman, eds., *United States Electoral Systems: Their Impact on Women and Minorities,* pp. 183–196. New York: Greenwood.

Surekha, K., and Bhaskara Rao, K.P.S. 2010. "May's Theorem in an Infinite Setting." *Journal of Mathematical Economics* 46: 50–55.

Taagepera, Rein. 1996. "STV in Transitional Estonia." *Representation* 34(1): 29–36.

Taagepera, Rein, and Mathew Shugart. 1989. *Seats and Votes: The Effects and Determinants of Electoral Systems.* New Haven, CT: Yale University Press.

Tideman, Nicolaus. 2006. *Collective Decisions and Voting: The Potential for Public Choice.* London: Routledge.

Tideman, Nicolaus, and Daniel Richardson. 2000. "Better Voting Methods through Technology: The Refinement-Manageability Trade-Off in the Single Transferable Vote." *Public Choice* 103(1-2 April): 13–34.

Tideman, Nicolaus. 1995. "The Single Transferable Vote." *Journal of Economic Perspectives* 9: 27–38.

Tolbert, Caroline J., and Kellen Gracey. 2018. "Changing How America Votes for President." In Todd Donovan, ed., *Changing How America Votes*, pp. 70–83. Rowman & Littlefield.

Trounstine, Jessica. 2008. *Political Monopolies in American Cities: The Rise and Fall of Bosses and Reformers.* Chicago: University of Chicago Press.

Wand, Jonathan N., et al. 2001. "The Butterfly Did It: The Aberrant Vote for Buchanan in Palm Beach County, Florida." *American Political Science Review* 95(4): 793–810.

Weaver, Leon H. 1971. "Representation of Minorities in At-Large Elections in City and Village Governments under Michigan Law." *Journal of Urban Law* 49: 131–162.

Weaver, Leon. 1984. "Semi-proportional and Proportional Representation Systems in the United States." In Arend Lijphart and Bernard Grofman, *Choosing an Electoral System*, pp. 191–206. Praeger: New York.

Weaver, Leon. 1986. "The Rise, Decline, and Resurrection of Proportional Representation in Local Governments in the United States." In Bernard Grofman and Arend Lijphart, eds. *Electoral Laws and Their Political Consequences*, pp. 139–153. New York: Agathon Press.

Weaver, Leon, and Judith Baum. 1992. "Proportional Representation on New York City Community School Boards." In Wilma Rule and Joseph F. Zimmerman, eds., *United States Electoral Systems: Their Impact on Women and Minorities*, pp. 197–205. New York: Greenwood.

Weeks, O. Douglas. 1937. "Summary of the History and Present Status of Preferential Voting in State Direct Primary Systems." *Southwestern Social Science Quarterly* 181: 64–67.

Wiggins, Charles W., and Janice Petty. 1979. "Cumulative Voting and Electoral Competition: The Illinois House." *American Politics Quarterly* 7(3): 345–365.

Williams, Benj. H. 1923. "Prevention of Minority Nominations for State Offices in the Direct Primary." *Annals of the American Academy of Political and Social Science* 106: 111–115.

Young, Lisa, and Keith Archer. 2002. *Regionalism and Party Politics in Canada*. Don Mills: Oxford University Press.

Zimmerman, Joseph F. 1994. "Alternative Voting Systems for Representative Democracy." *PS: Political Science and Politics* 27: 674–677.

Index

For the benefit of digital users, indexed terms that span two pages (e.g., 52–53) may, on occasion, appear on only one of those pages.

Tables and figures are indicated by an italic *t* or *f*.

Academy Awards. *See Academy of Motion Picture Arts and Sciences (AMPAS)*
Academy of Motion Picture Arts and Sciences (AMPAS), 5–6, 18–21, 20*f*, 149, 156, 176 n.19, n.21, 192 n.42
  Academy Award (Oscar) for Best Actress, 149
  Academy Award (Oscar) for Best Picture, 19–21
Adams, Adrienne, 71
Adams, Eric, 71–73, 192 n.41
African Americans. *See* racial and ethnic groups and group representation
Alabama, 66–67, 82
Alameda County, California, 116–117, 143, 144*t*, 150, 191 n.30
Alaska, 9*t*, 89, 149, 151–152, 154–156, 187 n.5
  Alaska, adoption of RCV and, 95–101
  Alaska, and electronic vote tabulation, 134–135
  Alaska, and top-four runoff, 161–162, 186 n.33, 192 n.43
  Alaska, voter education efforts in, 165
Alaskan Native people. *See* racial and ethnic groups and group representation
Alaskans for Better Elections Yes on 2, 97–98
Alberta, 83–84, 184 n.28
alternative vote (AV), 2, 31
American Academy of Arts & Science, 161–162
Andrae, Carl, 38–39, 178 n.24
Anglo-Irish Treaty of 1921, 39
Anuzis, Saul, 31, 67, 132, 154–155, 167, 182 n.73, n.75
Arnold, John, 71
Arrow, Kenneth, 14
Ashtabula, Ohio, 51, 53, 180 n.22, n.24, n.25
Asian Americans. *See* racial and ethnic groups and group representation
Aspen, Colorado, 63, 109, 156, 181 n.56

multiwinner ranked voting method of, 62–63
Associated Press Poll, and modified Borda count, 33–34
at-large elections, 15–16
Australia, 34, 36, 40–41, 47, 146, 168, 177 n.14, 178 n.21
  and ballot color, 36
  ballot completion and, 35–36
  ballot marking rules, 144
  House of Representatives in, 2, 31, 34, 37*f*, 146, 191 n.33
  and mandatory voting, 192 n.34
  Senate in, 38*f*, 191 n.33

Bailey, Kyle, 184 n.4
Ballon d'Or, and modified Borda count, 33–34
ballot design, for RCV ballots, 137
ballots with skipped rankings, 139–143, 142*t*, 166–167, 186 n.1, 191 n.28, n.29. *See also* cascade method, Minneapolis method, voter intent
Bangor, Maine, 189 n.7
Basalt, Colorado, 64, 187 n.4
batch elimination, 119, 148–149
Begich, Mark, 98–100, 185 n.29, 186 n.31
Bentham, Jeremy, 178 n.22
Berkely, California, 59, 111, 113–114, 150, 191 n.28
Bernier, Maxime, 86, 184 n.30
Beshear, Andy, 154
Biden, Joseph R., 103–104, 159–160
block voting, 16, 83, 167, 175 n.17, 180 n.32, 181 n.53, n.54, 182 n.75
Boebert, Lauren, 154
Bond, Tiffany L., 4*t*, 189 n.7
Borda count, 28–29, 32–33, 33*t*, 76–77, 177 n.6
Borda, Jean-Charles de, 28–29
Boston, Massachusetts, 66, 166
Boulder, Colorado, 53, 64, 136, 180 n.25

Brams, Steven, 67
Brautigam, John, 91, 151
British Columbia, 83–84
Brown, Jerry, 154–155, 193 n.50
Buckalew, Charles, 183 n.15
Bucklin voting, 49–51, 58–59, 68–69, 179 n.9, n.10, 181 n.42, 182 n.72, 190 n.11
    in Alabama primary, 76
    and differences from RCV, 49–51, 179 n.6
    use by Federal Reserve System, 50–51, 179 n.8
Bucklin, James W., 49–50
bullet voting. *See plunking*
Burlington Telecom, 61
Burlington, Vermont, 46*t*, 59–60, 156, 178 n.34, 181 n.52
    and non-monotonic mayoral race, 44–47, 178 n.35
Bush, George W., 137, 190 n.17

Calgary, Alberta, 54–56, 83–84
California, 2, 9*t*, 96–97, 154–155, 187 n.5
    and all-mail elections, 116–117
    and prohibition of STV, 53
    top two primary and, 12
California Ranked Choice Voting Coalition, 143
Cambridge, Massachusetts, 136–137, 149–150, 166, 168, 180 n.34, 181 n.41, 190 n.15, 192 n.39
    method of transferring surplus votes in, 56–57, 148–149
    name order on ballots in, 136
    number of choices allowed, 135–136
    Plan E proposal, 56
    proportionality of STV outcomes in, 56
    STV and, 2–3, 48, 111–113, 156, 189 n.34
    write-in votes in, 121–122
Canada, 48, 74, 155, 184 n.23
    electoral systems in western provinces, 84*t*
    House of Commons in, 82–83, 85, 184 n.26
    reform movement in, 54–56
    "ridings" as single member districts, 11
candidate name order on ballot, 190 nn.14–15
candidates, number of, with RCV, 109, 111–114, 127–128
Carbondale, Colorado, 64
Cary, North Carolina, 61–62, 157, 184 n.18
cascade method, for skipped rankings, 141–143, 146–147
cast vote records, 135, 148–149, 190 n.8
Center for Election Science, 67–68, 182 n.74

Center for Voting and Democracy, 59–60
Cincinnati method, 57–58, 148–149, 180 n.38
Cincinnati, Ohio, 51–53, 190 n.14
civility in elections, 156
classification of electoral systems, 27–34
Cleveland, Ohio, 53–54, 180 n.24, n.26
Clinton, Hillary, 105
Coghill, John, 98
Coleman, Norm, 137, 190 n.17
College Football Coaches Poll, and modified Borda count, 33–34
Collins, Doug, 160*t*, 160–161
Colorado, 48–50, 59, 154
Committee for Ranked Choice Voting (Maine), 90, 92, 185 n.15
Committee for Ranked Voting NYC, 71
Condorcet cycling, 41
Condorcet voting, 180 n.30
Condorcet winner, 27–28, 34, 41–42, 46, 185 n.18
    and presidential elections, 105
Condorcet, Marquis de, 14, 28
Conservative Party (Canada), 82–83, 85–87, 87*f*, 88*f*, 155
Constitution Act of 1867 (Canada), 85
Constitutional Convention (US), and presidential selection, 104
contingent vote, 32, 190 n.11
Coombs Rule, 175 n.8
coronavirus pandemic, 77–78, 158–159, 176 n.19, 193 n.2
COVID-19. *See coronavirus pandemic*
criticisms of RCV, 1, 23
cumulative voting, 31, 68–69, 132, 156, 167, 182 n.68, 187 n.2
    court responses to, 182 n.69, 183 n.13
    historical use of, 78, 183 n.14, n.15
    and minority voting blocs, 66, 78, 164, 183 n.15
cycling majorities, 14

Dáil Éireann, 2–3, 34–35, 39–40, 107, 177 n.16
de Valera, Eamon, 39–40
Democracy Maine, 90, 150, 184 n.3
Democratic Party. *See also presidential candidate nominations*
    and opposition to RCV, 154–155
    and support for RCV, 153–155, 192 n.37
Denmark, 38–39, 178 n.24
District of Columbia, 104, 154–155
    education level of residents in, 166

INDEX 211

Dowdall, Desmond, and modified Borda count, 32–33
Downs, Anthony, 176 n.1
Droop Quota, 18, 176 n.18, 180 n.34, n.35
Droop, Henry Raymond, 176 n.18
Duverger's Law, 176 n.23, 187 n.6, 194 n.18

Eastpointe, Michigan, and court-mandated use of RCV, 65
Edgmon, Bryce, 98, 185 n.24
Electoral College, 3, 104–105, 186 n.41, n.42, n.43, n.44, 190 n.18
Estonia, 35
exhausted ballots, 107, 118–122, 130, 138–139, 191 n.27
extremism, 23

FairVote, 59, 67–68, 90, 150, 161–162, 181 n.45, 192 n.44
  growth of, 59–60, 186 n.34
Fargo, North Dakota, 182 n.74, n.75
  and approval voting, 67–68
Federal Reserve System, 179 n.8
  use of Bucklin voting by, 50–51
Ferguson-Florissant School District, Missouri, 66–67
Fianna Fáil, 35, 39–40
Fiji, 34, 192 n.43
Fine Gail, 35
First Past the Post (FPTP). *See Single Member District Plurality (SMDP)*
Florida, 76, 137–138
Ford, Tanya, 149–150, 189 n.5
Franken, Al, 137, 190 n.17
Frantz, Don, 61–62, 157
full preferential voting, 146

Garcia, Kathryn, 71–73, 192 n.40
Georgia, 9*t*, 12, 183 n.5
  and 2020 Senate elections, 21, 159–161, 160*t*, 176 n.22
gerrymandering, 11, 15–16
Golden, Jared, 4*t*, 94*f*, 123, 125–126, 189 n.7
  and 2018 congressional election, 4–5, 93–95
Gore, Al, 137, 190 n.17
Grand Junction, Colorado, 49–50, 179 n.3, 182 n.72
Gregory method, 148–149
Griffith, Arthur, 39
Gross, Al, 99, 185 n.29, n.30

Hagenbach-Bischoff quota, 180 n.35

Hallett, George, 59–60, 181 n.43, n.45
Hampden, Maine, 189 n.7
Hare Quota, 18
Hare System, 49, 76, 183 n.13. *See also Single Transferable Vote (STV)*
  emergence in Ireland, 39
Hare, Thomas, 169, 176 n.18, 180 n.34
  Treatise on Election of Representatives, 36–38
Harper, Steven, 86, 184 n.26
Harris, Kamala, 103–104, 187 n.11
Hawaii, 100–101
Hazel, Shane, 159–160, 160*t*
Hendersonville, North Carolina, 62, 109
Hepburn, Katharine, 176 n.19
Heritage Foundation, 154
Hickel, Wally, 95–96
Hill, Steven, 59–60, 72, 181 n.46
Hispanics. *See* racial and ethnic groups and group representation
Hoag, Clarence, 58–60, 181 n.42
Hutchinson, Mike, 143–144, 144*t*, 191 n.31

Idaho, 154–155
Illinois, 78, 182 n.69
India, 29–31
  and elections to the Lok Sabha (India's House of the People) and Rajya Sabha (India's Council of States), 177 n.9
Initiative for Clean Elections (Maine), 90–91
Instant runoff voting (IRV), 2
  as a name for RCV, 48
  as original label for RCV, 58–59
Ireland, 2–3, 31, 34–36, 47, 56, 106–107
  2012 constitutional review of use of STV, 40
  election of presidents in, 32
  and multiparty system, 35
Irish Civil War, 39
Irish Free State, 39
Irish Home Rule, 39
Irish Parliament. *See Dáil Éireann*

Johnson, Gary, 105
Jones, Katherine, 191 n.21

Kellar, Anna, 90–91, 150
Kelley, Buzz, 100, 186 n.33
Kendall, Scott, 96–97, 98–99, 151–152, 185 n.18
Kentucky, 154, 175 n.14
King, Angus, 8–9, 174 n.3, 192 n.44
Kiss, Bob, 44–47, 46*t*, 60–61, 123

Las Cruces, New Mexico, 63
Laura and John Arnold Foundation, 59–60, 90
League of Women Voters (Alaska), 185 n.20
League of Women Voters (Maine), 89–90, 150
LePage, Paul, 90–92, 95
   writing "stolen election" on 2018 certificate, 93, 94*f*
Lewis, Leslyn, 87, 184 n.31
Liberal Party (Canada), 82–83, 85–87, 155
limited vote, 66–67, 68–69, 182 n.67, 188 n.28
list proportional system. *See proportional representation*
Lockhart, Stan, 154–155
Loeffler, Kelly, 160*t*, 160–161
London (England), 70, 190 n.11
Louisiana, 9*t*, 12, 77, 82, 175 n.7, 187 n.5

Madison, James, 186 n.42
Maine, 8–9, 9*t*, 89, 100–101, 149, 174 n.3, 191 n.26, 192 n.40
   2018 House elections in, 4–5, 4*t*
   adoption of RCV and, 1
   attitudes of election workers and administrators towards RCV in, 147, 192 n.37
   and electronic vote tabulation, 134–135
   handling of skipped rankings, 141–143, 191 n.27, n.29
   "people's veto", 92, 185 n.9, n.15
   reserved seats for Native Americans in state legislature, 175 n.9
   selection of presidential electors, 104
   variety of candidates from RCV, 187 n.5
   voter education efforts in, 165
Maine Citizens for Clean Elections (MCCE), 89–90, 150
Maine Clean Elections Act, 89–91
Majoritarianism. *See majority outcomes*
majority, defined, 3, 8, 174 n.2
majority outcomes, 9–10, 21, 27, 109, 125–127, 130–131
Malta, 31, 35–36, 40–41, 47, 56
Manigo, Pecolia, 143–144, 144*t*
Manitoba, 83, 184 n.28
Marquette, Michigan, 54, 180 n.30, 183 n.6
Maryland, 48, 76
Massachusetts, 57–58, 135–136, 180 n.33
McCormick, Cara, 184 n.4
McCullough, Doug, 79–82, 81*t*, 184 n.19, n.21
Merriam, Charles, 75–77
Michigan, 53–54, 154–155, 179 n.21, 182 n.69, 183 n.13

Mill, John Stuart, 178 n.22
   Considerations on Representative Government, 36–38
Mills, Janet, 92–94
Minneapolis, Minnesota, 48, 59, 113–114, 153, 166, 187 n.14, 188 n.22
   methods of transferring surplus in, 148–149
   "Minneapolis Method" of determining voter intent, 134, 146–147
   number of choices allowed, 135–136
   STV in, 48, 111, 187 n.8
   turnout in, before and after RCV, 116–118, 117*f*
   voter and poll workers, education about RCV for, 147
Minnesota, 2, 116–117, 130, 183 n.1
   Minnesota, and 2008 senate race, 137–138
   Minnesota, at-large congressional districts in, 175 n.14
   Minnesota, Supreme Court and Bucklin voting, 50
Mississippi, and RCV for UOCAVA voters, 82
Mixed Member Proportional System (for the German Bundestag), 31
monotonicity *See non-monotonicity*
Montroll, Andy, 44–47, 46*t*
multimember districts, 11, 15–18, 83
multiwinner ranked voting (MRV), 62–63, 78, 109, 176 n.3, 181 n.53
   limited utility of, 167
   in Portland, Maine, 64
Murkowski, Lisa, 95–96, 100, 185 n.18, 186 n.33
Myers, Robert, 98, 185 n.25

Nanson, Edward J, 34
   electoral method of (Nanson's method), 54, 181 n.42, 183 n.6
Native Alaskans. *See racial and ethnic groups and group representation*
Nauru, 31–33, 177 n.14
Nebraska, 74, 104
New America Foundation, 59–60, 161–162
New Jersey, 50, 179 n.10, 182 n.67
New Mexico, 2, 63
New York City, 66, 74, 190 n.19, 192 n.38
   Mayoral Election in 2021, 71–73, 134–135, 192 n.40
   number of rankings allowed in RCV, 135–136
New York State, 58
Newsom, Gavin, 154–155, 193 n.50

non-monotonicity, 23, 42–47, 44t, 45t, 178 n.33, 181 n.50. *See also* Burlington, Vermont
nontransferable ballots, 53–54, 118–122, 120f, 121f, 188 n.20
North Carolina, 59, 61–62, 174 n.4
   judicial elections in, 79, 81t, 184 n.18
no-show paradox, 47

Oakland, California, 187 n.8, 192 n.40
   adoption of preferential voting in, 48
   error in determining the winner of 2022 election, 143, 191 n.31
   and number of candidates, 113–114
   offices using RCV, 111
   RCV's impact on African-Americans in, 152–153
   turnout in, before and after RCV, 116–118, 117f
   voter education in, 150
Ohio, 50, 182 n.69
Oireachtas (Irish Parliament), 34–35, 39–40
Oklahoma, 32–33
   RCV primary ruled unconstitutional in, 75–77, 93–94
Olympics, 5–6, 158–159
One Member, One Vote (OMOV), 184 n.28
   and selection of Canadian Party Leaders, 85–86
Ontario, 70, 82–83, 190 n.20
optional preferential voting, 146
Oregon, 50–51, 154
Oscar Awards. *See* Academy of Motion Pictures Arts and Sciences (AMPAS)
Ossoff, Jon, 159–161, 160t
O'Toole, Erin, 86–87, 184 n.31
Otter, Butch, 154–155
Overacker, Louis, 75–77
overvotes, 107, 137, 139, 188 n.20, 190 n.19, 191 n.25, n.32
Owens, Monique, 65

Palin, Sarah, 99–100, 185 n.29, 186 n.31
Palm Desert, California, 65
Papua New Guinea, 31, 34, 35–36, 40–41
pareto dominant winner, 42–43
Payson, Utah, 63, 109, 181 n.60
Peltola, Mary, 99–100, 185 n.29, 186 n.32, n.33
Pennsylvania, 66–67, 182 n.67, 183 n.15
Perdue, David, 159–160, 160t
Pierce County, Washington, 59, 186 n.1
Pingree, Chellie, 4–5, 4t

plumping. *See* plunking
plunking, 70, 138–139, 149, 188 n.25, 191 n.26
plural at-large voting. *See* block voting
plurality, defined, 3, 8–9
plurality election, 26
   advantages of, 14–15
   objections to, 9–10
plurality winners, and RCV outcomes, 123–125, 130–131
Poliquin, Bruce, 4t, 99–100, 125–126, 189 n.7
   and 2018 congressional election, 4–5, 94–95
   legal motion to stop 2018 RCV, 93
Portland, Maine, 48, 59, 64, 187 n.8, 191 n.21, n.29
   number of rankings allowed for RCV ballots in, 135–136
   public counting of ballots in, 148
Portland, Oregon, 51, 179 n.11
preferential voting, 2–3, 31, 48
presidential candidate nominations (US), 85
   delegate selection rules and, 101–105, 186 n.39, n.40
   potential for use of RCV in, 105
Progressive Conservative Party (Canada), 87, 184 n.28
progressive movement, 48–49, 53–56, 57–58, 74, 83
proportional representation, 21, 29–31, 49, 58–59
   advantages of, 16–17
   and at-large multimember districts, 16–18
   and the single transferable vote (STV), 27
Proportional Representation League, 49, 58–60
Proportional Representation Society (Canada), 49, 181 n.43

Quebec, 82–83, 184 n.28

racial and ethnic groups and group representation, impact of RCV on, 71–72, 151–153, 164–165, 183 n.15, 192 n.43
Ramsey County, Minnesota, 134, 141–143, 189 n.3
ranking choices,
   advantages and disadvantages, 21–25
   number of choices allowed, 135–136
Raskin, Jamie, 153, 192 n.44
Republican Party. *See also presidential candidate nominations*
   and opposition to RCV, 153–155, 192 n.37
   and support for RCV, 154–155
Resnick, Nick, 143, 144t, 191 n.31

Richie, Robert, 59–60, 181 n.45
Riseborough, Andrea, 149
rules for breaking tie votes, 148–149, 189 n.31
runoff elections, 12, 21, 132, 159–161
   advantages of, 14–15
   cost of, as a rationale for RCV, 159
   as distinct from "top two" election, 193 n.3
   objections to, 12–13
   possible advantages over RCV, 23

San Francisco, California, 111, 120–121, 154–155, 166, 188 n.22
   adoption of preferential voting, 48
   and number of candidates, 111–112, 113–114, 187 n.11
   number of choices allowed in RCV elections, 135–136
   turnout in, before and after RCV, 116–118, 117f
   undervotes and overvotes in, 107
   and write-in votes for RCV elections, 121–122
San Leandro, California, 59, 150
Sanders, Bernie, 60, 181 n.49
Santa Fe, New Mexico, 63, 113–114
Scheer, Andrew, 86
Seanad Éireann (Irish Senate), 34–35, 39–40, 175 n.9
Simmons, LaTonda, 152–153
sincere voting, 21. *See also* strategic voting
Single Member District Plurality (SMDP), 3, 10–11, 29–31, 113, 118–119, 124–125, 130, 135, 168, 174 n.6
   in Canada, 82–83
   objections to, 16–17, 26–27
single non-transferable vote, 189 n.32
Single Transferable Vote (STV), 78, 132, 161–162, 164, 167–168, 189 n.36
   and distribution of surplus, 17, 57
   and exhausted ballots, 119
   and final round winners, 126
   and methods of transferring surplus, 56–57
   and proportionality, 17–18, 35, 65, 83–84, 102–103, 166–167
   and voter education, 166
   as a reform, 49
   Cambridge, Massachusetts and, 2–3, 187 n.7, n.8
   differences with and similarities to RCV, 2–3, 18
   Eastpoint, Michigan and, 187 n.7
   in Canada, 83

Ireland and, 2–3, 31, 34–35
Malta and, 2–3, 31, 35
Minneapolis, Minnesota and, 187 n.8
rounds of counting to select winner, 127, 189 n.34
single-member districts, 11
Smith, Dan, 44–45, 46t
Soga, Aki, 61
Spence, Catherine Helen, 39
Sri Lanka, election of national executive, 32
St. Louis, Missouri, 182 n.74
   and approval voting, 68
St. Paul, Minnesota, 134, 166, 189 n.2
   adoption of preferential voting in, 48, 59
   ballot design in, 136–137
   and cascade method of treating skipped rankings, 141–143
   hand counting of ballots in, 134, 189 n.3
   number of choices allowed in, 135–136
   turnout in, before and after RCV, 116–118, 117f
strategic voting, 21, 109, 176 n.23
   and RCV, 42, 124–125
Streisand, Barbra, 176 n.19
Sunnyvale, California, 64–65
supplementary vote, 32, 70, 79–80, 190 n.11
Supreme Judicial Court (Maine), 91–92

tabulation methods, when rankings are skipped in RCV. *See* ballots with skipped rankings
Tacoma, Washington, 59, 186 n.1
Takoma Park, Maryland, 59, 116, 166, 187 n.11
Telluride, Colorado, 64, 113–114, 189 n.31
Thigpen, Cressie, 79–80, 81t, 184 n.20
top four runoff, 97, 187 n.5, 193 n.3
Top-Four Ranked Choice Voting and Campaign Finance Laws Initiative (Alaska), 96
Triplett, Dave, 141–143, 189 n.3
Trudeau, Justin, 86–87, 155, 184 n.26
True, Jim, 62–63
Trump, Donald, 98, 105
Tshibaka, Kelly, 100–101, 186 n.33

undervotes, 107, 121–122, 137, 139, 188 n.20, 191 n.25, n.27
Uniformed and Overseas Civilians Absentee Voting Act of 1986 (UOCAVA), 82, 184 n.22
United Kingdom, 36–38, 70, 184 n.28
   elections to different parliaments of, 177 n.13

United States, state discretion of electoral methods and, 32
Utah, 63, 154–155, 181 n.60
   Municipal Alternative Voting Methods Pilot Project, 63
   use of RCV in state party conventions, 77–78
Utah County, Utah, 63

Vineyard, Utah, 63, 109, 181 n.60
Virginia, 77–78, 154–155
voter education, 149–151, 165–166
voter error, 137–138, 144, 146
voter intent, determining, when ballots poorly marked, 141–143, 146, 188 n.21. *See also* ballots with skipped rankings, cascade method, Minneapolis method
voter turnout, 21, 108, 114–118
   in Australia, 40–41
   and difficulty in comparing cities, 115–117
   in Malta, 40–41
   measuring after women's suffrage, 180 n.22
   in Papua New Guinea, 40–41
   and RCV, 106, 169
   and STV, 53–54

Wachlarowicz, Grace, 147–148
Walker, Lance, 93–94
Warnock, Raphael, 160*t*, 160–161
Washington (state), 9*t*, 50, 187 n.5
   top two primary and, 12, 96–97
wasted votes, 53–54, 108, 118, 176 n.1, 188 n.18
Waxman, Lesley, 149–150, 189 n.5
Weeks, Douglas, 77
Wiley, Maya, 71–72
   op-ed in the *Washington Post*, 72–73
William and Flora Hewlett Foundation, 59–60
Williams, Benjamin, 77
Winters, Robert, 180 n.38
Wright, Kurt, 44–47, 46*t*
write-in votes, 119, 121–122, 182 n.75, 188 n.26

Yang, Andrew, 71, 192 n.40, n.41
Young, Don, 99, 185 n.29
Youngkin, Glenn, 77–78, 154–155